Athens, 25/5/2020

To Professor Nigel Simmonds.

Best Wishes,

A. K

Private Law, Nudging and Behavioural Economic Analysis

Offering a fresh perspective on "nudging", this book uses legal paternalism to explore how legal systems may promote good policies without ignoring personal autonomy.

It suggests that the dilemma between inefficient opt-in rules and autonomy restricting opt-out schemes fails to realistically capture the span of options available to the policy maker. There is a third path, namely the 'mandated-choice model'. The book is mainly dedicated to presenting this model and exploring its great potential. Contract law, consumer protection, products safety and regulatory problems such as organ donation or excessive borrowing are the setting for the discussion. Familiarising the reader with a hot debate on paternalism, behavioural economics and private law, this book takes a further step and links this behavioural law and economics discussion with philosophical considerations to shed a light on modern challenges, such as organ donation or consumers protection, by adopting an openly interdisciplinary approach.

The book will be of interest to students and scholars of contract law, legal systems, behavioural law and economics, and consumer law.

Antonios Karampatzos is Associate Professor of Private Law at the Law School of National and Kapodistrian University of Athens.

Markets and the Law

Series Editor: Geraint Howells, City University of Hong Kong

Markets and the Law is concerned with the way the law interacts with the market through regulation, self-regulation and the impact of private law regimes. It looks at the impact of regional and international organizations (e.g. EC and WTO) and many of the works adopt a comparative approach and/or appeal to an international audience. Examples of subjects covered include trade laws, intellectual property, sales law, insurance, consumer law, banking, financial markets, labour law, environmental law and social regulation affecting the market as well as competition law. The series includes texts covering a broad area, monographs on focused issues, and collections of essays dealing with particular themes.

Other titles in the series

The Law and Economics of Enforcing European Consumer Law
A Comparative Analysis of Package Travel and Misleading Advertising
Franziska Weber

Consumer Protection, Online Shopping Platforms and EU Law
Christiana N. Markou

Private Law, Nudging and Behavioural Economic Analysis
The Mandated-Choice Model
Antonios Karampatzos

https://www.routledge.com/Markets-and-the-Law/book-series/ASHSER1252

Private Law, Nudging and Behavioural Economic Analysis

The Mandated-Choice Model

Antonios Karampatzos

Routledge
Taylor & Francis Group
LONDON AND NEW YORK

First published 2020
by Routledge
2 Park Square, Milton Park, Abingdon, Oxon OX14 4RN

and by Routledge
52 Vanderbilt Avenue, New York, NY 10017

Routledge is an imprint of the Taylor & Francis Group, an informa business

British Library Cataloguing-in-Publication Data
A catalogue record for this book is available from the British Library

Library of Congress Cataloging-in-Publication Data
A catalog record has been requested for this book

ISBN: 978-0-367-41032-2 (hbk)
ISBN: 978-1-003-01465-2 (ebk)

Typeset in Galliard
by codeMantra

MIX
Paper from responsible sources
FSC™ C013985
FSC www.fsc.org

Printed in the United Kingdom
by Henry Ling Limited

Contents

Preface

This book is, in essence, concerned with the traditional issue of legal paternalism and its boundaries. Its main focus, though, is on the recent findings of behavioral economics and their impact on designing efficient public policies that aim to protect individuals from certain self-harming or self-endangering activities. The root causes of such activities are specific rationality deficits or behavioral weaknesses that have a negative impact on the individuals' decision-making process. In this context, I attempt to provide a fresh approach that combines traditional and economic legal analysis with evidence from the behavioral sciences and philosophical argument. The main positions articulated in the book reflect and at the same time considerably expand some of the positions that I put forward in my extensive monograph in Greek under the title "Private Autonomy and Consumer Protection – A Contribution to Behavioral Economic Analysis of Law" (P.N. Sakkoulas Publishers, 2016); in this book I go into a much more detailed discussion of these positions following and incorporating recent developments in literature and the pertinent academic discourse.

The book is divided into two parts. The general Part A deals with 'Behavioral Economic Analysis of Law' (or 'Behavioral Law and Economics'—hereinafter *BEAL*), 'nudge theory,' and freedom of choice. Part B explores the possible scope of the practical application of an alternative regulatory tool, that is, the ***mandated-choice model***, under a BEAL approach; the particular cases examined in this part are the withdrawal right in distance contracts, the sale 'as is where is,' and the strict product liability. More specifically:

The book puts BEAL at the forefront. This new legal movement deserves attention because, based on the theory of ***bounded rationality***, it considers the real-world behavior of individuals and may thus greatly assist the quest for more appropriate—that is, efficient—regulatory tools. The movement began in the United States and has spread throughout Europe; it has particularly influenced modern German legal thinking and theory, on which I place considerable emphasis in an attempt to span both the U.S. and Continental way of thinking and the relevant literature. The practical application of the interdisciplinary assumptions of this new methodological movement is most common in the field of contract law, and more specifically, consumer protection law. Notwithstanding some legitimate concerns, it has been rightly suggested that "behavioral law is one of the most important developments — and probably *the most important* — in legal scholarship of the modern era" (Thomas Ulen, *The Importance of Behavioral Law*).

A characteristic BEAL approach offers the 'nudge theory' of Cass Sunstein and Richard Thaler (the 2017 Nobel laureate in economics). Specifically, in light of the various types of irrational decision-making due to behavioral foibles that the burgeoning field of behavioral economics has revealed over the past few decades, Sunstein and Thaler propose a fundamental paradigm shift: instead of teaching people to overcome their inertia and avoid its sometimes significant ramifications, the regulator could exploit this inertia in a positive and benevolent way by establishing default rules or options that improve individual well-being and societal welfare. The reshaping of the content of the default is famously what Sunstein and Thaler mean by the term 'nudge.' Admittedly, nudges can be very powerful. This is the case, for instance, with organ donation, when the government decides to make all citizens organ donors *by default*—unless they opt out. Such a legislative intervention may lead to a drastic increase in the number of organ donors.

Nonetheless, the 'mild' or 'libertarian' paternalism thus suggested by Sunstein and Thaler encounters some considerable objections, primarily philosophical ones. Rather more serious is the objection relating to the twofold violation of *human dignity* and *personal autonomy*, for which the nudge theory is criticized. It is argued that the central designing of individual choices, even in the form of default options, may entail a degradation of the value of the individual as a moral person capable of reflecting and acting in a sovereign and autonomous manner. This holds true especially for nudging interventions that fly below the radar of the individuals and thus influence their evaluations or preferences in a covert way so that other choices be promoted, choices that third persons deem more beneficial to the individual (and possibly the society as a whole).

I carefully examine this strong objection in the book and, up to a point, refute it. I further articulate a set of criteria that one may use to test the acceptability of a nudge that aims to defeat or limit systematic biases or rationality deficits of individuals. Those criteria chiefly reflect the demands of the proportionality principle.

In addition to the nudge theory, I examine a recent general trend toward *personalizing private law*. This thought-provoking idea has been initially advanced by eminent U.S. legal scholars such as Omri Ben-Shahar, Ariel Porat, and Lior Strahilevitz but has also found proponents in European academia—such as Philipp Hacker. These scholars claim that private law has much to gain from tailoring its regulatory apparatus to the needs of individual legal subjects. On the basis of the findings of behavioral economics and big data analytics, there is an attempt to personalize private law across different regulatory tools, such as disclosures, defaults, and mandates. I reach here the—rather self-evident—conclusion that with the advancement of algorithmic processing of big data and the general proliferation of artificial intelligence, personalized disclosures, defaults, or mandates will certainly become another hotbed of legal scholarship in the near future. This new personalization trend will have far-reaching effects on the general structure of law and, specifically, our right to privacy.

But there is more. In what follows, I support an alternative regulatory path that lies between the opt-out (default option) and opt-in models: namely, the aforementioned *mandated-choice model* (in German: *zwingendes Optionsmodell*), according to which the individual is, in some contexts, required to make a choice between two options. For example, with regard to organ donation: before submitting a tax declaration online, a citizen must first read about the social benefits as well as the implications of organ donation via hyperlink and then—obligatorily—check a box indicating whether they want to be an organ donor (otherwise, the submission of the tax declaration cannot be concluded).

In my opinion, the same concept may also prove very useful in the field of consumer protection law. Specifically, in Part B of the book, I primarily explore the possibility of applying the mandated-choice model to two important areas of EU regulation: withdrawal rights in distance contracts and the sale of a good '*as is where is*.' The conclusion I reach under a BEAL approach is that in such contexts, the adoption of the mandated-choice model would, *de lege ferenda*, be a more preferable, more efficient regulatory option than the existing mandates—which are dictated by EU Directives. For example, it would be better if in distance contracts, the law obligatorily provided the consumer with the possibility to choose between *a contract without a withdrawal right* and *a contract with a withdrawal right and a higher price*. From this perspective, the consumer is well aware of the additional cost she has to pay to enjoy enhanced legal protection by means of the withdrawal right and is in a position to weigh the pros and cons, and soberly reflect on whether the withdrawal right is worth the money. This model might enhance the consumer's freedom of choice and eliminate the socially unjust phenomenon of *cross-subsidization*—which is an often underappreciated flip side of the extended EU legal paternalism. It is, therefore, no coincidence that the mandated-choice path currently finds considerable resonance in German theory and is embraced by renowned legal scholars such as Horst Eidenmüller and Gerhard Wagner.

Another field in which the EU legislator has manifested their willingness to protect the consumer is product liability. The arresting question raised in this context is whether the mandated-choice model could also be applied to product liability; my answer, this time, is no.

All in all, examined on philosophical grounds, the mandated-choice model I advocate proves in many cases to be more compatible with private autonomy. As a specific form of 'mild' paternalism, it is more in line with a vision of private law as both modern and efficient. Interventions based on this model reinforce freedom of choice, which is indispensable in a free, liberal society.

By the end of my analysis, it should become evident that the mandated-choice model is situated in a middle zone between freedom of contract and mandatory law, that is, it constitutes a middle course. It is meant to function as a new type of mandatory law, which marries the advantages of the free shaping of the contractual content to the advantages of rules protecting the society as a whole as well as the need to remedy or at least limit cognitive or volitional weaknesses (or self-control problems) of the consumer in the transaction realm. In all events, though, I admit that the mandated-choice model is not a panacea, that is, a one-size-fits-all solution.

Of course, that's not the end of the story. There is still a long way to go in building a full-fledged alternative to traditional default and mandatory rules, such as the mandated-choice model. And although I am dipping my toe into the waters of the optimal drafting of legal norms, with this book I am just aiming to spur further methodological discussion, primarily within the realm of private law methodology.

This book has greatly benefited from the careful reading and insightful comments of my former student and now PhD candidate in law and economics, Ms. Paraskevi Stergiou; I am particularly grateful to her for encouraging me to try to make my thoughts more accessible. The book has also benefited from the editing of Janet Schilling Mower, the helpful comments and suggestions of the reviewers, as well as the careful formatting of the text and the bibliography carried out by my former student Filareti Kouimtzi-Filaretou. In addition, I would like to express my profound gratitude to my longtime friend and colleague Alexis Arvanitis, Assistant Professor of Social Psychology at the Department of Psychology of the University of Crete (Greece), who first introduced me to the world of cognitive psychology and the path-breaking findings of Amos Tversky and Daniel Kahneman. I have discussed with him repeatedly many ideas articulated in this book, and thus, I had the privilege to see many things the way psychologists see them. For similar discussions, I am also grateful to my friend and colleague Konstantinos Kalliris, Lecturer in Law at Essex Law School. Last but not least, my sincere thanks also goes to Omri Ben-Shahar, Leo and Eileen Herzel Professor of Law at the University of Chicago Law School, and Jonathan Masur, John P. Wilson Professor of Law at the University of Chicago Law School; their lectures and advice, especially during the 2019 Summer Institute in Law & Economics at the University of Chicago, enabled me to see the issues discussed in this book from new perspectives. Of course, any errors that remain herein are my sole responsibility.

The book is dedicated to my beloved brother John, whose passion for real science always inspires me.

Athens, November 2019
Antonios G. Karampatzos

About the author

Dr. iur. Antonios G. Karampatzos was born in Athens, Greece. He is Associate Professor of Private Law at the Law School of National and Kapodistrian University of Athens (initially appointed in 2007 as Lecturer). Between 2000 and 2004, he obtained his LL.M. and PhD at the Law School of University of Tübingen (Germany) under the supervision of Prof. em. Dr. iur. Dres. h.c. Harm Peter Westermann. His PhD thesis—which was unanimously accepted with *summa cum laude* (excellent)—concerned contracts with protective effects toward third parties and the liability of financial experts for pure economic loss (its title in German: "Vom Vertrag mit Schutzwirkung für Dritte zur deliktischen berufsbezogenen Vertrauenshaftung – Zugleich ein Beitrag zum Ersatz fahrlässig verursachter reiner Vermögensschäden," Nomos Verlag 2005). After his stay in Germany, he carried out his post-doctoral research (post-doc) in London at the Institute of Advanced Legal Studies of University College London. His post-doc research was presented in his paper under the title "Supervening Hardship as Subdivision of the General Frustration Rule: A Comparative Analysis with Reference to Anglo-American, German, French and Greek Law" [2 *European Review of Private Law* (2005), 105].

Dr. iur. Karampatzos has written five books and published a plethora of scientific papers in Greek, German, and English. His most recent book in Greek deals with behavioral economic analysis of law and consumer protection (title: "Private Autonomy and Consumer Protection – A Contribution to Behavioral Economic Analysis of Law," P. N. Sakkoulas Publishers, 2016). *Inter alia*, he is co-author of the following papers: "Negotiation as an Intersubjective Process: Creating and Validating Claim-Rights" [26 *Philosophical Psychology* (2013), 89], in cooperation with A. Arvanitis; "The Truth of Negotiation" [*World Financial Review* (July–August 2012), 30], in cooperation with A. Arvanitis; and "Negotiation and Aristotle's Rhetoric: Truth over Interests" [24 *Philosophical Psychology* (2011), 845], in cooperation with A. Arvanitis.

Dr. iur. Karampatzos has organized and participated in numerous domestic and international legal conferences. He is also a member of the Athens Bar Association. His professional interests are mainly focused on international arbitration and drafting legal opinions on private law issues. Last but not least, he is a regular newspaper columnist.

Part A

Behavioral economic analysis of law, nudge theory, and freedom of choice

1 Behavioral economic analysis of law (or behavioral law and economics) and paternalistic interference

I. The emergence of behavioral economic analysis of law and its instrumental value in the field of law

As is widely known, the burgeoning field of behavioral economics—initially based on the path-breaking work of psychologists Daniel Kahneman (the 2002 Nobel laureate in economics) and Amos Tversky—has over the past few decades revealed various instances of irrational decision-making due to behavioral foibles, mainly cognitive 'biases' or distortions. This field of scientific research has successfully challenged significant parts of the famous **rational choice theory**[1] and has brought forward the realistic and nowadays prevalent theory of **bounded rationality** that seems closer to *real-world human behavior.*[2] As a matter of fact,

1 On the basic content of *rational choice theory*, see Becker, *The Economic Approach to Human Behavior*, pp. 5 ff., esp. 14; Cooter/Ulen, *Law & Economics*[6], pp. 12 ff., 18 ff., 50, 230–231, 295; Mathis/Steffen, From Rational Choice..., pp. 32 ff.; White, 33 *J.Socio-Econ.* (2004), 89 ff., esp. 96 ff. *passim*, 211–212; Korobkin/Ulen, 88 *Cal.L.R.* (2000), 1060 ff.; Ghisellini/Chang, *Behavioral Economics...*, pp. 5 ff., esp. 9 ff., 20 ff.; Edwards, 51 *Psychol.Bull.* (1954), 380 ff.; Alchian, 58 *J.Polit.Econ.* (1950), 211 ff.; Friedman/Savage, 56 *J.Polit.Econ.* (1948), 287–288, 303–304. See also Kirchgässner, *Homo Oeconomicus*[4], *passim*, esp. pp. 13 ff., 319 ff.; Eidenmüller, *JZ* (2005), 217–218; the same, *Effizienz als Rechtsprinzip*[3], pp. 28 ff.; Schmolke, *Grenzen der Selbstbindung...*, pp. 106 ff.; Fleischer/Schmolke/Zimmer, Verhaltensökonomik als Forschungsinstrument..., pp. 12 ff.; Schäfer/Ott, *Lehrbuch der ökonomischen Analyse des Zivilrechts*[4], pp. 58 ff.; Englerth, Behavioral Law and Economics..., pp. 63, 66 ff.; Magen, Fairness, Eigennutz und die Rolle des Rechts..., pp. 262 ff., esp. 267 ff.; Lüdemann, Die Grenzen des homo oeconomicus..., pp. 12 ff.; Towfigh, Das ökonomische Paradigma, pp. 27 ff.; Mathis, *Effizienz statt Gerechtigkeit?*[3]..., pp. 21 ff.; Neumann, *Libertärer Paternalismus...*, pp. 20 ff.

2 For recent accounts of the growth of behavioral economics, see Richard Thaler himself in the lecture he delivered in Stockholm, on December 8, 2017, on receiving the Nobel Prize in economic sciences, entitled "From Cashews to Nudges: The Evolution of Behavioral Economics," 108 *Am.Econ.Rev.* (2018), 1265 ff.; the same, 125 *J.Polit.Econ.* (2017), 1799 ff.; Barberis, 120 *Scand.J.Econ.* (2018), 661 ff., who rightly concludes (*ibidem*, p. 680) that "[t]he rise of behavioral economics is one of the most prominent conceptual developments in the social sciences in the past 40 years." In detail (indicatively): Kahneman/Tversky, Choices, Values, and Frames; Dhami, *The Foundations of Behavioral Economic Analysis*; Cartwright, *Behavioral Economics*[2]; Ghisellini/Chang, *Behavioral Economics...*, esp. pp. 95 ff., where they deal extensively with the notion of 'bias,' in an attempt to determine in more precise terms what 'bias' actually is and, more importantly, which types of human behavior may legitimately qualify as irrational instances, namely,

the latter theory goes back to the seminal contribution of the great Herbert Simon (the 1978 Nobel laureate in economics).[3]

It is no wonder that the mind-boggling development of behavioral economics and, especially, the theory of bounded rationality have also become very influential in the field of law.[4] In particular, in recent years, legal science has used behavioral economics theory and findings to justify a series of paternalistic state interferences with a view to protecting individuals from the consequences of their own lack of prudence. The social planner is seen as someone who undertakes the task, through carefully designed regulatory tools, to steer people's behavior *gently*, aiming to protect them from their 'bad self' and the consequences of their own irrational decisions.[5]

This is, in essence, the focus of what we call nowadays *behavioral economic analysis of law* (or *behavioral law and economics*, hereinafter: ***BEAL***; in German: *verhaltensökonomische Analyse des Rechts, Verhaltensökonomik des Rechts*). This new legal movement began in the United States in the last decades and has since spread throughout Europe, particularly influencing modern German legal thought and theory (it suffices here to mention modern German legal scholars, such as Horst Eidenmüller, Klaus Ulrich Schmolke, and Anne van Aaken). The most popular field of practical application of the interdisciplinary assumptions of this new methodological movement is the law of contracts and, more specifically, *the law of consumer protection*, in all its special categories. Its influence has expanded, though, to the entire spectrum of private law covering, *inter alia*, capital markets regulation, competition law, and corporate law.[6]

---

as 'biases' (also *ibidem*, pp. 173 ff., where they undertake a similar attempt to accurately define the terminological pair 'rationality/irrationality'); Angner, *A Course in Behavioral Economics*[2]; Diamond/Vartiainen (eds.), *Behavioral Economics and Its Applications*; Tomer, *Advanced Introduction to Behavioral Economics*; also the same, *The Emergence and Progress of Behavioral Economics: Does It Constitute a New Paradigm?*; Stewart, 97 *The University of Chicago Magazine* (2005).

3 Simon, *Models of Man: Social and Rational…*, *passim*, esp. p. 198; the same, 69 *Quart.J.Econ.* (1955), 99 ff.; the same, 69 *Am.Econ.Rev.* (1979), 493 ff., esp. 499 ff.; the same, Bounded Rationality, pp. 15 ff.; the same, *Reason in Human Affairs*, *passim*, esp. chapter III; the same, 59 *J.Bus.* (1986), 209 ff.; the same, 83 *Am.Econ.Rev.* (1993), 156 ff. Cf., very indicatively, Ghisellini/Chang, *Behavioral Economics…*, *passim*, esp. pp. 51 ff.

4 See, indicatively, Sunstein, 1 *Am.L.&Econ.Rev.* (1999), 115 ff. *passim*, esp. 121, 133, 146 ff. Cf. also Ghisellini/Chang, *Behavioral Economics…*, *passim*, esp. p. 43.

5 See also Eidenmüller, *JZ* (2011), 814–815.

6 See Jolls/Sunstein/Thaler, 50 *Stan.L.Rev.* (1998), 1471 ff., *which may be regarded as the founding paper of BEAL*; Sunstein (ed.), *Behavioral Law & Economics*; Rachlinski (ed.), *Behavioral Law & Economics*; Zamir/Teichman (eds.), *The Oxford Handbook*, esp. pp. 91 ff., 193 ff.; Mathis (ed.), *European Perspectives on Behavioural Law and Economics*; Alemanno/Sibony (eds.), *Nudge and the Law—A European Perspective*; Shafir (ed.), *The Behavioral Foundations of Public Policy*; Sunstein, *1 Am.L.&Econ.Rev.* (1999), 115 ff.; the same, 64 *U.Chi.L.Rev.* (1997), 1175 ff.; Jolls, Behavioral Law and Economics, pp. 115 ff.; Arlen, 52 *Vand.L.Rev.* (1998), 1765 ff., coining the term "*behavioral economic analysis of law*"; Korobkin/Ulen, 88 *Cal.L.R.* (2000), 1051 ff., who use the term "*law and behavioral science*"; Issacharoff, 51 *Vand.L.Rev.* (1998), 1729 ff.; Rachlinski, 85 *Cornell L.Rev.* (2000), 739 ff.; the same, 73 *U.Chi.L.Rev.* (2006), 208 ff.; Bar-Gill, *Seduction*

In many countries around the world such an approach based on behavioral welfare economics has also penetrated other fields of public policy, such as the protection of people from excessive borrowing (e.g., after the U.S. subprime lending crisis of 2008[7]), the design of efficient social security or retirement systems, environmental protection (mainly through the design of energy efficiency policies, such as fuel economy labels on new motor vehicles), protection of health through the promotion of better nutritional choices (e.g., by restaurant menu calorie labeling), the saving of public resources, the design of efficient tax policies, and especially efficient taxpayer compliance strategies.[8] In this context, the European Union (EU) has also shown a particular interest: in 2013 a thesis paper entitled "Applying Behavioural Sciences to EU Policy-making" laid out an

---

by Contract...; the same, 92 *Minn.L.Rev.* (2008), 749 ff.; the same, 98 *Nw.U.L.R.* (2004), 1373 ff.; Camerer/Issacharoff/Loewenstein/O'Donoghue/Rabin, 151 *U.Penn.L.R.* (2003), 1211 ff.; Kelman, 97 *Nw.U.L.R.* (2003), 1347 ff.; Becher, 68 *La.L.Rev.* (2007), 123 ff.; Hacker, 2 *ERPL* (2016), 297 ff.; the same, 11 *ERCL* (2015), 299 ff.; Faure/Luth, 34 *J.Consum.Policy* (2011), 337 ff.; Tomer, *Advanced Introduction to Behavioral Economics*, pp. 92 ff., esp. 98–99; Herresthal, Consumer Law in the DCFR, pp. 200–201. From the German literature see Eidenmüller, *JZ* (2005), 216 ff., esp. 221 ff.; the same, *JZ* (2011), 814 ff.; Fleischer, in: *FS Immenga*, pp. 575 ff.; Englerth, Verhaltensökonomie..., pp. 169 ff.; Kirste, *JZ* (2011), 806 ff.; Steinbeck/Lachenmaier, 29 *NJW* (2014), 2086 ff.; Unberath/Cziupka, 209 *AcP* (2009), 71 ff.; Ringe, 213 *AcP* (2013), 116 ff.; Tscherner, 1 *ALJ* (2014), 144 ff.; in more detail in the German literature Engel/Englerth/Lüdemann/Spiecker-Döhmann (eds.), *Recht und Verhalten—Beiträge zu Behavioral Law and Economics* [where one can find the German terms *"Verhaltensökonomik des Rechts"* and *"verhaltensökonomische Analyse des Rechts"*]; Fleischer/Zimmer (eds.), *Beitrag der Verhaltensökonomie (Behavioral Economics) zum Handels- und Wirtschaftsrecht*; Bechtold, *Die Grenzen zwingenden Vertragsrechts*..., *passim*, esp. pp. 22 ff.; more recently Schmolke, *Grenzen der Selbstbindung*..., esp. pp. 176 ff., 212 ff.

7 *Cf.*, indicatively, Bar-Gill, *Seduction by Contract*..., pp. 116 ff.

8 See, indicatively, Shafir (ed.), *The Behavioral Foundations of Public Policy*, presenting, in detail, some impressive applications of the experimental findings and concepts emanating from behavioral research to the design and implementation of public policy (*'behavioral policy'*); Oliver (ed.), *Behavioural Public Policy*, a collection of contributions from academic economists, psychologists, and philosophers who "reflect on how behavioral economic findings can be used to inform the design of policy initiatives in the areas of health, education, the environment, personal finances and worker remuneration" (*ibidem*, preface); Sunstein/Reisch, 53 *Intereconomics* (2018), 5 ff., who also point to the various 'Behavioral Insights Teams' and 'Nudge Units' active in dozens of countries all over the world (see, e.g., the UK Behavioral Insights Team: www.gov.uk/government/organisations/behavioural-insights-team, www.behaviouralinsights.co.uk/about-us); Sunstein, 122 *Yale L.J.* (2013), 1832 ff.; the same, *The Cost-Benefit Revolution*; Benartzi/Beshears/Milkman/Sunstein/Thaler/Shankar/Tucker-Ray/Congdon/Galing, 28 *Psychol.Sci.* (2017), 1041 ff. *passim*; Ghisellini/Chang, Behavioral Economics..., pp. 206 ff.; Tomer, *Advanced Introduction to Behavioral Economics*, pp. 89–90; Feldman/Lobel, Behavioural Trade-Offs..., pp. 302 ff.; Alemanno/Sibony, Epilogue..., pp. 342 ff. See also the relevant Executive Orders of the U.S. President, no. 13707 dated 15.09.2015 (3 C.F.R. 56365) (www.whitehouse.gov/the-press-office/2015/09/15/executive-order-using-behavioral-science-insights-better-serve-american) and no. 13563 dated 18.01.2011 (76 F.R. 3821) (https://obamawhitehouse.archives.gov/the-press-office/2011/01/18/executive-order-13563-improving-regulation-and-regulatory-review, which ordered all federal agencies to consider using a number of *nudges*, including default rules, in their regulations.

initial framework for the integration of the behavioral findings into specific EU policies.[9]

In light of the above, it comes as no surprise that BEAL is considered as one of the most important developments in legal science in recent decades.[10] It is regarded as a "happy merger of cognitive psychology, experimental economics and the law," which has nowadays evolved into "one of the dominant paradigms of legal discourse in the US."[11] And as already pointed out, it is increasingly discussed in European legal academia as well.[12] It is true, though, that there is a differential implementation of BEAL in the United States and the EU: namely, while U.S. courts and regulatory agencies progressively take insights from behavioral economics into account, EU courts and agencies still remain reluctant and prefer to cling to the rational actor model (at least, in nominal terms).[13] The latter preference may be detected, for example, in the information disclosure scheme of the Consumer Rights Directive (2011/83/EU—see Chapter 4 below), or in the CJEU case law, which still clings to the 'reasonable consumer concept.'[14] Yet this picture on a normative EU level might change in the future.

Especially in the field of consumer protection law, the assumptions and findings of behavioral economics chiefly entail the articulation of *de lege ferenda* proposals for the introduction of better, more efficient regulatory instruments suitable for dealing with real-world consumer behavior.[15] Legal rules designed after careful examination of real people's behavior (by means of field evidence or laboratory data) may better serve consumer protection than policies drafted on the basis of theoretical economic paradigms or abstract doctrinal assumptions—which, of course, may still retain part of their value. The primary goal in this field—that is, efficient consumer protection[16] and bringing about a fairer balance

9 van Bavel/Herrmann/Esposito/Proestakis, *Applying Behavioural Sciences to EU Policy-making (EU 26033 EN)*, www.capire.org/capireinforma/scaffale/30092013_jrc_scientific_policy_report_en.pdf and http://ec.europa.eu/consumers/behavioural_economics/index_en.htm. See also Schmolke, *Grenzen der Selbstbindung...*, pp. 832–833; Engel/Stark, Buttons, Boxes, Ticks, and Trust..., p. 119.

10 See Ulen, European and American Perspectives..., p. 4; Tor, The Next Generation of Behavioural..., p. 17; Faure/Luth, 34 *J.Consum.Policy* (2011), *passim*, esp. 338–339.

11 Hacker, 11 *ERCL* (2015), 301; *cf.* also the same, 2 *ERPL* (2016), 322.

12 *Cf.* Hacker, 11 *ERCL* (2015), 301.

13 Hacker, 11 *ERCL* (2015), 299 ff., wherein extensive analysis of this differential implementation; see, *inter alia*, pp. 302–303: "While in the US, courts and regulatory agencies are increasingly willing to integrate findings from behavioral sciences into their opinions, the very inverse trend seems to be operating in the EU: Adjudication, first and foremost by the CJEU, is based on an ever more rational model of human behavior [...]. This finding is all the more astonishing at a time when academic scholarship in the EU increasingly takes behavioral insights into account. [...] While in the US a growing tendency to integrate bounded rationality both into the adjudication of cases and into policy analysis can be observed, the EU seems quite firmly and with few exceptions set on a course towards an ever more rational concept of human behavior."

14 See Hacker, 11 *ERCL* (2015), 315–316.

15 See Tscherner, 1 *ALJ* (2014), 145; *cf.*, more generally, Jolls/Sunstein/Thaler, 50 *Stan.L.Rev.* (1998), 1508 ff., 1522 ff.; further Note, 95 *Harv.L.R.* (1982), 1690.

16 See also Tscherner, 1 *ALJ* (2014), 145.

between the competing interests of consumers and sellers—is poorly served if legal rules are based on unrealistic and simplistic grounds, which might be solid doctrines but wrong conceptions of reality. On the other hand, though, within this process, we cannot exclude the possibility of—temporarily—endorsing behavioral assumptions that might later prove false, invalid, or at least equivocal; if this happens, such assumptions will have to be abandoned.[17]

All in all, it is nowadays acknowledged that behavioral economics, and by reflection BEAL, offer more accurate and realistic insight into human behavior and its motives[18] for they rest on the three fundamental assumptions of ***bounded rationality***, ***bounded self-control***, and ***bounded self-interest***; thus, they do not blindly subscribe to the classical yardsticks of rationality and efficiency.[19] BEAL brings forward cognitive and volitional weaknesses that systematically appear in groups of the population and in certain transactional situations. These weaknesses sometimes reach such an intensity, extent, or gravity that the legal order cannot turn a blind eye to them. To the contrary, it must take action with a view to securing individual and societal welfare, also given the fact that these weaknesses, owing to their systematic appearance, are by and large foreseeable and thus refer to regulatable instances.[20]

Of course, not everybody is happy with the aforementioned development. A large share of U.S. legal scholars are evidently critical of this shift to BEAL. Their main criticism focuses in general on the findings and assumptions of behavioral economics, which constitute the foundation for the development of BEAL.[21] Some scholars criticize—even vehemently—the growing contribution of behavioral economics to an "excessive rise of paternalistic interventions" and call for individual freedom and responsibility to be restored as central social values.[22] In particular, behavioral economics is considered as providing "foundations for much broader government interventions than before," facilitating "government attempts at regulating individual behavior in matters such as consumption, saving, education, risk taking, and speech," and thus as contributing

17 See also Sunstein, Introduction, p. 9, and 1 *Am.L.&Econ.Rev.* (1999), 151–152; extensively Englerth, Vom Wert des Rauchens..., pp. 231 ff. ***passim***.

18 See, indicatively, Arlen, 52 ***Vand.L.Rev.*** (1998), 1767–1768, 1770. In general, on the significant value of ***pragmatism*** in legal thinking see Posner, 63 *S.Cal.L.R.* (1990), 1653 ff., esp. 1661 ff.

19 In detail Jolls/Sunstein/Thaler, 50 ***Stan.L.Rev.*** (1998), 1473 ff. ***passim***.

20 See also Schäfer/Ott, *Lehrbuch der ökonomischen Analyse des Zivilrechts*[4], pp. 70–71; Fleischer/Schmolke/Zimmer, Verhaltensökonomik als Forschungsinstrument..., p. 44. Especially as regards this specific feature of ***predictable irrationality***, see Cooter/Ulen, *Law & Economics*[6], pp. 51 and 231; and in detail Ariely, *Predictably Irrational...*

21 See Wright/Ginsburg, 106 *Nw.U.L.R.* (2012), 1033 ff., esp. 1053 ff. and 1067 ff.; Mitchell, 99 *Nw.U.L.R.* (2005), 1245 ff.; the same, Alternative Behavioral Law and Economics, pp. 167 ff.; Klick/Mitchell, 90 *Minn.L.Rev.* (2006), esp. 1635 ff.; Bubb/Pildes, 127 *Harv.L.R.* (2014), 1594 ff., esp. 1601 ff.; R.Posner, 50 ***Stan.L.Rev.*** (1998), 1570–1571; Glaeser, 29 ***Regulation*** (2006), 33 ff. Cf. also in German theory, indicatively, Rittner, *JZ* (2005), 668 ff., who generally opposes such attempts, which allegedly threaten the doctrinal clarity of the law; see also, however, the reply delivered by Eidenmüller, *JZ* (2005), 670–671.

22 So recently and characteristically enough Saint-Paul, *The Tyranny of Utility...*

to "the foundation of the new paternalistic state."[23] As will emerge, though, in the following pages, these fears are rather exaggerated and may be partly attributed to a libertarian approach on steroids along with a false perception of personal autonomy—which is, in fact, nowadays in need of a rethink (see pp. 54 ff. below).

II. Do all individuals act irrationally?

The behavioral approach by no means suggests that all individuals show rationality deficits or that all individuals act irrationally on all occasions and everywhere (i.e., in any transactional situation); it only refers to some well-attested *deviations from the rational model.*[24]

More particularly, on the one hand, the behavioral approach does not deny that in many practical instances the *rational choice theory* proves to be correct, thus retaining a large part of its practical significance. On the other hand, this approach endorses the self-evident assumption that each person has different cognitive or perceptive abilities, faculties, experiences, and volitional weaknesses, which, in their turn, are formed under the influence of various specific factors, such as education, intelligence, family and social environment, financial circumstances, as well as demographics (e.g., age, gender, ethnicity). Given all of these influences, it is not possible that all people will behave in the same manner or direction, either rationally or irrationally. It is possible that people with high cognitive abilities will be less likely to make cognitive mistakes or to have biases (and *vice versa*), whereas it is equally possible for an individual who is aware of her own high cognitive abilities to be *over-confident* and thus undermine the rational character of her decisions herself.[25] Further, we should not overlook a non-negligible aspect of social inequality: not all people have equal access to the

23 Saint-Paul, *The Tyranny of Utility...*, p. 4—also *ibidem*, pp. 62 ff., 77 ff.

24 See, indicatively, Sunstein, *Nudging and Choice Architecture...*, p. 24; also Dorf, *Irrationality, Baselines, and Government "Intervention"*: "... behavioral economics [...] challenges the assumption that people always act rationally, which is important, but it accepts the hidden normative premise of neoclassical economics that people *ought* to act rationally." Besides, the above is also acknowledged by the opponents of BEAL; see mainly Rachlinski, 73 *U.Chi.L.Rev.* (2006), 208 ff. *Cf.* further Gary Becker's own acknowledgment, in his Nobel address [Nobel Lecture: The Economic Way of Looking at Behavior, 101 *J.Polit.Econ.* (1993), 402], regarding the limits of *rational choice theory*: "I have intentionally chosen certain topics for my research—such as addiction—to probe the boundaries of rational choice theory. [...] *My work may have sometimes assumed too much rationality, but I believe it has been an antidote to the extensive research that does not credit people with enough rationality*" (emphasis added). Thaler, in his turn, aptly remarks with respect to Becker's last sentence that it "suggests an alternative definition of behavioral economics: crediting people with just the right amount of rationality and human foibles. The trick is in figuring out what is just the right amount. The approach taken by most behavioral economists has been to focus on a few important ways in which humans diverge from *homo economicus*" [Thaler, 125 *J.Polit.Econ.* (2017), 1800].

25 See also Rachlinski, 73 *U.Chi.L.Rev.* (2006), 208 ff., 216 ff., esp. 217 ff., who finally reaches the following important conclusion (p. 219): "Cognitive ability is [...] no panacea for avoiding

economic, educational, and *cultural capital* of the society, which means that *some people's choices and possibilities are significantly limited*, even if their natural intellect is not.[26]

But even the same person does not always act in an expected, predetermined, rational, or irrational way for, as the perennial scientific research of Daniel Kahneman and his fellow scientists has shown,[27] in each of us there are *two different systems governing mind processes (two different 'processors')*. The two systems co-exist in harmony, and together, they both determine human behavior. In particular, System 1 thinks and (re)acts quickly, automatically, sentimentally, or intuitively to external signals and impulses and thus is characterized by limited self-control. System 2 is lazy and reacts slowly. But it is also analytical, calculative, reflective, and more logical; it is also distinguished by its ability to retain self-control and self-concentration, to make complex calculations, and to expend intensive spiritual effort. Even though System 2, the deliberative one, is also prone to mistakes and dysfunctions, System 1, the automatic or intuitive one, is the system that dovetails primarily with the behavioral 'anomalies,' weaknesses, or biases that lead to irrational choices.[28] So, System 1 is "*high risk in terms of probability of making mistakes.*"[29]

In all events, there is a clear, functional, and thus efficient division of labor between these two Systems. The Systems, though, are not completely distinct from each other; they interact, in the sense that when System 1 encounters difficulties it seeks the assistance of System 2. System 2 may then undertake the task to analyze and process more thoroughly and carefully the data it has been presented with. In this way, it assists in finding the solution to the problem that has come up or in validating a decision, choice, or conclusion already reached by System 1 (such as the outcome of a demanding mathematical calculation).

It would not be too far-fetched to suggest that System 2 effectively plays the role of the central commanding faculty as perceived in the Stoic philosophy of mind—that is, the so-called *hêgemonikon*, in which the higher cognitive functions take place.[30] Or further, System 2 may even be correlated with Plato's logical or *logistikon* (stemming from *logos*) part of the soul (*psyche*), which is the thinking part of the soul, loves the truth, and is thus capable of discerning what

---

cognitive errors. Smart people seem to have greater ability to identify cues to the underlying structure of some logical problems, but they remain vulnerable to errors."

26 So aptly Leggett, 42 *Policy Polit.* (2014), 11–12.

27 For a rather more popular synopsis of the basic findings of this extensive behavioral research, see Kahneman, *Thinking, Fast and Slow*.

28 See also Sunstein, 122 *Yale L.J.* (2013), 1838 ff.; the same, *Nudging and Choice Architecture*..., pp. 15–16, 37, 39–40, 47–48; the same, *Choosing Not to Choose*..., pp. 11 ff.; the same, *Fifty Shades of Manipulation*, pp. 12 ff.; Ghisellini/Chang, *Behavioral Economics*..., pp. 68 ff.; Rebonato, 37 *J.Consum.Policy* (2014), 361 ff. *passim*; Feldman/Lobel, Behavioural Trade-Offs ..., pp. 309 ff.; Alemanno/Sibony, Epilogue..., pp. 330 ff.; van Aaken, Judge the Nudge..., p. 93; Sibony/Helleringer, EU Consumer Protection and Behavioural Sciences..., p. 212.

29 Ghisellini/Chang, *Behavioral Economics*..., p. 69.

30 See, indicatively, www.iep.utm.edu/stoicmind/.

is real and true: namely, in Plato's tripartite theory of the soul, there is (a) the *logistikon*, which is juxtaposed to (b) the *spirited* or *thymoeides* (stemming from *thymos*), which normally represents our noble impulses, such as courage or passion, but can also cause people to experience strong emotions, particularly anger and temper, and (c) the appetitive or *epithymetikon* (stemming from *epithymia*), which largely corresponds with our coarsest impulses and is the part of the soul through which we experience carnal erotic love, hunger, thirst, and other desires.[31] In essence, the *logistikon* performs the function of a 'lazy controller'[32] since it often controls the instincts and impulses of System 1 or, in Platonic terms, the other two parts of the soul—sometimes successfully, sometimes not. This does not necessarily entail, though, that the *logistikon* always represents a constant of rationality, nor that it is meant to collide with the other two parts; for, at the end of the day, what is sought in Plato's thinking is a harmonical co-existence of the three parts. The platonic picture is rather familiar to all of us: the *logistikon* is viewed as the charioteer and the other two parts of the soul as two horses; as the charioteer is able to command the two horses, the soul is in harmony and justice is attained.[33]

III. Are all behavioral biases bad?

Let me now turn to another critical aspect: some of the phenomena typically labeled as negative by the behavioral approach may often also have a *positive side.* In other words, they may have a positive impact on the individual and society, which, in its turn, may impede a paternalistic intervention.[34]

First and foremost, it is rightly submitted that in the business field an *over-optimistic predisposition (or optimism bias)* can sometimes be very useful and represent a basic factor of success for a businessperson, who because of this predisposition is willing to assume great risks and thereafter to enjoy the fruits of this behavioral 'weakness.'[35] More specifically, it is true that in general *over-optimism* or *over-confidence* may sometimes have severe negative effects on our lives or health (e.g., making us drive recklessly or not quit smoking, thinking

31 Plato, *Republic*, Book IV *passim*, *Phaedrus*, 253c-254e, and *Timaeus*, 69a-72b—see https://en.wikipedia.org/wiki/Plato%27s_tripartite_theory_of_soul; *cf.* also Rebonato, 37 *J.Consum. Policy* (2014), 365.

32 Kahneman, *Thinking, Fast and Slow*, esp. pp. 39 ff.

33 See the references made in fn. 31 above.

34 *Cf.*, indicatively, Englerth, Vom Wert des Rauchens..., p. 241: "... viele der Effekte, welche Behavioral Law and Economics untersucht, ambivalent sind. Sie können positive und negative Konsequenzen haben. Dies ist personen- und kontextabhängig. Selten bergen sie eine *eindeutige* Rechtfertigung für paternalistisches Einschreiten im Hinblick auf das quasi-rational agierende Individuum."

35 So Rachlinski, 85 *Cornell L.Rev.* (2000), 759–760: "In the business setting optimism leads people to undertake the kind of risky, high-yield adventures that a company must endure in order to be successful. In fact, an excess of optimism may be an essential characteristic of a successful businessperson"; see also Englerth, Vom Wert des Rauchens..., p. 240. On *overconfidence bias* or *over-optimism*, see the authors referenced in fn. 104 of Chapter 4 below.

that we are the lucky ones who are going to get away with it). But on the other hand, more often than not, humanity and societies make significant progress, and the lives of people get better, because of the actions or initiatives of individuals who dare to move on when others stop or lose faith, who defy bad signs, who assume more risks than even they may think sensible, and who demonstrate cock-of-the-walk confidence instead of trembling self-doubt; those people are *overly optimistic by nature* (e.g., inventors, explorers, leaders, entrepreneurs).[36] Their behavior, though, may sometimes reach, or even cross, the boundary of the ancient Greek *hybris*,[37] which may be accompanied by greed, arrogance, or hauteur. In all events, it is beyond doubt that optimism is, in principle, a good thing: it drives us forward and gives us motivation, and, as relevant experimental research shows, it makes us live longer and happier (than when we succumb to a pessimistic stance on things); so, apart from its contribution to the general progress of humanity over the millennia, optimism has a clear survival value.[38]

A positive dimension may also be detected in our inherent *loss-aversion* and our tendency to stick with initial *reference points* or *anchors* (see Chapter 2, pp. 27 ff. below); for this rather conservative feature may, for instance, contribute to the observance of our various contractual undertakings (in accordance with the rule *pacta sunt servanda*).[39]

Further, without doubt, our positive behavioral traits such as *fairness* and *reciprocity* do not need to be eliminated or cured, even if they do not help maximize our utility (if narrowly defined as the one-dimensional pursuit of self-interest) and run contrary to the commonly held assumption that individuals are inherently selfish or seek to maximize their utility by any possible means.[40]

36 See also Kahneman, Thinking, Fast and Slow, pp. 255 ff., esp. 256; *cf.* further Alchian, 58 *J.Polit. Econ.* (1950), 213 and 218 ff. *passim*. So, next to the *risk-averse* people there are, on the other hand, those who are, by nature, *risk-seeking* (or *risk-preferring*, *risk-lovers*, such as, apart from the persons mentioned above, gamblers, mountaineers, or race drivers). See also Cooter/Ulen, *Law & Economics*[6], pp. 45–46, and *Posner*, *Economic Analysis of Law*[6], pp. 10–11. In general, on the distinction between *risk-seeking* and *risk-averse* people, see Schäfer/Ott, *Lehrbuch der ökonomischen Analyse des Zivilrechts*[4], pp. 408 ff.; also Haupt, 4 *Ger. Law J.* (2003), 1156.

37 See, indicatively, https://en.wikipedia.org/wiki/Hubris.

38 See Dubner, Here's Why All Your Projects Are Always Late—and What to Do About It (esp. 323 Rebroadcast), wherein further the following words of Tali Sharot, a cognitive neuroscientist at University College London, are quoted: "[Optimism] makes us explore different things. It's related to better health—both physical and mental health—because if you expect positive things, then stress and anxiety is reduced. So that's very good for both physical and mental health. [...] we know that people who are optimists live longer. So we survive more. We're more likely to find a partner. We're more likely to have kids and all of that. So there is a clear survival benefit [...]. However, [...] there are also these negative consequences. If we think everything's going to be OK or better than what we anticipate, we might not take precautionary action. We might [...] smoke when we shouldn't and that kind of thing. So there are the negative aspects to it. But what our research shows is that it's even better than what I just explained because the optimism bias is, in fact, flexible. So it changes in response to the environment. It can disappear under environments in a way that may be optimal."

39 See also Kahneman, *Thinking, Fast and Slow*, p. 305.

40 See also Sunstein, 1 *Am.L.&Econ.Rev.* (1999), 151.

A very illustrative example of our 'irrational' fairness feeling offers the famous ***ultimatum (bargaining) game***: it is reminded that in this game one player, the proposer, is given a sum of money and is tasked with splitting it with another player, the respondent. The proposer communicates a splitting offer; the respondent may accept the offer or reject it. If the respondent accepts, the money is split per the offer; if the respondent rejects, both players receive nothing. It is noted that both players know in advance the consequences of the respondent accepting or rejecting the offer.[41] In many experiments it has been attested that the respondent, in a rather irrational manner, rejects low offers of the proposer, feeling that she was treated unfairly by the proposer and preferring to having them both getting nothing than accepting an 'unfair' offer (*spite effect*).[42]

Furthermore, ***cognitive dissonance***, which is omnipresent in our daily lives, can also be viewed through a positive prism.[43] From an *evolutionary* viewpoint, cognitive dissonance might be counted as one of the mechanisms that help us adjust to the evolving circumstances of reality and that effectively protect us in our battle for survival. In other words, cognitive dissonance represents a mechanism with considerable *survival value*[44]; therefore it may be seen as sometimes having a positive impact on us.

However, caution is still in order here, since cognitive dissonance, as well as other irrational human behaviors, can have devastating effects on our lives. A good illustration of this is *Plato's allegory of the cave*[45]: the ascent of the former prisoner—who has been freed from his bonds—to the real world above offers him the ability to see everything in its real dimensions—that is, perceive reality as it is, see real objects (trees, flowers, houses) and not their mere reflections on

41 See, indicatively here, https://en.wikipedia.org/wiki/Ultimatum_game and the authors referenced in the next fn. 42.

42 In general, on the *ultimatum game* and the important lessons to be drawn therefrom, see Güth/Schmittberger/Schwarze, 3 *J.Econ.Behav.Organ.* (1982), 367 ff., esp. 371 ff.; Güth, 3 *J.Econ. Behav.Organ.* (1995), 329 ff.; Thaler, 2 *J.Econ.Persp.* (1988), 195 ff.; Jolls/Sunstein/Thaler, 50 *Stan.L.Rev.* (1998), 1489 ff.; Kahneman/Knetsch/Thaler, 59 *J.Bus.* (1986), 288 ff.; Sunstein, 1 *Am.L.&Econ.Rev.* (1999), 125 ff.; Thaler, *Misbehaving*..., pp. 140 ff., 266 ff.; Korobkin/Ulen, 88 *Cal.L.R.* (2000), 1135 ff.; Cooter/Ulen, *Law & Economics*[6], pp. 50–51; Georgakopoulos, *Principles and Methods of Law and Economics*..., pp. 51 ff.; Arlen, 52 *Vand.L.Rev.* (1998), 1775–1776, 1785 ff.; Magen, Fairness, Eigennutz und die Rolle des Rechts..., pp. 272 ff., 283 ff.; Englerth, Behavioral Law and Economics..., pp. 70 ff.; Bechtold, *Die Grenzen zwingenden Vertragsrechts*..., pp. 102 ff.

43 For more detail, see Festinger, *A Theory of Cognitive Dissonance*; Rabin, 23 *J.Econ.Behav.Organ.* (1994), 178 ff.; Akerlof/Dickens, 72 *Am.Econ.Rev.* (1982), 307 ff.; Elster, *Ulysses and the Sirens*..., pp. 178–179, who rightly highlights the relative notion of *selective exposure to information* in the context of our more general tendency to *self-deceive*; Ricciardi/Simon, 2 *Bus.Educ.&Tech.J.* (2000), 4–5; DellaVigna, 47 *JEL* (2009), 343–344; Becher, 68 *La.L.Rev.* (2007), 131; Saint-Paul, *The Tyranny of Utility*..., pp. 42–43. See also Eidenmüller, *Effizienz als Rechtsprinzip*[3], *passim*, esp. p. 380; the same, *JZ* (2005), 218; the same, 210 *AcP* (2010), 94; Tscherner, 1 *ALJ* (2014), 154.

44 See www.oxforddictionaries.com/definition/english/survival-value. *Cf.*, more generally, Englerth, Behavioral Law and Economics..., pp. 118 ff.

45 Plato, *Republic*, Book VII, 514a ff.

a wall. The critical point here is Plato's final assumption that, if that freed person were to return to the cave and attempt to explain to his former companions what he had seen in the real world above, he would have great difficulty convincing them *that the reality he encountered was completely different than they thought*; for those companions, suffering from an intense form of cognitive dissonance, would be so profoundly convinced of the accuracy of their own perceptions—seeing the shadows, the reflections on the wall, as *the only existing reality that is perceptible and comprehensible to them*—that they might even put to death the person who tried to free them from the chains of ignorance by dragging them out of the cave into the world above. This allegory effectively sheds light on why, in many cases, it is a proper task of the state to adopt policies that will drag people as far out of the cave of ignorance as possible, that will reduce cognitive dissonance, mainly through proper educational policies, for there is no survival value in ignorance; to the contrary, ignorance diminishes the chances of survival, and at the very least the chances of a decent way of living.[46] In all events, Plato rightly sees in the allegory the fatal repercussions that grave cognitive dissonance can have.[47]

46 The fact that cognitive dissonance may even cost the lives of many people is also shown through the so-called *Our Boys Didn't Die in Vain syndrome*, which has urged many nations in the past to keep on fighting wars that lead to even more pointless sacrifices, simply because people cannot acknowledge the pointless character of the initial losses and base their faith in the just cause *merely on the casualties they have suffered* [in this instance, the *sunk cost fallacy* might also be at work: this fallacy, namely, exists when individuals continue a behavior or endeavor merely because of previously invested resources, such as time, money or effort, without looking at future costs and benefits (as rational choice theory would demand)—on the *sunk cost fallacy*, see, indicatively, Thaler, 1 *J.Econ.Behav.Organ.* (1980), 47 ff., 59, Jolls/Sunstein/Thaler, 50 *Stan.L.Rev.* (1998), 1482–1483, 1490 ff., Becher, 68 *La.L.Rev.* (2007), 125 ff., Korobkin/Ulen, 88 *Cal.L.R.* (2000), 1073–1074, 1124 ff.]. On this fatal syndrome, see Harari, *Homo Deus...*, pp. 349 ff., referring, for instance, to Italy's participation in the First World War with the aim to liberate Trento and Trieste, a participation which, after twelve gory battles lasting more than two years, ended up in a bloodbath for Italy, since by the end of the war almost 700,000 Italian soldiers lost their lives and more than a million were wounded. In this case Harari (*ibidem*, p. 351) rightly discerns the element of cognitive dissonance: "While it's difficult for a politician to tell parents that their son died for no good reason, it is far more painful for parents to say this to themselves—and it is even harder for the victims. A crippled soldier who lost his legs would rather tell himself, 'I sacrificed myself for the glory of the eternal Italian nation!' than 'I lost my legs because I was stupid enough to believe self-serving politicians.'" And Harari goes on to conclude (*ibidem*, p. 353) that "[e]ventually, if we want to come clean about past mistakes, our narrating self must invent some twist in the plot that will infuse these mistakes with meaning."

47 In general, on the close affinity between Plato's thought and behavioral economics as well as his keen interest in various human fallacies and mental errors, see Romeo, *Platonically Irrational*, who aptly identifies such traits in Plato's work: "... many of his insights are remarkably similar to the descriptions of the cognitive biases found by Kahneman and Tversky. [...] Plato not only identified various specific weaknesses in human cognition, he also offered powerful proposals for how to overcome these biases and improve our reasoning and behaviour. [...] Many of Plato's dialogues dramatise the habits and processes that lead humans to false conclusions. He depicts people believing what they want or what they are predisposed to believe (confirmation bias); asserting whatever comes most readily to mind (availability bias); reversing their opinions about

In general, though, a basic objection of those who oppose a BEAL approach, the most prominent of whom is, of course, *Richard Posner*,[48] is that many behavioral biases on which the behavioral analysis relies, such as cognitive dissonance, may be explained mainly through the lens of evolutionary biology, in the sense that such behaviors or practices have been adopted over the long evolutionary process—that is, they are imprinted in humans through evolution to allow us to survive in various circumstances. Thus they have been beneficial to humans and bear, in principle, a 'rational' character.[49] In this respect, characteristically enough, an evolutionary origin has also been ascribed to our *loss-averse behavior*, which, considered in terms of evolutionary success, is supposed to make perfect sense: "*Most animals, including our ancestors [...], lived very close to the margin of survival. Paleontologists who study early human civilizations have uncovered evidence that our ancestors faced frequent periods of drought and freezing. When you are living on the verge of starvation, a slight downturn in your food reserves makes a lot more difference than a slight upturn. [...] Although we may not be living under the same conditions as our Ice Age progenitors, we did inherit our brains from them.*"[50] In a similar vein, a possible evolutionary explanation is given to the 'irrational' behavior of the players in the ultimatum game as well.[51]

---

identical propositions based on the language in which the propositions are presented (framing); refusing to relinquish current opinions simply because these happen to be the opinions they currently possess (a cognitive version of loss aversion) ..." See also fn. 166, Chapter 2, below especially in relation to Plato's concern with the *framing effect.*

48 See esp. Posner, 50 *Stan.L.Rev.* (1998), 1564 ff.

49 This view is also endorsed by Foka-Kavalieraki/Hatzis, 12 *Rev.phil.écon.* (2011), 33 ff.; Rebonato, 37 *J.Consum.Policy* (2014), 392. For the relevant debate, see also Thaler, *Misbehaving...*, pp. 260 ff.; Englerth, Behavioral Law and Economics..., pp. 118 ff.

50 Kenrick/Griskevicius, *The Rational Animal...*, chapter "Loss Aversion in Monkeys and Men." See also Ghisellini/Chang, *Behavioral Economics...*, pp. 110–111.

51 See, instead of others, Harari, *Homo Deus...*, pp. 163–164: "The Ultimatum Game made a significant contribution to undermining classical economic theories and to establishing the most important economic discovery of the last few decades: Sapiens don't behave according to a cold mathematical logic, but rather according to a warm social logic. We are ruled by emotions. These emotions [...] are in fact sophisticated algorithms that reflect the social mechanisms of ancient hunter-gatherer bands. If 30,000 ago I helped you hunt a wild chicken and you then kept almost all the chicken to yourself, offering me just one wing, I did not say to myself: 'Better one wing than nothing at all.' Instead my evolutionary algorithms kicked in, adrenaline and testosterone flooded my system, my voice. In the short term I may have gone hungry, and even risked a punch or two. But it paid off in the long term, because you thought twice before ripping me off again. We refuse unfair offers because people who meekly accepted unfair offers didn't survive in the Stone Age. / Observations of contemporary hunter-gatherer bands support this idea. Most bands are highly egalitarian, and when a hunter comes back to camp carrying a fat deer, everybody gets a share. The same is true of chimpanzees. When one chimp kills a piglet, the other troop members will gather round him with outstretched hands, and usually they all get a piece." Nonetheless, it has to be noted that these contemporary observations do not seem to explain the behavior of the respondent to the offer in the ultimatum game, since they focus on the 'altruistic' behavior of the proposer. However, in the ultimatum game the main focus is on the decisive behavior of the respondent, who actually is the only one who acts 'irrationally' in classical economic terms when she rejects offers under a certain threshold in order to punish the

Still, it is hard to tell and, moreover, to scientifically prove that some of our behavioral biases or weaknesses can indeed be explained *in evolutionary terms.*[52] It has been suggested that evolutionary biology may explain *why and how* some types of 'rational' human behavior emerged and evolved through time; today, however, some of those same behavioral patterns might not be considered 'rational.' For example, when you are alone reading a book and your partner taps you on the shoulder to offer you a cup of coffee, you jump up from the chair, startled by their touch. This reaction would have been 'rational' when humans lived in the jungle surrounded by animals, but not today after thousands of years, when we live in houses and are protected from wild animals lurking in bushes.[53] Consequently, it seems rather problematic to attempt to present as 'rational,' on the basis of the assumptions of evolutionary biology, some of the

---

proposer; for she should accept even a dollar ('*a penny is better than nothing*') and not succumb to the spite effect by punishing the proposer and thus losing a dollar—see Posner, 50 *Stan.L.Rev.* (1998), 1564 (who eloquently points out that "[t]he offer of the penny should signal to the respondent the proposer's belief that the respondent holds a low supposal of his own worth, that he is grateful for scraps, that he accepts being ill-used, that he has no pride, no sense of honor"), the same, 9 *J.Leg.Stud.* (1980), 71 ff., Jolls/Sunstein/Thaler, 50 *Stan.L.Rev.* (1998), 1493 ff., and Sunstein, 1 *Am.L.&Econ.Rev.* (1999), 122, 125 ff., esp. 128. On the other hand, the proposer who adjusts her behavior to the possible acceptance threshold of the respondent [*"anticipated spite"*; see once again Sunstein, 1 *Am.L.&Econ.Rev.* (1999), 125 ff., esp. 126)] acts 'rationally,' since she seeks the acceptance of the offer so that she will be able to keep the rest of the available money for herself—see Korobkin/Ulen, 88 *Cal.L.R.* (2000), 1135–1136, and *Magen*, Fairness, Eigennutz und die Rolle des Rechts..., pp. 283–284. By contrast, in the so-called *dictator game* the 'irrational' behavior is limited to the first player—that is, the player who donates an amount of money—since her counterparty is not able to reject the former's decision to offer her a certain portion of the money and thus is no position to interact—see Englerth, Verhaltensökonomie..., p. 175, DellaVigna, 47 *JEL* (2009), 336, and Gächter, Human Prosocial Motivation..., p. 32. Furthermore, on the suggestion that, also in the context of negotiations, fairness and reciprocity assumptions may gain the upper hand by virtue of the driving force of *Aristotelian truth* and the intersubjective validation of the claims raised during the negotiations, both of which may prevail over the immediate (selfish) interests of the negotiating parties, see Arvanitis/Karampatzos, 24 *Philos.Psychol.* (2011), 845 ff.; in the same direction *cf.* also the same, 26 *Philos.Psychol.* (2013), 89 ff.

52 *Cf.* Thaler, *Misbehaving...*, p. 261; also Schmolke, *Grenzen der Selbstbindung...*, p. 209 (: "Solche Reparaturversuche des Rationalwahlmodells vermögen indes nicht zu überzeugen"). *Cf.*, once again, though, the anthropologist viewpoint of Harari, *Homo Deus...*, pp. 91 ff. *passim*, esp. 94: "Why do modern humans love sweets so much? Not because in the early twenty-first century we must gorge on ice cream and chocolate in order to survive. Rather, it is because when our Stone Age ancestors came across sweet fruit or honey, the most sensible thing to do was to eat as much of it as quickly as possible. Why do young men drive recklessly, get involved in violent arguments and hack confidential Internet sites? Because they are following ancient genetic decrees that might be useless and even counterproductive today, but that made good evolutionary sense 70,000 years ago. A young hunter who risked his life chasing a mammoth outshone all his competitors and won the hand of the local beauty; and we are now stuck with his macho genes."

53 See Farber, 68 *U.Chi.L.Rev.* (2001), 294–295; Schmolke, *Grenzen der Selbstbindung...*, p. 209; Eidenmüller, *JZ* (2005), 220.

behavioral biases or weaknesses identified by virtue of the empirical and experimental research of behavioral economics.[54]

In all cases, one thing should be made clear: many of the behavioral phenomena that have been recognized and widely used by behavioral economics and BEAL *may allow for a double (or even multiple) reading*; that is, they may have both negative and positive repercussions for individual and societal welfare. The position of the pendulum will be determined each time by the person or the situation affected by the behavioral bias or weakness, while at the same time the existence of a behavioral bias or weakness will rarely justify *beyond any doubt* the need for paternalistic interference.[55]

At the end of the day, the decision to proceed or not to a regulatory intervention will ultimately hinge on the predisposition of the regulator—that is, usually the legislator—against private autonomy and the assumption of risks by the individuals. That is, if she deems it appropriate to protect *urbi et orbi* the citizens from their inability to discern the existence of some risks, obvious or not, then it is almost certain that she will interfere easily and without giving it a second thought. If, on the other hand, she is imbued with the spirit that the legal order must accord to the citizens as much individual freedom as possible, while at the same time accepting the price of an eventual failure (along with its further individual and social repercussions), then she will generally be hesitant to adopt paternalistic interventions and refrain, in principle, from doing so.[56] However, this crucial decision is not related to assessments that fall within the realm of BEAL, as strictly defined, but is dependent on the *fundamental evaluations and considerations* of each legal system, which are regularly entrenched in their constitutional charters (even in only a rudimentary way).[57] I hereby primarily refer to the basic concepts adopted with respect to private autonomy, a person's well-being, and the general welfare promotion. Such concepts guide the more specific value judgments that have to be made by legislative, judicial, or administrative bodies (e.g., whether increasing organ donations or protecting animal rights are goals that should be pursued, and so forth).[58] Of course, that's not the end of the story; however, the full coverage of the fundamental evaluations and considerations that permeate each legal system would surely require far more pages than this book can contain.

54 See Eidenmüller, *JZ* 2005, 217, 220; Farber, 68 *U.Chi.L.Rev.* (2001), 294–295, who characterizes the relevant argumentation of R.Posner as a "*pretty desperate defense*"; Schmolke, *Grenzen der Selbstbindung*..., p. 209; *cf.* further Korobkin/Ulen, 88 *Cal.L.R.* (2000), 1055.

55 See Englerth, Vom Wert des Rauchens..., pp. 241 ff. *passim*, esp. 241 (: "... Dies ist personen- und kontextabhängig"); *cf.* also Bar-Gill, 92 *Minn.L.Rev.* (2008), 749.

56 So, once again, Englerth, Vom Wert des Rauchens..., p. 241.

57 See also Englerth, Vom Wert des Rauchens..., pp. 241, 253, 256.

58 *Cf.* Lichtenberg, Paternalism, Manipulation, Freedom, and the Good, p. 497: "... the clear implication of behavioral economics and psychology (not to mention philosophy) is that we cannot avoid making value judgments. [...] we have no alternative but to shape choice environments in accordance with some values or other. [...] / From the recognition that we need a conception of a person's good it is not much of a step to the conclusion that we need a conception of the general good."

IV. Undermining the learning effect or experience through state interference: a moral hazard issue

Notwithstanding the above, in a liberal society the state should, in principle, refrain—as much as possible—from interfering with people's individual decisions or choices. For extended state interference with individual choices creates a significant *moral hazard*, that is, it may deprive people of the positive effects of the so-called *learning effect or experience*—that is, our ability to learn from our mistakes and not repeat them in the future.[59] In particular, not allowing free choice or preventing mistakes may lead to "infantilisation, and learning effects are an important means of progress (individually as well as for societies)."[60] An extended state interference can cause people to live in a state of constant state protection or custody, in which personal autonomy is gradually given away.[61] This is the 'nanny-state concern,' and it is the most prominent argument of those who generally oppose paternalism and regulation. It speaks to the great practical importance of each individual's *freedom* to err. The *assumption of individual responsibility* for our own actions is key to our development and to our interactions with other people.[62]

This deontological aspect of the learning experience goes back to the philosophy of the Enlightenment, and more specifically to the great Immanuel Kant; it is premised on the idea that freedom and autonomy do not come without *individual responsibility* for the consequences of one's actions and decisions.[63] The idea that liberty and responsibility are woven inextricably together may also be encountered in the work of Friedrich Hayek, where it is related to the learning experience; thus, according to Hayek too, the individual must bear the

59 See Eidenmüller, Widerrufsrechte, p. 128 (: "„Aus Fehlern lernt man" bzw. „Aus Schaden wird man klug", sagt der Volksmund zu Recht."); the same, *Effizienz als Rechtsprinzip*[3], pp. 331–332, 384–385; Schmolke, *Grenzen der Selbstbindung...*, pp. 164–165, 244–245, 822 ff.; Wright/Ginsburg, 106 *Nw.U.L.R.* (2012), 1070 ff.; Sunstein, 122 *Yale L.J.* (2013), 1869–1870; Conlisk, 34 *JEL* (1996), 683–684; Cherednychenko, 10 *ERCL* (2014), 419; Rekaiti/van den Bergh, 23 *J.Consum.Policy* (2000), 377. *Cf.* further the Popperian approach on *trial and error*: Popper, *The Poverty of Historicism*, *passim*, esp. pp. 52, 58 ff., 80 ff. (where *inter alia*, p. 80: "... we make progress if, and only if, we are prepared to *learn from our mistakes*").

60 van Aaken, Judge the Nudge..., p. 91—see also *ibidem*, p. 95.

61 See, mainly, Wright/Ginsburg, 106 *Nw.U.L.R.* (2012), 1070 ff.; Klick/Mitchell, 90 *Minn.L.Rev.* (2006), 1626, 1635 ff.; Glaeser, 29 *Regulation* (2006), 33 ff.; more recently, Ghisellini/Chang, *Behavioral Economics...*, p. 213.

62 See, once again, Wright/Ginsburg, 106 *Nw.U.L.R.* (2012), 1072, wherein *inter alia*: "If individuals are to realize their full potential as participants in the political and economic life of society, then *they must be free to err in large ways as well as small*" (emphasis added). Precisely this freedom to err is vividly expressed in Huxley's *Brave New World*, p. 163, by the Savage, when he breaks the chains of protectivism and renounces the totalitarian state and the 'convenient' default options that the latter has predecided for its subjects: "*But I don't want comfort. I want God, I want poetry, I want real danger, I want freedom, I want goodness. I want sin. [...] I'm claiming the right to be unhappy.*"

63 See Kant, Beantwortung der Frage: Was ist Aufklärung?, pp. 53–54; also Flume, *AT des BürgR—Das Rechtsgeschäft*[4], pp. 59 ff., and Reuter, 189 *AcP* (1989), 220.

consequences of their own choices.[64] In a similar vein, Amartya Sen relates freedom of choice to our moral obligation to assume responsibility for our actions.[65] In a nutshell, it is important to realize that freedom always comes at a price. A liberal society cannot but consciously accept the cost of a vital source of creativity and both individual and social progress, that is, the price of freedom.

Here, however, we have reached a point where a significant reservation is due: even if our capacity for autonomous rationalization through learning experiences exists in principle, it does not seem to be present all the time.[66] Apparently, this ability depends chiefly on the specific capacity of each transacting party. Natural and legal persons may go separate ways. More specifically:

On the one hand, companies do indeed draw lessons from markets and competition based on previous mistaken or irrational entrepreneurial decisions. They sometimes even go bankrupt. Thus they succumb to the powerful evolutionary rule of the *survival of the fittest*, in the sense that the fight for survival tends to drive away from the market companies that fail to adjust their behavior on the basis of lessons learned from past mistakes, to act rationally, and to obey the demand for profit maximization. Nonetheless, even this view has been challenged by prominent economists.[67] It has been suggested, *inter alia*, that for such a process to develop a state of *perfect competition* is, in principle, assumed. In practice, though, perfect competition is a rare phenomenon. Practical experience shows that irrational entrepreneurial decisions do not necessarily lead to bankruptcy, at least in the short run and by themselves.[68] Though, as reasonable as these objections might be, I believe that it cannot be questioned that the model of rational choice properly captures the economic activity of companies, which normally do indeed function as rational maximizers of their utility.[69]

64 Hayek, *The Constitution of Liberty*..., pp. 82, 133 (: "... Liberty and responsibility are inseparable"), 139. See also Saint-Paul, *The Tyranny of Utility*..., *passim*, esp. pp. 8 ff. (who concludes that "[f]reedom without responsibility is extortion"—*ibidem*, p. 10), 115 ff.

65 Sen, *The Idea of Justice*, *passim*. *Cf.* also Buchanan, 124 *Public Choice* (2005), esp. 23 ff.; Dworkin, 7 *Midwest Stud.Philos.* (1982), 51.

66 See Fleischer/Schmolke/Zimmer, Verhaltensökonomik als Forschungsinstrument..., p. 39: "Heute kann wohl als sicher gelten, dass Marktkräfte die beobachteten Verhaltensanomalien nicht gänzlich beseitigen. Zwar können Erfahrung und Lernverhalten anomales Entscheidungsverhalten verringern. Jedoch folgt auf bestimmte Entscheidungen nur selten oder aber uneindeutiges *feedback*, so dass Lernerfolge ausbleiben"; also Schmolke, *Grenzen der Selbstbindung*..., p. 207: "Die von vorneherein wenig realistische Annahme, dass sämtliche Anomalien durch Lerneffekte tatsächlich neutralisiert werden könnten, kann [...] als widerlegt gelten" (further, *ibidem*, pp. 822 ff.); Englerth, Behavioral Law and Economics..., p. 119: "Es wäre [...] unrealistisch anzunehmen, dass sämtliche Anomalien durch Lerneffekte de facto eingeebnet werden."

67 For a critical approach on this view, see the classic paper by Winter, 4 *Yale Econ.Essays* (1964), 225 ff.; also Elster, *Ulysses and the Sirens*..., pp. 135 ff.

68 See Korobkin/Ulen, 88 *Cal.L.R.* (2000), 1070; Conlisk, 34 *JEL* (1996), 684; Englerth, Behavioral Law and Economics..., p. 118; Schmolke, *Grenzen der Selbstbindung*..., p. 208.

69 See also, indicatively, Fleischer/Schmolke/Zimmer, Verhaltensökonomik als Forschungsinstrument..., p. 44.

But what about natural persons and especially consumers? Their decisions are much different; for the aforementioned argument relating to mistaken entrepreneurial decisions and mechanisms of market punishment cannot be automatically transferred to the activity of natural persons. In particular, individuals daily make a plethora of transactional and other decisions that have a (large or small) impact on their lives, health, bodily integrity, freedom, or property. And they may systematically repeat the same mistakes, without being put off or deterred by them, simply accepting that those mistakes will lead to a lower quality of life or consumption.[70] Individuals are notoriously bad at learning about or from the biases affecting their behavior—especially when the stakes are low, which is the case, though, in most consumer transactions. In other words, unlike companies, individuals, who indeed often act irrationally, will continue to make bad or 'unfortunate' decisions. Despite doing so, they may still remain active in the transaction realm, with some of them leading less happy lives or adjusting to poorer conditions than individuals who usually think and act rationally.[71]

The possible impact and extent of the learning effect is dependent upon the frequency with which individuals, especially in their capacity as consumers, use a good or service, in conjunction with the frequency with which they experience unfortunate incidents therefrom. For instance, an individual's frequent use of certain consumer goods renders her a *repeat player*, who increasingly risks exposure to the goods' defects; thus she might be able to enrich her own learning experience and avoid repurchasing goods that have proven defective. Under this scenario, consumers may indeed learn over time and become savvier. In contrast, for example, taking out a mortgage loan is a transaction that an individual engages in only once or twice in a lifetime. For *one-shotters* in the mortgage lending world, the learning experience will have hardly any impact.[72] In other words, few people buy enough houses for learning to be effective, in the terms described above. And more generally, transactions with high stakes are infrequent enough to have little learning—although it might be true that consumers use costly mental effort to increase their computing accuracy (e.g., with respect to opaque prices) when the stakes increase.[73]

In the same vein, a learning experience will be valuable to an individual only if the consequences of an unfortunate transactional decision are not devastating to

70 See Eidenmüller, *JZ* (2005), 220, and Schmolke, *Grenzen der Selbstbindung*..., p. 208. Characteristic of the often limited impact of a previous negative experience on our present behavior is an old saying about one's second marriage, which is attributed to Samuel Johnson, according to which the second marriage represents "*the triumph of hope over experience*"*(!)*; see Thaler/Sunstein, *Nudge*..., p. 32, and Kahneman, *Thinking, Fast and Slow*, p. 256.

71 In more detail, see Korobkin/Ulen, 88 *Cal.L.R.* (2000), 1070 ff.; also Conlisk, 34 *JEL* (1996), 684; further Russell/Thaler, 75 *Am.Econ.Rev.* (1985), 1074.

72 See Bar-Gill, 92 *Minn.L.Rev.* (2008), 755–756, and Seduction by Contract, pp. 26 ff.; also Schmolke, *Grenzen der Selbstbindung*..., pp. 164–165, 244, 823 ff.; Möslein, *Dispositives Recht*..., p. 325; Cserne, *Freedom of Contract*..., p. 53; the same, Making Sense of Nudge-Scepticism..., p. 292; Tversky/Kahneman, Rational Choice and the Framing of Decisions, p. 222.

73 *Cf.* Morrison/Taubinksy, *NBER Working Paper No. 26180* (August 2019).

that individual for if the individual's life is destroyed by an irrational transactional or other decision, she will not be able to repeat the disastrous transaction (or decision) in the future. Consider an overly optimistic borrower. Her optimistic predisposition causes her to borrow more than she can afford, which leads her into a financial catastrophe. She learns a lesson, but can she apply this valuable lesson to future decision-making? If the damage to her livelihood is too great, the overly optimistic borrower might not have a second chance to apply the learning.[74] In such a case there is no learning effect, and the lesson is of no value to the individual.[75]

All in all, for an unfortunate experience to have a beneficial impact on an individual and thus be capable of teaching and functioning as a debiasing

74 More generally, on the five main types of consumers' financial ignorance (i.e., ignorance of financial concepts; ignorance of contract terms; ignorance of financial history; ignorance of self; and ignorance of incentives, strategy, and equilibrium), which lead them to make (repeated) financial mistakes, and in particular on the widely acknowledged, and very concerning, problem of consumers' 'financial illiteracy'—that is, their lack of understanding of even the most basic concepts needed to solve a financial choice problem—see Campbell, 106 *Am.Econ.Rev.* (2016), 10 ff., who further points out that "[l]ow financial literacy scores are associated with low income, wealth, and education, implying that financial illiteracy — like suboptimal investment behavior — is a particular problem among people with low socioeconomic status" and that "a complex financial system particularly disadvantages poorer people and contributes to wealth inequality" (*ibidem*, p. 12). It is also an equally alarming finding, falling under the category of 'ignorance of contract terms,' that mortgage borrowers with adjustable-rate mortgages (ARM) underestimate the extent to which their mortgage rate can change (*ibidem*, p. 12—see also 22 ff.). The above findings become more troubling if we also take into account that at the same time consumers usually express high confidence in their financial knowledge (*ibidem*, p. 13). Especially, on the failure of the U.S. subprime mortgage market in 2008 and the two critical design features that the subprime mortgage contracts exhibit—that is, complexity and cost deferral—*cf.*, extensively, Bar-Gill, *Seduction by Contract...*, pp. 116 ff. Further, on the crucial behavioral biases that affect potential borrowers and the specific countervailing tools that may be used against them in a conceptual framework for 'behaviorally informed financial regulation' (e.g., full information disclosure to debias borrowers, ex post standards-based truth in lending, restructuring mortgage brokers' duties to borrowers, and reform of compensation schemes that provide incentives to brokers to mislead borrowers), *cf.* Barr/Mullainathan/Shafir, Behaviorally Informed Regulation, pp. 440 ff., 447 ff.; also Ghisellini/Chang, *Behavioral Economics...*, pp. 77 ff.

75 In the same direction, see Eidenmüller, Widerrufsrechte, pp. 128, 144, and *Effizienz als Rechtsprinzip*[3], pp. 331, 384–385; also Englerth, Vom Wert des Rauchens..., p. 251 (: "In vielen Fällen [...] wird Adaption nicht möglich sein, da die Individuen keine Wiederholungsmöglichkeit haben"); Schmolke, *Grenzen der Selbstbindung...*, pp. 165, 244; Bar-Gill, Consumer Transactions, p. 471; Thaler/Sunstein, *Nudge...*, pp. 74–75, 241; Cserne, *Freedom of Contract...*, p. 53. It is no accident that the validity of the aforementioned assumptions is also recognized by scholars who were initially rather sceptical of the approach of behavioral economics, such as Arlen, 52 *Vand.L.Rev.* (1998), 1783, who, especially in relation to the phenomenon of *over-optimistic predisposition*, rightly points out that, insofar as an individual does not often repeat a certain choice, the learning experience does not have, in principle, any value: "Many important decisions—such as the decision whether to undergo a particular medical procedure, or purchase a product with a risk of fatality, or commit a crime—*do not occur in situations where the individual decision maker is a repeat player who will have the opportunity to learn from her mistakes.* [...] Thus the decision maker *does not learn* ..." (emphasis added).

instrument,[76] some basic pre-conditions must be met: (a) the individual must have repeated chances to exercise a choice (if the choice is rare or the decision is made once in a lifetime, then there will be no beneficial learning effect), (b) there should be low reflection costs each time the choice is repeated, (c) the individual must have access to ***good feedback*** after an unfortunate or mistaken choice, and (d) there must be no material change in the circumstances of decision-making after each repetition.[77]

The above suggestions on the limits and dangers of paternalistic interventions already convey the flavor of what follows: namely, we are going to examine some special regulatory means of interference and, above all, test their efficiency and compatibility with individual autonomy.

76 *Cf.* van Aaken, Judge the Nudge..., p. 95, wherein it is also concluded that "[f]rom an autonomy point of view, enabling learning is crucial. It is hard to justify a state keeping its citizens in the 'fast thinking' mode in cases where a 'slow thinking' mode can be initiated."

77 Conlisk, 34 *JEL* (1996), 683; Tversky/Kahneman, Rational Choice and the Framing of Decisions, p. 222. See also DellaVigna, 47 *JEL* (2009), 365; Schmolke, *Grenzen der Selbstbindung...*, p. 207.

2 Sunstein and Thaler's nudge theory, the steering of people's behavior by means of default or opt-out rules, and the promotion of a 'mild' or 'libertarian' paternalism

I. Introductory remarks

Cass Sunstein and Richard Thaler (the 2017 Nobel laureate in economics) offer a characteristic BEAL approach, which justifies various ways of state interference. They are the founders of a new theory of public policy (or public decision-making)—namely, the famous '*nudge theory*.'[1] Their main line of reasoning is that people can be induced to make proper or right decisions through sector-specific, carefully designed state interventions, which fall under the umbrella term '*nudges*.'[2] Nudges lead to individually and collectively beneficial decisions and thus they promote both individual and societal welfare. Such interventions usually take the form of *default options or rules (ius dispositivum)*. The latter generally have a crucial steering function.[3] As a matter of fact,

1 On the basis, initially, of their much-acclaimed book *Nudge*.... See also, indicatively, Sunstein/Thaler, 70 *U.Chi.L.Rev.* (2003), 1159 ff.; Sunstein, *Nudging and Choice Architecture*..., pp. 1 ff.; the same, *Nudging: A Very Short Guide*, pp. 1 ff.; Schlag, 108 *Mich.L.Rev.* (2010), 913 ff.; Neumann, *Libertärer Paternalismus*..., *passim*.

2 For the precise meaning of the term, see Thaler/Sunstein, *Nudge*..., esp. pp. 4, 6, 8, 65; Sunstein, *Nudging and Choice Architecture*..., pp. 7 ff.; the same, *Nudging: A Very Short Guide*, pp. 1 ff.; the same, 127 *Harv.L.R. Forum* (2014), 210 ff.; the same, *Misconceptions about Nudges*. Sunstein/Reisch, 53 *Intereconomics* (2018), *Thaler*, 108 *Am.Econ.Rev.* (2018), 1280 ff.; Benartzi/Beshears/Milkman/Sunstein/Thaler/Shankar/Tucker-Ray/Congdon/Galing, 28 *Psychol.Sci.* (2017), 1041 ff.; Congdon, Phychology and Economic Policy, pp. 466–467; see also Ghisellini/Chang, *Behavioral Economics*..., pp. 201 ff.; Cartwright, *Behavioral Economics*[2], pp. 519 ff.; Mols/Haslam/Jetten/Steffens, 54 *EJPR* (2015), 81 ff., esp. 83 ff.; Hacker, 2 *ERPL* (2016), 299 ff. *passim*; Szaszi/Palinkas/Palfi/Szollosi/Aczel, 31 *J.Behav.Dec.Making* (2018), 355 ff.; Tomer, *Advanced Introduction to Behavioral Economics*, pp. 82 ff.

3 See also, indicatively, Willis, 80 *U.Chi.L.Rev.* (2013), 1157, pointing out that: "... intestacy rules that can be overridden by a will, marital property rules that can be overridden by a prenuptial agreement, and gap-filling contract rules that can be overridden by explicit contract language are common examples. But these have largely been put in place because the law needs *some* rule when the parties have not specified otherwise, rather than with an explicit purpose to alter the ultimate position of the parties" (emphasis in the original).

default rules constitute the "mother of all nudges"[4] and they are ubiquitous in the law.[5] Especially in private law, they represent a very common regulatory technique.

The basic claim of Sunstein and Thaler is that nudges steer people in certain directions, while maximally preserving people's freedom of choice. This is in contrast with ***mandates (ius cogens)***, which entail open but transparent coercion. The overriding goal of nudging is to increase the likelihood that people's free choices will improve their welfare and thus to tightly link freedom of choice with well-being. And this comes at relatively little cost, because, in terms of policy making, changing the default is relatively cheap to do.[6]

Through mild state or private interventions, employees may, for instance, be encouraged to save more money in order to ensure for themselves a decent pension in the future: in particular, an employer may offer its employees an additional pension plan (a "retirement savings plan"), which is to be funded through the automatic extraction of a certain percentage (e.g., 5%) from the employees' wage, insofar as the employees do not object to this automatic extraction—thus automatic enrollment of the employees in the retirement savings plan is the ***default option***. If, however, the employees do not wish to be automatically enrolled in this program, they may elect to opt out of it and choose another pension program, or simply follow the path of saving money on their own.[7]

Even a dramatic increase in the organ donation percentage—a very desirable goal, which mainly serves the interests of people in need of a transplant[8]—may be achieved if the regulator imposes an ***opt-out system (presumed-consent***

4 Schlag, 108 *Mich.L.Rev.* (2010), 915: "... this kind of nudge is the mother of all nudges – the default rule. Picking smart default rules is a key way of nudging people." *Cf.* also Johnson/Goldstein, Decisions by Default, pp. 417 ff.

5 See also Möslein, *Dispositives Recht...*, p. 482; Cziupka, *Dispositives Vertragsrecht...*, pp. 486 ff.; Eidenmüller, *JZ* (2005), 217, 220; *cf.* further Engel, *JZ* (1995), 215–216.

6 See Cartwright, *Behavioral Economics*², p. 524.

7 Relevant surveys in the United States reveal that the introduction of such an opt-out system does indeed considerably increase participation rates in retirement plans, although the possibility of opting out is associated with very low transaction costs. See Sunstein/Thaler, 70 *U.Chi.L.Rev.* (2003), 1159 ff., 1172 ff., 1190–1191; the same, *Nudge...*, pp. 103 ff.; Benartzi/Peleg/Thaler, *Choice Architecture and Retirement Saving Plans*, pp. 245 ff., esp. 247 ff.; Congdon, *ibidem*, pp. 465 ff. *passim*; Camerer/Issacharoff/Loewenstein/O'Donoghue/Rabin, 151 *U.Penn.L.R.* (2003), 1227 ff.; DellaVigna, 47 *JEL* (2009), 322 ff.

8 See, indicatively, Sunstein/Thaler, 70 *U.Chi.L.Rev.* (2003), 1192–1193; Sunstein, 64 *Duke L.J.* (2014), 26, 42–43; the same, 162 *U.Penn.L.R.* (2013), 35–36; Chouhan/Draper, 29 *J.Med. Ethics* (2003), 157 ff.; Siegal/Bonnie, 34 *J.L.Med.&Ethics* (2006), 415 ff.; Cooter/Ulen, *Law & Economics*⁶, p. 163. See also recital 1 of the Preamble to Directive 2010/53/EU (initially 2010/45/EE) of the European Parliament and of the Council of 07.07.2010 on standards of quality and safety of human organs intended for transplantation (O.J. L 207): "Over the past 50 years organ transplantation has become an established worldwide practice, bringing immense benefits to hundreds of thousands of patients. The use of human organs (hereinafter 'organs') for transplantation has steadily increased during the last two decades. Organ transplantation is now the most cost-effective treatment for end-stage renal failure, while for end-stage failure of organs such as the liver, lung and heart it is the only available treatment."

system) instead of an *opt-in system (explicit-consent system)*; in an opt-out system every person is presumed to be an organ donor unless she explicitly opts out. The presumption here is that the individual consents to organ donation.[9] In general, under an opt-out system the addressee of the statutory regime can be freed from it if she chooses to opt out, whereas under an opt-in system the statutory regime is activated only if the addressee explicitly opts in.[10] In practice, especially in the field of organ donation, it has been proven that shifting from an opt-in system to an opt-out system may indeed have impressive results[11]: in particular, in countries where the opt-out system has been adopted, more than 90% of the population are organ donors (e.g., in Austria it is close to 100%), whereas in countries with an opt-in system fewer than 20% are organ donors (e.g., Germany and the United States).[12] It is no coincidence that from spring 2020 the UK is also going to adopt an opt-out system due to shortage of donors.[13] For the same reasons, there is nowadays in Germany a wide public debate over whether it would be appropriate to switch from the opt-in to an

9 See Thaler/Sunstein, *Nudge*..., pp. 175 ff.; the same, 70 *U.Chi.L.Rev.* (2003), 1191 ff.; Sunstein, 73 *U.Chi.L.Rev.* (2006), 264–265; the same, 162 *U.Penn.L.R.* (2013), 4; Johnson/Goldstein, 302 *Science* (2003), 1338 ff.; the same, 78 *Transplantation* (2004), 1713 ff.; the same, Decisions by Default, pp. 417 ff.; Siegal/Bonnie, 34 *J.L. Med. & Ethics* (2006), 415 ff.; Chouhan/Draper, 29 J. Med. Ethics (2003), 157 ff.; Ulen, The Importance of Behavioral Law, pp. 98 ff. *Cf.* also recital 21 of the Preamble to the Directive 2010/53/EU (Directive 2010/53/EU (initially 2010/45/EE) of the European Parliament and of the Council of 07.07.2010 on standards of quality and safety of human organs intended for transplantation (O.J. L 207): "Several models of consent to donation coexist in the Union, including opting-in systems in which consent to organ donation has to be explicitly obtained, and opting-out systems in which donation can take place unless there is evidence of any objection to donation. In order to enable individuals to express their wishes in this regard, some Member States have developed specific registries where citizens record them. This Directive is without prejudice to the broad diversity of the systems of consent already in place in the Member States. In addition, by means of its Action plan on Organ Donation and Transplantation the Commission aims to increase public awareness of organ donation and in particular to develop mechanisms to facilitate the identification of organ donors across Europe."

10 For detail on this distinction, see Bachmann, *JZ* (2008), 14 ff.; Bechtold, *Die Grenzen zwingenden Vertragsrechts*..., pp. 120 ff., 225 ff.; Ringe, 213 *AcP* (2013), 102 ff.; Kähler, *Begriff und Rechtfertigung*..., pp. 42 ff., esp. 50 ff.; Kirchgässner, *Homo Oeconomicus*[4], pp. 279–280.

11 See, indicatively, Johnson/Goldstein, 78 *Transplantation* (2004), 1713 ff. *Cf.* also the more general observation of DellaVigna, 47 *JEL* (2009), 322: "... the findings of large default effects is one of the most robust results in the applied economic literature of the last ten years."

12 See Johnson/Goldstein, 302 *Science* (2003), 1338–1339; Sunstein/Thaler, 70 *U.Chi.L.Rev.* (2003), 1191–1192; Sunstein, 73 *U.Chi.L.Rev.* (2006), 264–265; Thaler, *Misbehaving*..., pp. 327–328; Lichtenberg, Paternalism, Manipulation, Freedom, and the Good, p. 496; Siegal/Bonnie, 34 *J.L. Med. & Ethics* (2006), 419; Cooter/Ulen, *Law & Economics*[6], p. 163; van Aaken, Begrenzte Rationalität..., p. 127; Altmann/Falk/Marklein, Eingeschränkt rationales Verhalten..., p. 81; Neumann, *Libertärer Paternalismus*..., pp. 43–44; Tscherner, 1 *ALJ* (2014), 147–148. *Cf.* further, though, Becker/Elias, Cash for Kidneys..., who express their doubts about the practical effectiveness of such a twist in the default rule.

13 See www.organdonation.nhs.uk/helping-you-to-decide/about-organ-donation/faq/what-is-opt-out/.

opt-out system, or even adopt other solutions—such as the ***mandated-choice model***, which is going to be discussed in the next chapters of this book.[14]

It is rather evident that in general the legislative choice between an opt-out and opt-in system is a crucial one.[15] The practical implications of each regulatory path are non-negligible, as the regulation of organ donation clearly manifests. In a nutshell: predesigned "menus matter"[16]—sometimes a lot. It is noteworthy, though, than in practice both systems may sometimes co-exist and mingle with each other: if, for instance, in a legal system, such as the Greek one, the default rule for assets acquired during the marriage is separate ownership, a couple's decision to *opt in* the alternative system of joint ownership will at the same time mean *opting-out* of the default system of separate ownership.

Sunstein and Thaler propose a 'choice architecture' scheme based primarily on the introduction of default rules or options.[17] The scheme emblematizes an initial, desired, welfare-promoting frame of choice; the individual may choose to opt out of it.[18] The basis of this proposal is the fundamental assumption that very often we are bound by default rules mainly owing to inertia, laziness, idleness, procrastination, distraction, limited time, or further, *ignorance of the very existence of such rules.* More particularly, despite the fact that we enjoy having choices, and thus they are a basic ingredient of well-being, in many situations we find it more convenient not to make a decision than to carefully reflect on the optimal choice (*a preference for inaction over action*), which would remove us from our comfort zone and would demand from us an *effort tax* (or *effort cost*).[19]

14 See, indicatively, www.bundesgesundheitsministerium.de/fileadmin/Dateien/3_Downloads/O/Organspende/Gesetzentwurf_zur_Sta__rkung_der_Entscheidungsbereitschaft_bei_der_Organspende.pdf.

15 See also Kähler, *Begriff und Rechtfertigung*..., pp. 50–51.

16 *Cf.* Ayres, 73 *U.Chi.L.Rev.* (2006), 3; Fleischer, 76 *RabelsZ* (2012), 239.

17 See Thaler/Sunstein, *Nudge*..., *passim*, esp. pp. 2 ff., 81 ff. and 252–253, who underline the fact that the mission of the 'choice architect' is to determine the framework within which people make their choices, while also clarifying, and rightly so, in principle, that there can be no axiologically neutral design (or ordering) of this choice framework; Thaler, 108 *Am.Econ.Rev.* (2018), 1283 ff., esp. 1283: "Choice architecture is the environment in which people make decisions. Anyone who constructs that environment is a choice architect. Menus are the choice architecture of restaurants, and the user interface is the choice architecture of smart phones..."; Sunstein, *Nudging and Choice Architecture*..., pp. 4 ff.; Thaler/Sunstein/Balz, Choice Architecture, pp. 428 ff.; Benartzi/Peleg/Thaler, *Choice Architecture and Retirement Saving Plans*, pp. 245 ff.; *cf.* also Bubb/Pildes, 127 *Harv.L.R.* (2014), 1596 ff., *passim*; Schlag, 108 *Mich.L.Rev.* (2010), 915 ff.; further Ringe, 213 *AcP* (2013), 98 ff.

18 See, indicatively, Sunstein, Introduction, p. 2. For more detail on the general importance of the framework within which decisions are made that entail legal effects, see Kelman/Rottenstreich/Tversky, Context-Dependence..., pp. 61 ff., esp. 71 ff., as well as later on in the text with respect to the so-called *framing effect.*

19 See Sunstein/Thaler, 70 *U.Chi.L.Rev.* (2003), 1172 ff., 1180 ff., esp. 1181, 1193 and 1198–1199; Thaler/Sunstein, *Nudge*..., *passim*, esp. pp. 7–8, 43, 83 ff., 109, 229; Thaler/Sunstein/Balz, Choice Architecture, p. 430; Sunstein, 162 *U.Penn.L.R.* (2013), 1 ff., esp. 17 ff., 38, 41, 43; the same, 64 *Duke L.J.* (2014), 1 ff., esp. 5 ff., 20 ff. and 38; the same, *Behaviorally Informed Health Policy?*..., pp. 3 ff., esp. 10 ff.; the same, 122 *Yale L.J.* (2013), 1843–1844, 1896; the same, 127

So, *people often choose not to choose*[20] simply because they are unmotivated or bored, are afraid of change, or tend to stick with the *status quo*, heavily relying on convenient *heuristics or rules of thumb*.[21] Default rules or options have this "sticky" function, and as a result, we tend not to abandon them. Along this same line of reasoning, though, the aforementioned practically crucial parameter of the *ignorance of the existence of a default rule* seems to receive little attention or to be somehow downplayed in the relevant discussion; the problem is here that when an individual is not aware—or cannot be easily informed—of the default rule, that individual ***does not make a decision*** to delegate the decision-making authority to someone else or to accept a pre-determined default option.[22] This significant parameter, however, is discussed in more detail in a later chapter.

The influence that inertia exerts on us may be viewed, in some circumstances, as an instance of our *bounded rationality*. In particular, if the costs (i.e., time, effort, money) of opting out of a default rule or a given state of things are trivial or very low and opting out would better serve our interests, then sticking with the rule or the state of things is irrational.[23] On the other hand, though,

---

Harv.L.R. Forum (2014), 212–213; the same, *Choosing Not to Choose…*, *passim*, esp. pp. 34 ff., 85–86, 96–97; Korobkin, 51 *Vand.L.Rev.* (1998), 1583 ff.; the same, Behavioral Economics…, pp. 123 ff.; Bubb/Pildes, 127 *Harv.L.R.* (2014), 1596 ff., 1604 ff., *passim*, esp. 1625; Elster, *Ulysses and the Sirens…*, pp. 139, 148–149; Camerer/Issacharoff/Loewenstein/O'Donoghue/Rabin, 151 *U.Penn.L.R.* (2003), 1225; Ayres, 73 *U.Chi.L.Rev.* (2006), 4–5, 13; Mols/Haslam/Jetten/Steffens, 54 *EJPR* (2015), 84, 89. See also *World Development Report 2015: Mind, Society, and Behavior*, pp. 202–203, wherein *inter alia*: "People may […] get stuck in habits, succumb to inertia, and repeatedly procrastinate despite intentions to do otherwise" (p. 202). In particular, on the phenomenon of *procrastination* and the specific ways to deal with it, see Camerer/Issacharoff/Loewenstein/O'Donoghue/Rabin, *op.cit.*, pp. 1248 ff.; Akerlof, 81 *Am.Econ.Rev.* (1991), 1 ff.; Ariely, *Predictably Irrational…*, pp. 141 ff.; also Sunstein, 73 *U.Chi.L.Rev.* (2006), 251–252, and 122 *Yale L.J.* (2013), 1843–1844, 1858; DellaVigna, 47 *JEL* (2009), 323.

20 See Sunstein, 64 *Duke L.J.* (2014), 1 ff.; the same, *Choosing Not to Choose…*, *passim*, esp. pp. 34 ff.; the same, *Behaviorally Informed Health Policy?…*, pp. 3 ff., esp. 10 ff.; the same, *Nudging and Choice Architecture…*, pp. 30–31; the same, *Forcing People to Choose is Paternalistic*, 13 ff.; Dinner/Johnson/Goldstein/Liu, 17 *J.Exp.Psychol.-Appl.* (2011), 332 ff.; Thaler, 1 *J.Econ.Behav. Organ.* (1980), 51 ff.

21 Indicatively, recently, once more Sunstein, *Forcing People to Choose Is Paternalistic*, esp. 13–14: "People might decline to choose for multiple reasons. Their choice not to choose is, in their view, the best way to promote their welfare, and they want that choice to be treated with respect. They might have a kind of intuitive framework: They want to minimize decision costs and error costs. When choosing would impose high decision costs, they might not want to do it […]. And if they think that someone (a cab driver, an employer, a public official) would be more likely to make the right decision, they might think that the best way to reduce error costs is not to choose. […] / […] They might find it a relief, or even fun, to delegate. They might not want to take responsibility. […] Active choosing saddles the chooser with responsibility for the choice, and reduces the chooser's welfare for that reason."

22 *Cf.* Sunstein, *Forcing People To Choose Is Paternalistic*, 14 ff., and the same, *Misconceptions About Nudges*, 5–6.

23 See Sunstein/Thaler, 70 *U.Chi.L.Rev.* (2003), 1181; for more detail, Sunstein, 64 *Duke L.J.* (2014), 1 ff.; Ben-Shahar/Pottow, 33 *Fla.St.U.L.Rev.* (2006), 651 ff.; Willis, 80 *U.Chi.L.Rev.* (2013), 1155 ff.; esp. 1161 ff.

if the costs of opting out are prohibitive, or even just somewhat greater than the benefits of opting out (and thus shaping the state of things autonomously), then sticking with the default rule or a given state of things may be rightly characterized as 'rational apathy' (in German: *rationale Apathie*[24]). Under the rational choice theory (see also Chapter 1), for opting out to make sense, the benefits of an alternative shaping of the legal state of things (e.g., of a contractual arrangement) or a life-related issue should be greater than the costs of the opting-out process.[25]

II. The pervasiveness of loss aversion and the endowment effect

Delving further into the decision-making mechanism, one may ascertain that, apart from inertia, our tendency to treat default rules as sticky may also be attributed to another significant behavioral glitch, namely: *loss aversion*. This is our *psychological tendency to give losses more weight (typically, twice as much)* than equivalent gains (for example, for most individuals the *pain* for a loss of 5€ is greater than the *pleasure* of a profit of 5€). It is no wonder that we prefer the avoidance of loss over the attainment of an equivalent gain, since the amount of *pleasure* we draw from a gain is smaller than the pain of a loss. This function is in contrast with the orthodox economic assumption that one's evaluations of equal gains and losses should coincide. In the same vein, stickiness might also be related to *status quo bias*—that is, our tendency to favor the current state of affairs; or it could be related to the *anchoring effect*, which draws us to initial *reference points* (e.g., we measure how the outdoor temperature feels in comparison with the indoor temperature, and so forth). In this context, the default rules are viewed by individuals as reliable regulatory instruments that reflect a fair *status quo*, and thus they become attractive *reference points* that we do not feel comfortable detaching ourselves from.[26] And it is natural to think that, especially in the

24 On this notion, see Bechtold, *Die Grenzen zwingenden Vertragsrechts...*, p. 191.

25 So Möslein, *Dispositives Recht...*, pp. 281, 302; see also Unberath/Cziupka, 209 *AcP* (2009), 49; Bechtold, *Die Grenzen zwingenden Vertragsrechts...*, pp. 191–192, 256–257, 259; Grundmann/Möslein/Riesenhuber, Contract Governance..., p. 46.

26 For the above assumptions associating the stickiness of default rules with *loss aversion*, *status quo bias*, and *anchoring effect*, see Korobkin/Ulen, 88 *Cal.L.R.* (2000), 1104 ff., esp. 1112: "... default rules are more difficult to contract around than rational choice theory explanations suggest. This is because contracting parties are likely to see default terms as part of the status quo and, consequently, prefer them to alternative terms"; Korobkin, 83 *Cornell L.Rev.* (1998), 608 ff., esp. 637 ff.; the same, 51 *Vand.L.Rev.* (1998), 1583 ff., esp. 1588; the same, Behavioral Economics..., pp. 116 ff., esp. 118 ff.; Sunstein/Thaler, 70 *U.Chi.L.Rev.* (2003), 1171 ff.; Sunstein, Introduction, pp. 4, 5–6; the same, 1 *Am.L.&Econ.Rev.* (1999), 123–124, 131 ff., esp. 134–135; the same, 162 *U.Penn.L.R.* (2013), 21 ff.; the same, *Choosing Not to Choose...*, pp. 44 ff.; Thaler, 1 *J.Econ.Behav.Organ.* (1980), 42–43; the same, 125 *J.Polit.Econ.* (2017), 1801–1802; Ben-Shahar/Pottow, 33 *Fla.St.U.L.Rev.* (2006), 651 ff., esp. 655 ff.; Willis, 80 *U.Chi.L.Rev.* (2013), 1155 ff., esp. 1161 ff.; Zamir, Law's Loss Aversion, pp. 268 ff., esp. 272 ff., 279–280, 289, 290–291 (: "Loss aversion is a robust behavioral phenomenon"); Kahneman/

field of contracts, the desire to maintain the *status quo* might, ultimately, attach a *quasi* or *de facto mandatory force* to the contractual default rules.[27]

Further, our tendency to stick with default rules may also be justified by the considerable influence that exerts on us a more specific expression of our inherent loss aversion—that is, the *endowment effect* that we develop in relation to a legal right or an object.[28] Under that emotional bias, "*once we own something (or*

Knetsch/Thaler, Experimental Tests of the Endowment Effect..., pp. 211 ff. *passim*, esp. 226 ff.; the same, 5 *J.Econ.Persp.* (1991), 193 ff., esp. 197 ff.; Tversky/Kahneman, Loss Aversion in Riskless Choice..., pp. 143 ff.; the same, 47 *Econometrica* (1979), esp. 279; the same, 107 *Quart.J.Econ.* (1991), 1039 ff.; Kahneman, 93 *Am.Econ.Rev.* (2003), 1454 ff.; the same, 58 *Am.Psychol.* (2003), 697 ff.; Cohen/Knetsch, 30 *Osgoode Hall L.J.* (1992), 737 ff.; Camerer/Issacharoff/Loewenstein/O'Donoghue/Rabin, 151 *U.Penn.L.R.* (2003), 1224 ff.; Samuelson/Zeckhauser, 1 *J.Risk Uncertainty* (1988), 7 ff.; Dinner/Johnson/Goldstein/Liu, 17 *J.Exp.Psychol.-Appl.* 2011, 332 ff.; Graddy/Loewenstein/Mei/Moses/Pownall, Anchoring or Loss Aversion?..., 1 ff.; Arlen, 52 *Vand.L.Rev.* (1998), 1771–1772; Ghisellini/Chang, *Behavioral Economics...*, pp. 109 ff., 190–191, esp. 209; Noll/Krier, Some Implications of Cognitive Psychology..., p. 329. See also the relevant German literature: van Aaken, Begrenzte Rationalität..., pp. 115 ff., esp. 117, 123, 126–127, 132, 138; the same, Das deliberative Element juristischer Verfahren..., pp. 195 ff.; Englerth, Behavioral Law and Economics..., pp. 85 ff.; Bechtold, *Die Grenzen zwingenden Vertragsrechts...*, pp. 230 ff.; Kähler, *Begriff und Rechtfertigung...*, pp. 170–171; Eidenmüller, *JZ* (2005), 219, 222; Schäfer/Ott, *Lehrbuch der ökonomischen Analyse des Zivilrechts*[4], pp. 68–69; Ringe, 213 *AcP* (2013), 119–120; Tscherner, 1 *ALJ* (2014), 147. Especially on the *anchoring effect*, see Tversky/Kahnenman, 185 *Science* (1974), 1128 ff.; Feldman/Schurr/Teichman, 13 *J.Emp.Leg.Stud.* (2016), 298 ff.; Korobkin/Ulen, *op.cit.*, pp. 1100 ff.; Sunstein, 1 *Am.L.&Econ.Rev.* (1999), 118–119, 123, 141; Sunstein/Thaler, 70 *U.Chi.L.Rev.* (2003), 1177–1178.

27 Korobkin, Behavioral Economics..., pp. 137; see also Bar-Gill, Consumer Transactions, p. 483. *Cf.* further Willis, 80 *U.Chi.L.Rev.* (2013), 1155 ff., esp. 1161 ff., who, in general, partly challenges the idea of defaults' *stickiness* (or '*magnetism*') and thus the effectiveness of nudge theory, positing that policy defaults will not be sticky when (a) motivated firms (i.e., private organizations) oppose them, (b) these firms have access to the consumer, (c) consumers find the decision environment confusing, and (d) consumer preferences are uncertain.

28 For detail, see Thaler, 1 *J.Econ.Behav.Organ.* (1980), 43 ff.; the same, 108 *Am.Econ.Rev.* (2018), 1272 ff.; Kahneman/Knetsch/Thaler, 5 *J.Econ.Persp.* (1991), 193 ff.; the same, Experimental Tests of the Endowment Effect..., pp. 211 ff.; Knetsch, 79 *Am.Econ.Rev.* (1989), 1277 ff.; Cohen/Knetsch, 30 *Osgoode Hall L.J.* (1992), 745 ff.; Kahneman/Tversky, Choices, Values, and Frames, pp. 13 ff.; the same, Loss Aversion in Riskless Choice..., pp. 145 ff., 155 ff.; Kahneman, 93 *Am.Econ.Rev.* (2003), 1457; Jolls/Sunstein/Thaler, 50 *Stan.L.Rev.* (1998), 1482 ff., 1497 ff., 1505 ff.; Jolls, Behavioral Law and Economics, pp. 116 ff.; Thaler, *Misbehaving...*, pp. 12 ff., 148 ff., 263 ff.; Sunstein, 73 *U.Chi.L.Rev.* (2006), 265; the same, 1 *Am.L.&Econ.Rev.* (1999), 119, 132–133, 144; Korobkin/Ulen, 88 *Cal.L.R.* (2000), 1107 ff.; Korobkin, Wrestling with the Endowment Effect..., pp. 300 ff., esp. 323 ff.; the same, Behavioral Economics..., pp. 116 ff.; *the same*, 97 *Nw.U.L.R.* (2003), 1227 ff.; Cartwright, *Behavioral Economics*[2], pp. 49 ff.; Hochma, *Endowment Effect...*; DellaVigna, 47 *JEL* (2009), 326 ff.; Graddy/Loewenstein/Mei/Moses/Pownall, Anchoring or Loss Aversion?..., 1 ff., esp. 7–8; Ariely, *Predictably Irrational...*, pp. 167 ff., esp. 173 ff.; Cooter/Ulen, *Law & Economics*[6], p. 87; Arlen, 52 *Vand.L.Rev.* (1998), 1771–1772, 1777 ff.; Smith, Economics in the Laboratory, pp. 345–346. See also the relevant German literature: Eidenmüller, *JZ* (2005), 218–219, 222, 224; the same, *JZ* (2011), 817, 818, 819· the same, *Effizienz als Rechtsprinzip*[3], pp. 125 ff., 341 ff., 379–380; the same, Widerrufsrechte, p. 136; van Aaken, Begrenzte Rationalität..., pp. 117–118· the same, Das deliberative

have a feeling of ownership) we irrationally overvalue it, regardless of its objective value."[29] The endowment effect may even appear immediately after a legal right or an object is bestowed on us; in such a case there is an *instant endowment effect* at work,[30] which might be significant in explaining the impact of default rules, since they may often come to our attention only instantly (with the exception, of course, of repeated transactions).[31] A legal right or an entitlement thus often becomes "our precious" in the same way that Gollum, the famous character in the "Lord of the Rings" movie, was influenced in his decision-making by the ring.[32]

In addition, still with respect to default rules, there is today reliable experimental evidence on the so-called 'Coase theorem' showing that in its basic version it may often prove false. According to the 'Coase theorem,' the initial (legislative or judicial) allocation of goods or rights—in other words, the *initial endowment of property rights or entitlements*—does not determine their final allocation insofar as the transaction costs are null or very low.[33] This may not always be true, though. Frequently, the endowment effect—along with the other aforementioned factors—exerts such an influence on the parties to a transaction that they do not opt out of the default option; even when the transaction costs of opting out are low, the initial allocation of goods or rights pursuant to the default rule may often be the final one.[34]

Element juristischer Verfahren..., pp. 197–198; Kähler, *Begriff und Rechtfertigung*..., pp. 179 ff.; Bechtold, *Die Grenzen zwingenden Vertragsrechts*..., pp. 226 ff.; Unberath/Cziupka, 209 *AcP* (2009), 72 ff.

29 Hochma, *Endowment Effect*...

30 See the path-breaking research of Kahneman/Knetsch/Thaler, Experimental Tests of the Endowment Effect..., pp. 213 ff., esp. 225 ff.; also Tversky/Kahneman, Loss Aversion in Riskless Choice..., pp. 145–146; Thaler, *Misbehaving*..., pp. 154, 274; Ariely, *Predictably Irrational*..., p. 174. *Cf.* Eidenmüller, *JZ* (2005), 218–219, 221–222; Zamir, Law's Loss Aversion, p. 275.

31 *Cf.* further Bechtold, *Die Grenzen zwingenden Vertragsrechts*..., pp. 234 ff.

32 Hochma, *Endowment Effect*....

33 On the 'Coase theorem,' see in detail Coase, 3 *J.L.&Econ.* (1960), 1 ff.; Cooter/Ulen, *Law & Economics*[6], pp. 74 ff., 81 ff., esp. 84–85, 87, 291–292; R.Posner, *Economic Analysis of Law*[6], pp. 7, 49 ff.; Wittman, *Economic Foundations of Law*..., chapter 5 (pp. 33 ff., esp. 34 and 38), chapter 6 (pp. 42 ff.); Georgakopoulos, *Principles and Methods of Law and Economics*..., pp. 96 ff.; Jolls/Sunstein/Thaler, 50 *Stan.L.Rev.* (1998), 1483–1484, 1497; Kahneman/Knetsch/Thaler, Experimental Tests of the Endowment Effect..., pp. 211, 223, 226–227; Cohen/Knetsch, 30 *Osgoode Hall L.J.* (1992), 744 ff.; Hoffman/Spitzer, 71 *Wash.U.L.Q.* (1993), 62 ff.; Korobkin, Wrestling with the Endowment Effect..., pp. 300 ff. *passim*; Bix, *Jurisprudence: Theory and Context*[7], pp. 214 ff. See also Eidenmüller, *Effizienz als Rechtsprinzip*[3], pp. 59 ff.; Schäfer/Ott, *Lehrbuch der ökonomischen Analyse des Rechts*[4], pp. 5–6, 102 ff.; Mathis, *Effizienz statt Gerechtigkeit?*[3], pp. 71 ff.; Drexl, *Die wirtschaftliche Selbstbestimmung*..., pp. 191 ff.; Oechsler, *Gerechtigkeit im modernen Austauschvertrag*..., pp. 133 ff.; Bechtold, *Die Grenzen zwingenden Vertragsrechts*..., pp. 228 ff.

34 See also Eidenmüller, *JZ* (2005), 219: "Die Existenz von Besitzeffekten stellt das Coase-Theorem und damit die Grundlage der ökonomischen Analyse des Rechts in Frage. Wenn die Bewertung einer bestimmten Rechtsposition von deren Allokation abhängt, dann bedeutet dies, dass Verhandlungen auf Märkten auch bei Nicht-Existenz von Transaktionskosten keineswegs zwingend zu einem invarianten Ergebnis führen werden. Die Anfangsallokation einer Rechtsposition determiniert vielmehr möglicherweise die Endallokation." For more detail, see Bechtold,

III. The case for 'mild' or 'libertarian' paternalism and the proposed paradigm shift

As already alluded to above, Sunstein and Thaler propose, in essence, a paradigm shift: instead of teaching people how to overcome their inertia and avoid its sometimes significant ramifications, which would mean inducing them to use their freedom of choice, the regulator—chiefly the government—could exploit this inertia in a positive, benevolent way and set default rules or options that would contribute to individual well-being and societal welfare.

Resetting the starting point—that is, reshaping or restructuring the content of the default rule—is exactly what Sunstein and Thaler mean by the term "nudge." This is how it is currently understood in the United States and elsewhere. Nudge is rightly distinguished from *incentive*, since the nudged individual does not receive any *direct* financial benefit or advantage in exchange for showing a certain conduct.[35] Nudges take advantage of the structure of the decision-making process to direct people, especially consumers, and society as a whole *toward easy and cost-effective decisions* that will lead them to more desirable 'destinations,'[36] to better choices for themselves.[37]

More often than not, consumers do not adequately consider the costs they impose on their future selves. They often turn a blind eye to the welfare of that future self, falling prey to *present-bias*, that is, *hyperbolic discounting* and *temporal myopia*; such qualities constitute a sort of future blindness due to which individuals show too little concern about the future (e.g., by borrowing or spending excessively).[38] This should come as no surprise for many people suffer from a lack of self-control or, in Aristotelian terms, 'akrasia.'[39]

Under a nudging scheme, the regulator purports to defeat this sort of future blindness. However, the final decision does not escape the control of the

---

Die Grenzen zwingenden Vertragsrechts..., pp. 234 ff., esp. 236–237, 264–265; Korobkin, 83 *Cornell L.Rev.* (1998), 638 ff., 660, 665, 679 ff.; the same, 97 *Nw.U.L.R.* (2003), esp. 1257 and 1273; Sunstein, 77 *N.Y.U.L.Rev.* (2002), 113.

35 See also Thaler/Sunstein, *Nudge*..., p. 8; Sunstein, The Ethics of Nudging, p. vi.

36 See also Waldron, It's All for Your Own Good, chapter 1.

37 See also Camerer/Issacharoff/Loewenstein/O'Donoghue/Rabin, 151 *U.Penn.L.R.* (2003), 1220–1221.

38 On *present-bias, hyperbolic discounting*, and the like, see Laibson, 112 *Quart.J.Econ.* (1997), 443; Dasgupta/Maskin, 95 *Am.Econ.Rev.* (2005), 1290 ff.; Frederick/Loewenstein/O'Donoghue, 40 *JEL* (2002), 351 ff.; Strotz, 23 *Rev.Econ.Stud.* (1955–1956), 165 ff., esp. 177 ff.; Benhabib/Bisin/Schotter, 69 *GEB* (2010), 205 ff.; *Korobkin/Ulen*, 88 *Cal.L.R.* (2000), 1119 ff.; Bubb/Pildes, 127 *Harv.L.R.* (2014), 1640 ff.; Sunstein, 1 *Am.L.&Econ.Rev.* (1999), 122–123, 129 ff., 131; the same, 122 *Yale L.J.* (2013), 1842 ff.; Benartzi/Peleg/Thaler, *Choice Architecture and Retirement Saving Plans*, pp. 247 ff.; Ghisellini/Chang, *Behavioral Economics*..., pp. 151 ff.; Cartwright, *Behavioral Economics*^{2}, pp. 172 ff.; Thaler, *Misbehaving*..., pp. 88 ff.; DellaVigna, 47 *JEL* (2009), 318 ff.; Elster, *Ulysses and the Sirens*..., pp. 65 ff.; Schelling, 60 *The Public Interest* (1980), 94 ff., esp. 99 ff.; Saint-Paul, *The Tyranny of Utility*..., pp. 43 ff.; van Aaken, Begrenzte Rationalität..., pp. 120–121, 137; Englerth, Behavioral Law and Economics..., pp. 80–81; Schmolke, *Grenzen der Selbstbindung*..., pp. 815 ff.; Bechtold, *Die Grenzen zwingenden Vertragsrechts*..., pp. 73 ff.

39 See, indicatively, https://en.wikipedia.org/wiki/Akrasia.

individual (consumer or not), who is still able to alter the starting point (i.e., the default option) and choose, for example, not to participate in the retirement savings plan offered by her employer or not to become an organ donor. In this opting-out scenario, the individual must overcome the hurdle of inertia by paying the necessary effort tax.[40]

In light of the above, Sunstein and Thaler are considered proponents of a *'libertarian or mild, soft paternalism,'* which purports to advance individual well-being and societal welfare. Libertarian paternalism employs nudges to achieve these noble goals. It promotes a *light-touch* regulatory intervention[41] that encompasses carefully designed default options which seek to constrain self-harming conduct.[42] The golden rule of libertarian paternalism, its core tenet, is to "*offer nudges that are most likely to help and least likely to inflict harm.*"[43]

It is a form of paternalism devoid of coercion (at least of a direct form), which still preserves the freedom of choice of the individual: the regulator sets as the starting point the choice *that the individual herself would make if she possessed the analytical abilities of a rational decision-maker and had adequate time and optimal information at her disposal*; the individual is still free, however, to opt out of the default option.[44]

40 *Cf.* also Jolls/Sunstein/Thaler, 50 *Stan.L.Rev.* (1998), 1522 ff.

41 See Bubb/Pildes, 127 *Harv.L.R.* (2014), 1596 and *passim*.

42 In other words, such a mild paternalism allows state interferences with individuals' choices that aim at constraining self-harming conduct, but regularly without the consent of the people they are meant to protect "*when but only when that conduct is substantially non-voluntary*" (Feinberg, *Harm to Self*, p. 12). And, as Voorhoeve aptly puts it (Response to Rabin, p. 140), "[c]onduct is substantially non-voluntary [...] when it is insufficiently informed or performed by someone insufficiently capable of rational self-governance with respect to the conduct in question."

43 See Thaler/Sunstein, *Nudge...*, *passim*, esp. pp. 4 ff. and 72; Sunstein/Thaler, 70 *U.Chi.L.Rev.* (2003), 1159 ff., esp. 1162; Sunstein, 73 *U.Chi.L.Rev.* (2006), 254 ff., esp. 256–257, 263 ff.; the same, 127 *Harv.L.R. Forum* (2014), 210 ff.; the same, 122 *Yale L.J.* (2013), 1861 ff., 1867 ff.; Thaler, *Misbehaving...*, *passim*, esp. pp. 323 ff.; Hausman/Welch, 18 *J.Polit.Philos.* (2010), 124 ff.; Schlag, 108 *Mich.L.Rev.* (2010), 913 ff., esp. 919 ff.; Cserne, *Freedom of Contract...*, pp. 57 ff.; Sturn, 1 *ALJ* (2014), 48 ff., esp. 53 ff.; Glaeser, 29 *Regulation* (2006), 32 ff.; Englerth, Vom Wert des Rauchens..., pp. 232 ff.; van Aaken, Begrenzte Rationalität..., pp. 123 ff.; Kirchgässner, *Homo Oeconomicus*[4], pp. 269 ff.; Schmolke, *Grenzen der Selbstbindung...*, pp. 219 ff.; Karampatzos, Rechtspaternalismus im Europäischen Verbraucherschutzrecht..., pp. 208 ff.; also recently in detail Neumann, *Libertärer Paternalismus...* On the similar theory and notion of *asymmetric (or cautious) paternalism*, see Camerer/Issacharoff/Loewenstein/O'Donoghue/Rabin, 151 *U.Penn.L.R.* (2003), 1212 and 1219 ff.; see also Sunstein, 73 *U.Chi.L.Rev.* (2006), 256–257; Thaler/Sunstein, *Nudge...*, pp. 72, 249–250; Congdon, Psychology and Economic Policy, pp. 467–468; Schmolke, *op.cit.*, pp. 221 ff.; Englerth, *op.cit.*, pp. 245 ff.

44 See Rebonato, 37 *J.Consum.Policy* (2014), 357 ff., esp. 359; for more detail, Thaler/Sunstein, *Nudge...*, *passim*, esp. p. 5.: "... Libertarian paternalists want to make it easy for people to go their own way; they do not want to burden those who want to exercise their freedom. The paternalistic aspect lies in the claim that it is legitimate for choice architects to try to influence people's behavior in order to make their lives longer, healthier, and better"; also *ibidem*, p. 237: "Our proposals are emphatically designed to retain freedom of choice"; Sunstein/Thaler, 70 *U.Chi.L.Rev.* (2003), 1159 ff., 1170, 1173, 1182; Sunstein, 73 *U.Chi.L.Rev.* (2006), 254 ff., esp. 256–257, 263 ff.; the same, 122 *Yale L.J.* (2013), 1835 ff., 1859 ff., 1883 ff., 1894; the same, *Nudging and Choice Architecture...*, pp. 4 ff., 27 ff., 49–50; the same, 127 *Harv.L.R. Forum* (2014), 210

The *libertarian* paternalism of Sunstein and Thaler, even though a seeming terminological oxymoron, does not entail, *prima facie* at least, severe restrictions to individual freedom; and this is probably the reason it echoes so strongly in European legal thinking as well, especially amongst German legal scholars.[45] Besides, the choice of the term 'libertarian' was obviously meant to appeal to libertarians, who generally favor minimal state intervention. Based on the assumption that we often rely on rules of thumb or available regulatory tools, this kind of paternalism is typically harnessed to mend, or at least limit, the systematic rationality deficits that permeate and influence our decision-making process. Thus it is also meant to appeal to paternalists, who generally want to help people make the 'right' decisions.

In effect, the approach of Sunstein and Thaler is in line with a more general shift in the modern role of jurisprudence, a shift that is being discussed worldwide, but more intensely, and sometimes more enthusiastically, in Germany. This shift has been considerably reinforced by the advancement in the BEAL. Especially in the field of private law, jurisprudence is lately viewed more and more not so much as a science relating to the proper interpretation and application of law (in German: *Rechtsanwendungswissenschaft*) but rather as a science relating to the proper design or drafting of legal norms, to achieve *better regulation* (in German: *Rechtsetzungswissenschaft*). In this latter form, it examines (a) how the legislator (or in more general terms, the *social planner*) can achieve a regulatory goal by using a specific regulatory tool or, in a similar vein, (b) which undesired implications, deriving from the use of a specific regulatory tool, she must take into account (in German: *Gesetzesfolgenabschätzung*).[46]

In light of the above, the libertarian paternalism of Sunstein and Thaler seems to be more of a *means-paternalism* than an *ends-paternalism*, although the boundaries between the two are not always clear.[47] As they argue, nudges respect people's goals; they do not quarrel with people's judgments about the right destination but help them find the path that will get them there; so, nudges offer

---

ff.; also Frey/Gallus, Beneficial and Exploitative Nudges, pp. 11 ff.; Zamir, Law's Loss Aversion, p. 291; Sturn, 1 *ALJ* (2014), 48 ff., esp. 53 ff.; Wright/Ginsburg, 106 *Nw.U.L.R.* (2012), 1039 ff. *passim*; Glaeser, 29 *Regulation* (2006), 32 ff.; Neumann, *Libertärer Paternalismus…*, *passim*, esp. pp. 3–4, 37 ff., 84 ff., 98; Englerth, Vom Wert des Rauchens…, pp. 232 ff.; *Karampatzos*, Rechtspaternalismus im Europäischen Verbraucherschutzrecht…, pp. 208 ff.

45 See Eidenmüller, *JZ* (2011), 814 ff.; the same, *JZ* (2005), 216 ff.; the same, Widerrufsrechte; van Aaken, Begrenzte Rationalität…, pp. 123 ff.; recently, for more detail, Neumann, *Libertärer Paternalismus…*

46 On this important paradigm shift, see Bechtold, *Die Grenzen zwingenden Vertragsrechts…*, passim, esp. pp. 3 ff., 318–319, 326–327, 331 ff.; Eidenmüller, *JZ* (1999), 53 ff. *passim*, esp. 54 and 60; the same, *JZ* (2007), 490–491; the same, *JZ* (2005), 671; the same, *Effizienz als Rechtsprinzip*[3], pp. 2 ff., 489–490, 597–598; Wagner, 206 *AcP* (2006), 352 ff., esp. 422 ff.; Bachmann, *JZ* (2008), 11; the same, *Private Ordnung…*, pp. 359 ff.; Fleischer, 76 *RabelsZ* (2012), 235 ff., esp. 236–237; the same, 168 *ZHR* (2004), 673; Engel, *JZ* (1995), 213; Unberath/Cziupka, 209 *AcP* (2009), 37.

47 See Sunstein, *Nudging and Choice Architecture…*, pp. 27 ff., and 122 *Yale L.J.* (2013), 1835 ff., 1855 ff., 1898–1899, where he expressly refers to a *means-paternalism*.

navigability. Sunstein and Thaler's fundamental claim is that the liberal political tradition has placed too little emphasis on the pervasive challenge of navigability. Nudges, such as automatic enrollment in a retirement savings plan, increase our navigability and get us where we would like to get ourselves, just like a GPS device. The social planner's interventions, the nudges, lead us where we want to go, *at least upon reflection*; in that sense, they promote freedom, since freedom is seen as a 'navigability problem.'[48]

Sunstein and Thaler's means-paternalism seeks to select the means that is least burdensome to private autonomy, in order to attain ends that are, more or less, seen by the majority of society as welfare-promoting and contributing to the public good (by increasing the number of organ donors, for example).[49] Regulatory interventions are measured against the benchmark of people's well-being.[50]

Now we have reached the point where some further clarifications are necessary: whereas behavioral economics may, in general, justify the need for some form of regulatory interference, Sunstein and Thaler, as has already emerged, focus on the proper *specific* design of each regulatory intervention—that is, mainly the design of the default rule. They are not much concerned with the evaluation of the "objective" or "basic good" (*Finnis*[51]) they purport to promote or protect, since they usually take that for granted. For instance, the significance and intrinsic value of health as an "objective good" is not questioned. This does

48 On the immense importance of the notion of 'navigability' within Sunstein and Thaler's nudge theory, see Sunstein, *Misconceptions about Nudges*, 3 ff. *passim*, esp. 7: "As the GPS example suggests, many nudges have the goal of *increasing navigability* – of making it easier for people to get to their preferred destination. Such nudges stem from an understanding that life can be either simple or hard to navigate, and a goal of helpful nudging is to promote simpler navigation. I wish that *Nudge* had made this point clearer, and had connected nudging to the central idea of navigability"; the same, "Better Off, As Judged by Themselves": A Comment on Evaluating Nudges, 1 ff. *passim*; the same, The Ethics of Nudging, pp. vi, viii.

49 So, in essence, Möslein, 1 *ALJ* (2014), 140 ff.

50 Recently, in an interesting and enlightening paper, the authors calculated ratios of impact to cost for nudge interventions and for traditional policy tools, such as tax incentives and other financial inducements. They found that "nudge interventions often compare favorably with traditional interventions," thus concluding that "nudging is a valuable approach that should be used more often in conjunction with traditional policies," yet "more calculations are needed to determine the relative effectiveness of nudging"; see Benartzi/Beshears/Milkman/Sunstein/Thaler/Shankar/Tucker-Ray/Congdon/Galing, 28 *Psychol.Sci.* (2017), 1041 ff. In another relevant paper the authors presented a *domain-general scoping review* of the nudge movement, by reviewing 422 choice architecture interventions in 156 empirical studies, and offered directly applicable recommendations for future research to support the evidence accumulation *on why and when nudges do actually work*—that is, whether choice architecture techniques indeed provide, as they promise, "generally applicable and easily implementable solutions to important societal problems"; see Szaszi/Palinkas/Palfi/Szollosi/Aczel, 31 *J.Behav.Dec.Making* (2018), 355 ff.

51 See *Natural Law and Natural Rights*. In general, on Finnis's natural law theory, which is based on the acknowledgement of a list of 'basic goods' [: life (and health), knowledge, play, aesthetic experience, sociability (friendship), practical reasonableness, and religion], see, indicatively Bix, *Jurisprudence: Theory and Context*[7], pp. 77 ff.

not mean, though, that Sunstein and Thaler are indifferent to moral or welfare evaluations; rather, the objective of their theory is different. In this respect they *seem* to honor the sacred liberal principle that the state should be neutral toward people's conception of what a good life consists in—this is the so-called *neutrality principle.*[52] As is correctly clarified, though, by this principle liberals do not actually support a kind of *evaluative* neutrality (if there is such a thing); rather, they only object to "the state forcing individuals to make choices, merely on the basis that their life will go ethically better."[53]

Nevertheless, the above do not go to suggest that normative assumptions about the nature of human well-being (welfare, interests, happiness, etc.) can be separated from the conceptual groundwork of behavioral research.[54] If the claim of Sunstein and Thaler is that the idea of 'libertarian paternalism' can obviate political and ideological disagreements on core issues such as well-being, it cannot be endorsed.[55] More generally, normative assumptions and moral imperatives deriving from fundamental constitutional principles cannot be set aside. Law also offers normative guidance, which must always be taken into account.[56] As Cserne eloquently puts it, "[l]aw is more than a simple technique of command and control; legal doctrines are interwoven with common sense moral intuitions about human agency."[57] To top it all, even Sunstein himself adheres to a specific normative idea of good, when he repeatedly maintains that the maximization of welfare is the guiding principle of nudging.[58] It rather goes without saying that this idea points to the—nowadays, highly contestable—philosophy

52 See, indicatively, Letsas, 10 *L.& Ethics Hum. Rights* (2016), 322.

53 Letsas, 10 *L.& Ethics Hum. Rights* (2016), 328, who further goes on to conclude that "liberal neutrality prohibits the state from violating what Dworkin calls the right to ethical independence; liberal neutrality does not prevent the state from recognizing and regulating aspects of the good life (e.g. marriage and parenthood), when doing so does not violate the right to ethical independence. So by recognizing and accommodating certain commitments, the state does not necessarily violate liberal neutrality, in so far as the rationale for its coercive intervention (e.g. forcing the employer to accommodate religious employees, forcing parents to care for their children, or forcing promisors to perform) is not solely premised on the view that the life of those coerced (e.g., the employer, the parents, or the promisor) will go ethically better." On the key notion of 'ethical independence,' see R.Dworkin himself in *Justice for Hedgehogs*, pp. 368 ff., 385, 418.

54 See Cserne, Making Sense of Nudge-Scepticism…, p. 291, also p. 292.

55 *Cf.* Cserne, Making Sense of Nudge-Scepticism…, p. 299.

56 *Cf.* also Hacker, 2 *ERPL* (2016), 315–316, who aptly talks about the "necessary normativity" of behavioral analysis of law: "The lack of genuine debate of the aims and normative principles underlying behavioural analysis seems all the more surprising since most proposals openly aim at changing individual behavior. When doing so, the legislator or regulator should have a firm normative compass in order to know in which direction she intends to steer the people that are affected by behavioural strategies. On another occasion, I have called this the 'necessary normativity' of the behavioural analysis of law."

57 Cserne, Making Sense of Nudge-Scepticism…, p. 299—see also *ibidem*, pp. 293 ff.

58 See, for example, Sunstein, *Why Nudge?: The Ethics of Libertarian Paternalism*, *passim*, esp. pp. 87, 142.

of utility maximization that from a normative perspective cannot go unnoticed and certainly is "worthy of critical discussion."[59]

In all events, paternalism of means cannot be clearly separated from paternalism of ends. And there is a great deal of justified criticism here. For example, in White's opinion[60] "modern paternalism does not respect people's true interests but instead adopts a perfectionist or objective conception of well-being"—which may infringe on people's personal autonomy. White articulates his thesis against 'benevolent nudges' eloquently, stressing the crucial importance of respecting people's individual interests and thus challenging the above basic assumptions of Sunstein and Thaler: "A new employee may choose not to enrol in a retirement program because he wants to have more money for a down payment on a home, to support her parents, or simply to enjoy her youth in a new city. A person who chooses the huge slice of chocolate cake in the cafeteria may be doing so to celebrate a colleague's birthday, to flirt with the person at the dessert counter, or simply because he likes chocolate cake, each in full knowledge of the adverse health consequences."[61] In a similar vein, according to Mitchell's critical concerns, "Sunstein and Thaler's welfarist approach will inevitably result in the imposition of some conception of welfare on irrational people that some subset would surely find objectionable under conditions that permit rational evaluation."[62]

IV. Beyond default rules: informational nudges and cooling-off periods

Within the aforementioned pursuit of the optimal regulatory tool, mild or libertarian paternalism is not limited to the design of proper default rules but also propounds some types of *informational or educative nudges* that can draw the attention of people to the dangerous consequences of an action or transaction (e.g., "smoking can cause cancer," "read carefully the General Contract Terms before signing")[63]; even in this case, however, the individual's freedom of choice is still

59 See Hacker, 2 *ERPL* (2016), 315.

60 White, The Crucial Importance of Interests..., pp. 21 ff., esp. 21 and 26 ff.

61 White, The Crucial Importance of Interests..., p. 23.

62 Mitchell, 99 *Nw.U.L.R.* (2005), 1268–1269, wherein it is concluded that "[t]hus, when Sunstein and Thaler avoid the issue of what exactly welfare enhancement should look like under their version of libertarian paternalism, they avoid the hardest but most important question raised by their welfare-focused paternalism." On the fact that, in general, in such discussions the emphasis should actually be on how we define welfare and well-being, see Fallon, 101 *Mich.L.Rev.* (2003), 979 ff., esp. 983.

63 See Thaler/Sunstein, *Nudge..., passim*, esp. pp. 4, 65 ff., 243 ff.; Sunstein, *Nudging and Choice Architecture...*, pp. 7 ff., esp. 18 and 24 ff.; the same, 122 *Yale L.J.* (2013), 1887 ff., 1898–1899; more recently, Sunstein/Bar-Gill, *Regulation As Delegation*, pp. 1 ff. *passim*. For their part, Hausman/Welch (18 *J.Polit.Philos.* (2010), 127) are critical of such a broadening of the notion of nudge suggesting that in this case there is no paternalism at all, since the provision of information or advice presupposes that people are fully capable of making decisions. *Even though this*

preserved, in principle.[64] It is true, though, that even informational nudges may carry with them a certain moral evaluation; in many cases, information is not neutral.[65] It is also true that one who provides a piece of information is also, in effect, providing advice.[66]

Therefore, in its attempt to cure or limit people's rationality deficits, mild paternalism does not only employ ***default rules***—"the mother of all nudges"—but also ***informational nudges***, chiefly in the form of mandatory ***disclosure rules***. In particular, mandatory disclosure rules may be addressed either to public authorities (e.g., with a view to promoting a healthy way of life by limiting smoking) or to contracting parties. They are especially important when businesses conclude contracts with consumers. For example, with a view to strengthening responsible lending—'***know before you owe***'—and particularly countering the influence of ***hyperbolic discounting*** that affects the behavior of a would-be borrower, mandatory disclosure rules can help prevent instances of excessive borrowing and resulting financial disaster.[67]

But there is more in the quiver of mild paternalism. A third (c) regulatory tool that might be included is the so-called ***cooling-off period*** or ***period for sober reflection***: a party, after concluding a consumer contract, is given the right to free herself from her initial decision to contract within a certain period of time—under EU consumer protection law, the period is normally 14 days. This is the so-called ***withdrawal right*** of the consumers. For example, this right protects a consumer who has purchased a product impulsively, such as from a door-to-door salesperson; in such a context the consumer may have concluded the contract under psychological pressure from the salesperson, a state that usually leads to sub-optimal-irrational transactional decisions.[68] The same also holds for distance selling or e-commerce, where, however, the problem lies with the fact that the goods (products or services) acquired are ***experience goods***, whose quality and utility to the consumer cannot be ascertained until after the consumer receives the good—in detail Chapter 4.

---

criticism is, in principle, justified, I will keep referring to the term 'informational nudge,' since it has nowadays been established in the relevant discussion.

64 *Cf.* also van Aaken, Begrenzte Rationalität..., p. 126; Tscherner, 1 *ALJ* (2014), 148.

65 *Cf.* also van Aaken, Judge the Nudge..., p. 97: "The way information is presented also matters for decision-making. In other words: information is never neutral. It is sometimes difficult to differentiate between warning and preference formation (due to a campaign's inherent educational aim)"; the same, Begrenzte Rationalität..., p. 126.

66 So Jolls/Sunstein/Thaler, 50 *Stan.L.Rev.* (1998), 1534–1535.

67 On the above, see Sunstein/Thaler, 70 *U.Chi.L.Rev.* (2003), 1159 ff.; the same, ***Nudge...***, pp. 133 ff., esp. 137–138; Sunstein, 122 *Yale L.J.* (2013), 1826 ff. ***passim***, esp. 1887 ff., 1898–1899; the same, ***Nudging and Choice Architecture...***, pp. 7 ff., 14 ff.; the same, 127 ***Harv.L.R. Forum*** (2014), 213 ff.; the same, ***Nudging: A Very Short Guide***, pp. 3 ff.; Sunstein/Bar-Gill, ***Regulation As Delegation***, pp. 1 ff.; Camerer/Issacharoff/Loewenstein/O'Donoghue/Rabin, 151 *U.Penn.L.R.* (2003), 1211 ff., esp. 1224 ff. and 1232 ff.; Bubb/Pildes, 127 *Harv.L.R.* (2014), 1596 ff.; Oliver (ed.), ***Behavioural Public Policy, passim.***

68 See, indicatively, Schmolke, ***Grenzen der Selbstbindung*** ..., pp. 219 ff., 256 ff., esp. 258–259, 260–261, 861 ff.

This type of regulatory tool is also called 'regret mechanism,' and it is rightly praised in relevant literature for "making it possible for individuals to think their decision through and let them decide afterwards whether the decision was based on a 'bias' and was therefore wrong."[69]

V. Main objections to nudging through default rules and arguments in favor of it

Despite its positive features and apart from the criticism already delineated above with regard to its being labeled as a 'means-paternalism,' the mild paternalism brought forward by Sunstein and Thaler, especially in the form of nudging through default rules, also encounters considerable, primarily philosophical, objections, which may be summarized as follows.

1. The deficiencies of centralized regulation

In general, one may reasonably wonder whether there are indeed social planners that know better what is in the best interest of the rest of the people and should be able to determine the optimal way of shaping their choices, thus assuming the role of a *supreme elite of experts or lodestars.* Are they law professors or professors of behavioral economics? Do legislative, judiciary, and administrative bodies comprise people endowed with supernatural, rational capabilities? Is their thinking always rational, in contrast to that of the rest of us? What about their own biases and ignorance? What are the distinct characteristics that empower them to intervene in order to enhance the "common people's" rational exercise of freedom of choice if those common people are adults and of sound mind?[70]

69 van Aaken, Judge the Nudge..., p. 98. Apart from the above, we could also add the possibility of a *fourth* kind of nudge, namely, *temporary law*: According to its proponents Ginsburg/Masur/McAdams (81 *U.Chi.L.Rev.* (2014), 291 ff.), this different kind of nudge "may have a significant advantage over permanent law. When the rationale for regulation is to overcome path dependence, there is no need for a permanent restriction on liberty" (*ibidem*, p. 294). Ginsburg/Masur/McAdams thus "propose imagining regulations that include an expiration date" (*ibidem*, p. 294); their principal example for illustrating their point is the regulation of smoking in public places. They assert that temporary law is less intrusive than permanent regulation, and is particularly attractive in situations in which it is believed that path dependence has produced the *status quo.* "Given path dependence, it may be desirable to use law to shift society from the high-smoking to the low-smoking equilibrium. Across a large domain of issues besides smoking, the best argument that can be made for legal intervention and the most charitable interpretation of the arguments that are made is exactly this point: that the status quo is trapped in an inefficient equilibrium and that law will shift the system to a more desirable equilibrium, one that is also consistent with individual choice to satisfy existing preferences" (*ibidem*, p. 295).

70 On this critical aspect, see Waldron, It's All for Your Own Good, chapter 3; Mols/Haslam/Jetten/Steffens, 54 *EJPR* (2015), 87, 95; Brest, Quis custodiet ipsos custodies?..., pp. 481 ff.; Sunstein, *The Cost-Benefit Revolution*, *passim*, esp. p. xi; the same, *Forcing People To Choose Is Paternalistic*, 3; the same, The Ethics of Nudging, pp. xvi-xvii; Ghisellini/Chang, *Behavioral Economics...*, pp. 213 ff., esp. 216 (: "Who will nudge the nudgers?"); Frey/Gallus, Beneficial

These critical questions would seem to pertain generally to any kind of paternalistic intervention.[71] It is rightly suggested that "experts' judgment can become prey to two types of distortive mechanisms: misaligned incentives due to external economic pressures and economically-independent cognitive failures."[72] The second category of judgment failure means that experts are also susceptible to various cognitive (or volitional) biases.[73] It is, in fact, true that all sorts of social regulators—legislators, judges, and administrative officials—are humans too, and therefore they themselves may also err from time to time (or even systematically). This means, in particular, that even their own regulatory choices and judgments are fallible, and they may be influenced by behavioral biases, rationality deficits, or lack of self-control (e.g., hindsight bias, availability bias, lack of foresight, over-optimism, hyperbolic discounting, temporal myopia, emotional influences), exactly as the choices and behaviors of common people are.[74] In a nutshell, the problem of '*who will guard the guards themselves*' *(quis custodiet ipsos custodes)*[75] refers to any kind of regulatory intervention and transfer of powers to legislative, administrative, or judicial bodies in modern liberal democracies. And although we generally hope that 'experts' will be less subject to behavioral biases, we can never be sure.

In addition, according to Hayek, social planners typically make worse decisions than ordinary people (i.e., the addressees of regulatory intervention). Flawed decision-making processes can lead social planners to ignore the precise parameters of reality and the available information—which, by contrast, the choosers possess. At least hypothetically, ordinary people '*know better*'—that is, they are the best judges of what is in their own interest, and of what fosters their individual welfare. This is, in rather amplified terms, the so-called *knowledge problem.* For this reason, according to Hayek's approach, we should prefer a decentralized

---

and Exploitative Nudges, pp. 14 ff.; Perez, Can Experts be Trusted..., pp. 115 ff.; Sturn, 1 *ALJ* (2014), 52, 56–57; van Aaken, Begrenzte Rationalität..., pp. 134–135, esp. fn. 85; Bachmann, *Private Ordnung*..., p. 176.

71 See, indicatively, Buckley, *Fair Governance*, p. 19, and Husak, 10 *Phil.&Pub.Aff.* (1981), 41. *Cf.* also Sunstein, *Misconceptions about Nudges*, 3.

72 Perez, Can Experts be Trusted..., p. 117.

73 *Cf.* also Perez, Can Experts be Trusted..., pp. 117 ff.

74 See Jolls/Sunstein/Thaler, 50 *Stan.L.Rev.* (1998), 1541, 1543 ff.; Kuran/Sunstein, 51 *Stan.L.Rev.* (1999), 683 ff.; Sunstein/Thaler, 70 *U.Chi.L.Rev.* (2003), 1200–1201; Sunstein, 1 *Am.L.&Econ.Rev.* (1999), 146; the same, 122 *Yale L.J.* (2013), 1871–1872, 1878; the same, *Nudging and Choice Architecture*..., p. 44; Brest, Quis custodiet ipsos custodes?..., pp. 481 ff.; Wright/Ginsburg, 106 *Nw.U.L.R.* (2012), 1063 ff.; Bubb/Pildes, 127 *Harv.L.R.* (2014), 1605; Zamir, Law's Loss Aversion, p. 291; Englerth, Behavioral Law and Economics..., pp. 121–122; Schmolke, *Grenzen der Selbstbindung*..., pp. 239–240. See also the characteristic words of R.Posner, Treating Financial Consumer as Consenting Adults, p. A15: "Behavioral economists are right to point to the limitations of human cognition. But if they have the same cognitive limitations as consumers, should they be designing systems of consumer protection?"

75 *Cf.* Brest, Quis custodiet ipsos custodes?..., pp. 481 ff., who focuses, *inter alia*, precisely on strategies for mitigating biases and other errors in the decision-making process of the policy makers themselves.

system of decision-making, within which priority is, in principle, to be given to *active choice/choosing* on the part of the individual. Under such a scheme, there would be no default option designed by a 'benevolent' government planner.[76]

In the same vein, another argument sharpens the aforementioned point about the unreliability of the choices of central planners and favors recognizing the freedom of choice of individuals. This argument is derived from the well-known *public choice theory*, advanced most notably by James Buchanan. According to this theory, regulatory choices that are made by public or central authorities (i.e., primarily by legislative and governmental bodies) are inherently flawed, since such bodies are aggregates of individuals that struggle with each other to satisfy private interests rather than public ones, within, of course, the institutional and fiscal policy constraints in force. Thus regulation and public policy reflect the interaction between selfishly acting individuals. Regulation is the outcome of strong private interests over others, or at least the conflation of interests that conflict with each other. This may result in the adoption of regulations and policies that lack rationality or economic efficiency. For instance, businesses may obtain legislative or governmental approval for products deemed to be safe for consumers, even if they are not; strong pressure groups, unions, or syndicates might secure for themselves tax immunity schemes or guaranteed minimum fees to the detriment of the rest of society, which cannot benefit from price competition in the market; and so forth. From this viewpoint, in principle, it is preferable for individuals to make their own choices so that their own interests are satisfied, instead of those of other entities or persons, either overt or covert.[77]

76 Hayek, 35 *Am.Econ.Rev.* (1945), 519 ff.; see also Bubb/Pildes, 127 *Harv.L.R.* (2014), 1605; Sunstein, *The Cost-Benefit Revolution*, pp. xv–xvi, esp. 79 ff.; the same, *Choosing Not to Choose...*, pp. 94–95, 97 ff., 191–192; the same, 64 *Duke L.J.* (2014), 36–37; the same, 162 *U.Penn.L.R.* (2013), 8, 43–44; the same, 127 *Harv.L.R. Forum* (2014), 211; Sunstein/Bar-Gill, *Regulation as Delegation*, p. 8. *Cf.* further Bentham, *An Introduction to the Principles of Morals and Legislation*, chapter 17, para. XV, p. 319: "It is a standing topic of complaint, that a man knows too little of himself. Be it so: *but is it so certain that the legislator must know more?* It is plain, that *of individuals the legislator can know nothing*: concerning those points of conduct which depend upon the particular circumstances of each individual, *it is plain, therefore, that he can determine nothing to advantage*" (emphasis added). For detail, on the *knowledge problem* as a factor impeding, in principle, paternalistic state interventions, see Rizzo/Whitman, 2009 *B.Y.U.L.Rev.* (2009), 905 ff., esp. 908 ff., who criticize the 'new paternalism' of Sunstein and Thaler precisely from the perspective of the *knowledge problem*; this criticism is also endorsed by Wright/Ginsburg, 106 *Nw.U.L.R.* (2012), esp. 1065 ff., as well as Saint-Paul, *The Tyranny of Utility ...*, *passim*, esp. pp. 56 ff.

77 For the whole argument, which rests on the *public choice problem*, see Glaeser, 29 *Regulation* (2006), 34 ff.; Rebonato, 37 *J.Consum.Policy* (2014), 360, 389 ff.; Arlen, 52 *Vand.L.Rev.* (1998), 1769–1770, 1785; Sunstein/Thaler, 70 *U.Chi.L.Rev.* (2003), 1200; Jolls/Sunstein/Thaler, 50 *Stan.L.Rev.* (1998), 1509 ff. *passim*, 1543–1544; Sunstein, 64 *Duke L.J.* (2014), 36–37; the same, 127 *Harv.L.R. Forum* (2014), 211; the same, *Choosing Not to Choose...*, pp. 99 ff., 192; also R.Posner, *Economic Analysis of Law*^{6}, pp. 535 ff.; Schmolke, *Grenzen der Selbstbindung...*, pp. 240, 246; for more detail, Becker, 98 *Quart.J.Econ.* (1983), 371 ff. For a more authentic and precise picture of the public choice theory, see Buchanan, *Public Choice: The Origins and Development of a Research Program*, esp. pp. 4 ff.; the same, 1 *Const.Polit.Econ.* (1990), 1 ff.;

In a nutshell, the argument against the theory of Sunstein and Thaler deriving from the above may be summarized as follows: the imposition of heteronomous regulations—even in the form of simple default options—and thus the deprivation of individuals' freedom to choose actively and autonomously, is the manifestation of an ***elitistic paternalism.*** The necessity for and the rational foundations of such elitist paternalism are questionable, however noble the motives for each intervention might be.[78]

This argument, though, is not at all new. It reproduces the traditional discussion about the well-known, inherent defects of modern systems of representative democracy and, more particularly, the main reasons to reject the deliberate transfer of power from the people to legislative and governmental bodies, and in turn to groups of experts and technocrats who act chiefly as 'cost-benefit analysts.'[79] Yet this process represents a fundamental and not easily debatable trait of the constitutional order of modern liberal democracies; up till now, no better system of democratic division of powers has been discovered. However, the extent of state interference and central regulation is a matter of controversy and debate, giving rise to different possible responses from various points of view, still within a democratic order.

This argument also touches on the general ***principal-agent problem.*** This problem is typically present in any trust or agency relationship. It is developed either in the public sphere, such as the relationship between the electorate and its national representatives (whereby the control of the former over the latter is effectuated mainly by elections every four years, or by the exercise of citizens' political rights and freedoms, such as freedom of speech), or in private entities (such as between the shareholders-owners of a Société Anonyme and its board of directors, which determines the course of the Société Anonyme). In fact, very often we encounter abuse of power by an agent who cannot resist the temptation to exploit its privileged position for personal gain. In particular, the agent may exploit the principal's objective inability to properly monitor her and in addition use her informational superiority against her principal, who is usually remote from mission the agent has undertaken, whereas the agent is close to the source of information and the facts relating to the decision-making.[80] These ***agency risks and costs***, which are normally assumed by the principal, are in general the

Buchanan/Tullock, *The Calculus of Consent*; Formaini, 8 *Economic Insights* (2003), 1 ff.; Hill, 34 *Faith & Economics* (1999), 1 ff.; Towfigh/Petersen, Public Choice Theorie und Social Choice Theorie, pp. 133 ff., esp. 135 ff.; Bix, *Jurisprudence: Theory and Context*[7], pp. 227–228.

78 See, especially, the criticism by Waldron, It's All for Your Own Good, chapter 3.

79 For detail on this specific capacity of various government officials, see Sunstein, *The Cost-Benefit Revolution*, *passim*, esp. pp. 79 ff.

80 On the *principal-agent problem*, see, indicatively, Falk/Kosfeld, 96 *Am.Econ.Rev.* (2006), 1611 ff., esp. 1612; R.Posner, *Economic Analysis of Law*[6], pp. 407–408, 426 ff., esp. 547–548; Cooter/Ulen, *Law & Economics*[6], p. 138; Wittman, *Economic Foundations of Law*..., chapter 33 (pp. 313 ff.), chapter 36 (pp. 341 ff.); Sunstein, *Choosing Not to Choose*..., pp. 8–9; Thaler, *Misbehaving*..., pp. 105, 109, 291; Rebonato, 37 *J.Consum.Policy* (2014), 390; Schäfer/Ott, *Lehrbuch der ökonomischen Analyse des Zivilrechts*[4], pp. 645 ff.; Nicklisch/Petersen, Vertragstheorie,

necessary price that a person (the principal) who benefits from delegating tasks to other people (agents) has to pay.[81]

Put differently, the possibility of trust being disenchanted is a risk inherent in politics, policy making, transactions, and life relationships in general. This risk is consciously assumed by the person who places her trust in other people or grants them powers of management or representation relating to her own economic and other interests. This risk assumption is justified by the fact that the conferring of those powers entails, in principle, a division of labor that is desired by and beneficial to the principal, who is now free to devote herself to other activities.[82]

It is also worth mentioning that an agent may act opportunistically or irresponsibly because she does not have *skin in the game* when conducting other people's business and thus is not herself exposed to serious economic risk (e.g., a fund manager does not risk losing her own money).[83] And it is no coincidence that the legal system often seeks to *align the interests* of principal and agent, through various means, with a view to cracking down on such behavior. The general rule here is to create a link between the agent and the tasks delegated to her in a way that the agent herself is affected by the decisions she reaches in conducting those tasks. In a nutshell, the agent must have *skin in the game* or, to put it crudely, must be forced to *eat her own cooking*. This is the case, for instance, when the remuneration of a company's board of directors is linked to the company's economic course, or when there is a system of bonus clawbacks to dissuade a CEO from taking too many risks to the detriment of the shareholders.[84]

2. *Undermining human dignity and personal autonomy through manipulation*

a. Main points of the objection

Rather more seriously, the nudge theory is criticized for the twofold violation of *human dignity and personal autonomy*—the latter being "generally understood to refer to the capacity to be one's own person, to live one's life according to reasons and motives that are taken as one's own and *not the product of manipulative*

pp. 122 ff.; Bechtold, *Die Grenzen zwingenden Vertragsrechts...*, pp. 35 ff., 160 ff.; Schmolke, *JZ* (2015), 124, 128, 129.

81 See, indicatively, Bechtold, *Die Grenzen zwingenden Vertragsrechts...*, p. 36, and Schmolke, *JZ* (2015), 124.

82 For detail, see Sunstein/Bar-Gill, *Regulation as Delegation*, pp. 1 ff.

83 See Taleb/Sandis, 1 *Rev.Behav.Econ.* (2014), 1 ff.

84 See Taleb/Sandis, 1 *Rev.Behav.Econ.* (2014), 1 ff.: "... anyone involved in an action which can possibly generate harm for others, even probabilistically, should be required to be exposed to some damage, regardless of context. [...] ... one should be the first consumer of one's product, a cook should test his own food, helicopter repairpersons should be ready to take random flights on the rotorcraft that they maintain, hedge fund managers should be maximally invested in their funds." *Cf.* also Jensen/Meckling, 3 *JFE* (1976), 308; Schmolke, *JZ* (2015), 124, 128, 129.

or distorting external forces."[85] Specifically, it is argued that the central designing of individual choices, even in the form of default options, entails a degradation of the value of the individual as a moral person capable of reflecting and acting in a sovereign and autonomous manner, making her own evaluations and choices, and shaping her own life plans. Human dignity and personal autonomy are undermined when the evaluations or the preferences of the individual, even if false or mistaken, are influenced ***in a covert, intransparent way*** to promote other choices, choices that third persons deem more beneficial to the individual (or to the society as a whole). The individual is somehow 'programmed,' 'choice-architected,' or 'intervened on' to choose what the central planner considers ***a priori*** as right. In this respect, there is a reproachable ***manipulation*** of the behavior of the individual.[86] By the same token, other authors argue that the nudge theory offers only the ***illusion of choice***, because the choices available to the individual have been drastically chipped away in a nearly undetectable way.[87]

Thus there is an assault on the very core of private autonomy—that is, the freedom of individuals to self-determination, their privilege to determine and control their own lives and preferences, to decide which choices are desirable or important to them and which are not. In philosophy, ***autonomy*** is traditionally defined as regulation by the self and is distinguished from ***heteronomy***, that is, regulation by forces outside the self.[88] The nudge theory appears to strike at the

85 Christman, Autonomy in moral and political philosophy, Introduction. This definition is also endorsed by Schweizer, Nudging and the Principle of Proportionality..., pp. 98–99 (who rightly infers that "[a]t the heart of the debate whether nudging interferes with personal autonomy lies therefore the question whether nudges – some or all of them – are 'manipulative and distorting external forces'"), and van Aaken, Judge the Nudge..., p. 90.

86 On this objection, see Mitchell, 99 *Nw.U.L.R.* (2005), 1245 ff., esp. 1260 ff., who suggests precisely that the libertarian paternalism of Sunstein and Thaler is an 'oxymoron,' since it ultimately significantly restricts personal autonomy and thus does not deserve to be called 'libertarian'; Waldron, It's All for Your Own Good, chapter 4; Wright/Ginsburg, 106 *Nw.U.L.R.* (2012), 1033 ff. ***passim***, esp. 1067 ff.; Goodwin, 32 *Politics* (2012), 85 ff.; Wilkinson, 61 *Polit. Stud.* (2013), 341 ff.; Rebonato, 37 *J.Consum.Policy* (2014), 367 ff. ***passim***; Alemanno/Sibony, Epilogue..., pp. 325 ff., 333 ff.; van Aaken, Judge the Nudge..., pp. 91–92 (wherein ***inter alia***: "The blind spot of liberal paternalism is the notion of autonomy"), 94 ff.; Feldman/Lobel, Behavioural Trade-Offs..., pp. 314 ff. (wherein ***inter alia***, p. 314: "Under a nudge approach, the law operates behind the scenes, in the background of private decision-making"); Conly, ***Against Autonomy***..., p. 30; G.Dworkin, Paternalism, chapter 3 (esp. ***in fine***); cf. also Hausman/Welch, 18 *J.Polit.Philos.* (2010), 128 ff.; Feldman/Lobel, Behavioural Trade-Offs..., pp. 305 ff. Further, in general on the notion of ***manipulation***, *cf.* Wilkinson, 61 *Polit.Stud.* (2013), 342 and 345, as well as Raz, *The Morality of Freedom*, pp. 377 ff.

87 This is the basic tenet of the criticism exercised by Bubb/Pildes, 127 *Harv.L.R.* (2014), 1596 ff., who, characteristically, refer to an ***artificial truncation*** of the available options by means of the default rules or options.

88 Arvanitis, 47 *New Ideas in Psychology* (2017), 57 ff., esp. 58, who, further, eloquently presents a motivational theory called "Self-Determination Theory" (SDT), which surely deserves our attention: SDT is, namely, one of the most comprehensive psychological theories of autonomy and well-being; it has been at the forefront of the study of autonomy and self-authorship for more than 45 years. Specifically, this theory distinguishes autonomy from independence, defining "autonomous acts [...] in terms of a person's endorsement of the act itself." SDT views (a) behavior

heart of *self-authorship*, our sacred ability to ***autonomously shape our own lives*** and to remain authors of the book of our life without falling victim to manipulative regulatory tools that surreptitiously limit the choices we have.[89]

Self-authorship is highly valued, and rightly so, in the realms of legal and political philosophy. As is nowadays widely acknowledged, this influential notion is primarily attributable to the eminent Oxford philosopher Joseph Raz.[90] For him, we are namely pursuing a culture in which the value of personal autonomy or self-authorship is perceived to be the core value.[91] Raz describes personal autonomy as follows: "autonomy is opposed to a life of coerced choices. It contrasts with a life of no choices, or of ***drifting through life without ever exercising one's capacity to choose.***"[92] He further explains that "the autonomous person is a (part) author of his own life" and that "the ideal of personal autonomy is the vision of people controlling, ***to some degree***, their own destiny, fashioning it through successive decisions throughout their lives."[93] In this regard, "[a] person who has never had any significant choice, or was not aware of it, or never exercised choice in significant matters but ***simply drifted through life*** is not an autonomous person."[94] Furthermore, in a similar vein, according to Finnis's autonomy-supportive line of reasoning,[95] we should live, or at least have the opportunity to live, fully reasonable or even flourishing lives, lead them

as the result of the interaction between person and environment, and (b) autonomy as a psychological need, arguing that "an autonomous act is defined as regulation by the self, the self being a central process that regulates behavior and experience. It is an organismic theory that accepts that humans have a natural propensity to grow and assimilate aspects of their environment. Behavior is essentially the product of the interaction between the organism and the environment" (Arvanitis, *ibidem*, p. 58). On SDT, see also Arvanitis/Kalliris, 30 *Philos.Psychol.* (2017), 763 ff.; further, more recently, for an examination of nudges, especially defaults, through the lens of SDT, see Arvanitis/Kalliris/Kaminiotis, *The Social Science Journal* (2019).

89 See Kalliris, *Autonomy, Well-Being and the Law*, *passim*, esp. pp. 14 ff., 32 ff., 40 ff., 59 ff., 84–85, 153 ff., 164–165, 207 ff., who considers the existence of ***an adequate range of options*** as a fundamental prerequisite of self-authorship; the same, 8 *Jurisprudence* (2017), 23 ff.; also White, The Crucial Importance of Interests…, p. 23, wherein *inter alia*: "One of the bedrock principles of a liberal society is that each person may pursue his or her own idea of the good life, provided no one interferes wrongfully with others doing the same. In steering people's choices away from their true interests, however, nudges deny people this self-directedness." In a similar vein, see Sneddon, 33 *CRITICA* (2001), 105 ff., who also draws the interesting distinction between *deep* and *shallow* autonomy; in this regard the latter may be restricted in favor of the former with a view to securing the *self-rule* of individuals, which involves shaping and acting on a plan for one's life. *Cf.* further Enderlein, *Rechtspaternalismus…*, *passim*, esp. pp. 52 ff., 232 ff., 266, 286 ff., 306 ff., 552, who supports a paternalism that maximizes freedom (*freiheitsmaximierender Paternalismus*)—that is, paternalistic interventions that aim at securing or even enhancing individuals' future freedom (*freiheitsmaximierend paternalistische Eingriffe*).

90 Raz, *The Morality of Freedom*, *passim*, esp. pp. 204–205, 369, 371 ff., 391 ff., 407 ff.

91 Raz, *The Morality of Freedom*, *passim*; see also Gardner, 9 *Oxf.J.Leg.Stud.* (1989), 17 ff., esp. 20.

92 Raz, *The Morality of Freedom*, p. 371—emphasis added.

93 Raz, *The Morality of Freedom*, p. 369—emphasis added.

94 Raz, *The Morality of Freedom*, p. 204—emphasis added.

95 See Finnis, *Natural Law and Natural Rights*, *passim*, and Simmonds, *Central Issues in Jurisprudence*[5], pp. 123 ff.

in accordance with our own values, and not have them imposed upon us by authority. There can be no single ideal way of life that we should all aim to live, or that the state should aim to impose or encourage; in other words, individuals should have the capacity to choose for themselves from among the widely different life plans that may count as 'reasonable,' such a capacity being *an objective good in itself*.[96] Similar philosophical accounts of personal autonomy or self-authorship (or, further, 'self-ownership,' 'self-sovereignty') may also be found in the writings of other great political philosophers, such as Rawls, R.Dworkin, and Nozick.[97]

The aforementioned points do a lot of work in the direction of fleshing out the core idea of self-authorship—or personal autonomy—as the ability to live "a life in accordance with the principles, values, and choices of the person whose life it is. It requires freedom from undue external interference (*negative* freedom) but, more importantly, it requires actively making autonomous choices (*positive* freedom). A possible qualification for this kind of life is the *mental capacity* for adopting principles, endorsing values, and making choices."[98] The nudge theory sometimes seems, indeed, to pose an assault on both aspects of self-authorship (*negative* and *positive* freedom), mainly by devising manipulative techniques, that is, practices that distort the way we see our options and lead us to make choices that are not self-endorsed.[99]

From this critical perspective, the nudge, instead of teaching us how to think and choose actively, usurps our right to make certain transactional or life choices. It succeeds primarily because it takes advantage of our inertia or ignorance, since our decisions are channeled in a particular direction, sometimes without our knowing that we are being nudged or choice-architected.[100] It may thus undermine our capacity to choose for ourselves the lives we wish to lead. And it is evident that in this regard, it also infringes on Immanuel Kant's second version of categorical imperative relating to the protection of human dignity, according to which no individual can be treated as a *means or object* for the attainment of an end (whatever that end might be),[101] for, although

96 Simmonds, *Central Issues in Jurisprudence*[5], p. 127, wherein Simmonds elucidates Finnis's line of reasoning as follows: "The liberal aspect of the theory depends in part upon Finnis's insistence that the capacity of individuals to choose for themselves is itself (under the heading of 'practical reasonableness') an objective good. [...] It is true that people who were simply coerced into conformity would not themselves be leading flourishing lives: for, in being the outcome of coercion, their lives would not be manifestations of the capacities for deliberation and choice that constitute the good of 'practical reasonableness'...."

97 See, indicatively, Arvanitis/Kalliris, 30 *Philos.Psychol.* (2017), 763 ff.

98 Arvanitis/Kalliris, 30 *Philos.Psychol.* (2017), 773.

99 *Cf.*, once again, Arvanitis/Kalliris, 30 *Philos.Psychol.* (2017), 773 ff., esp. 775 and 776.

100 See Waldron, It's All for Your Own Good, chapter 4.

101 Kant, *Grundlegung zur Metaphysik der Sitten*, esp. para. 429 (pp. 54–55): "*Handle so, daß du die Menschheit, sowohl in deiner Person als in der Person eines jeden anderen, jederzeit zugleich als Zweck, niemals bloß als Mittel brauchest.* [...] Der Mensch [...] ist keine Sache, mithin nicht etwas, das *bloß als Mittel* gebraucht werden kann, sondern muß bei allen seinen Handlungen jederzeit als *Zweck an sich selbst* betrachtet werden" (see also paras. 430, 433, 434–435). *Cf.* Wolf/

the regulatory intervention is meant to serve the individual's (and possibly the society's) best interests, by virtue of the heteronomously determined default option the individual seems to become ***a mere means for attaining objectively desirable purposes.***[102]

As is rather evident, the criticism leveled above emphasizes, in essence, the ***non-transparent character*** of defaults. Defaults sometimes ***(but not always)*** fly, indeed, below the radar of the individual. They are not easily detectable and they influence our behavior in a covert way without our realizing, thus promoting a 'governance by stealth.'[103] This might be the very purpose of nudges, though, in the sense that transparency would undermine their efficiency.[104] In this regard, mild or libertarian paternalism, along with its strong political popularity, may easily become an instrument that clever politicians (or social planners) will systematically exploit. Consider, for instance, the illustrative example of "distorting mirrors" offered by Blumenthal-Barby: someone wishes to convince his overweight roommate to lose weight by replacing all mirrors in the house with distorting mirrors that make the person look fatter.[105] Such a nudging interference, though, is unacceptable not only because it is nontransparent but also because it evidently provides false information.[106]

By contrast, it is argued that hard or coercive paternalism interventions, which consist in overt, explicit prohibitions and mandatory rules as well as all sorts of sanctions (such as fines or imprisonment), may be preferable because they are

---

Neuner, *AT des BürgR*[10], § 10 paras. 3 ff.; Heun, *JZ* (2005), 853; White, 33 *J.Socio-Econ.* (2004), 93; Wagner, Mandatory Contract Law..., p. 10; Nozick, *Anarchy, State, and Utopia*, pp. 30 ff.

102 See also G.Dworkin, Paternalism, chapter 3; Waldron, It's All for Your Own Good, chapter 4; Raz, *The Morality of Freedom*, p. 378: "... by coercing or manipulating a person one treats him *as an object rather than as an autonomous person*" (emphasis added), 410.

103 See, indicatively, Mols/Haslam/Jetten/Steffens, 54 *EJPR* (2015), 87–88, 94–95: "This mode of governance enables governments *to 'fly below the radar,'* to influence behaviour covertly, and is in our view therefore best described as *governance by stealth*" (emphasis added); Schweizer, Nudging and the Principle of Proportionality..., pp. 99 ff.; also Lichtenberg, Paternalism, Manipulation, Freedom, and the Good, pp. 495 ff., wherein *inter alia* (p. 496): "The idea that someone is attempting to influence our choices without our knowledge or consent is troubling [...]. We tend to call this kind of influence-creation *manipulation*; its connotations are negative"; van Aaken, Judge the Nudge..., pp. 94–95.

104 *Cf.* also Ghisellini/Chang, *Behavioral Economics...*, p. 213: "... As a matter of fact, if it were true that the substance of freedom to choose is preserved, nudges would be ineffective in the first place. *So, paradoxically, in order to be effective, nudges are required to reduce freedom of choice*" (emphasis added).

105 Blumenthal-Barby, Choice Architecture..., p. 190; see also Schweizer, Nudging and the Principle of Proportionality..., pp. 100, 101.

106 Schweizer, Nudging and the Principle of Proportionality..., p. 100, who further rightly points out (*ibidem*, p. 102) that *on the other hand* "the provision of purely factual information will enhance rather than diminish personal autonomy. Nudges aimed merely at increasing the awareness and information of citizens do not lead to constitutional concerns. Reminding students to enrol in higher education by sending them text messages, for example, is no interference with private autonomy."

more transparent, in both their means and their ends,[107] for, in that case, people are well aware that the state is attempting to control them or influence their behavior or choices—for example, when it prohibits riding a motorcycle without a helmet by providing, at the same time, a relevant fine for the offenders, whereas this is not the case, for example, when people are presented with an arrangement of food in the cafeteria, whose influence on their behavior they cannot regularly perceive.[108]

b. Rebuttal

aa The particular nature and function of default rules and the benefit from their legislative use

It is true, at least *prima facie*, that the drafting of a specific choice architecture scheme—that is, the design of a certain set of default rules—constitutes a form of individual choice 'manipulation' (even of a mild character) that reflects the wishes and expectations of the social regulator. It seems to rest on a usurpation of the power of the individual to make decisions autonomously by means of carefully putting away (or even concealing) some set of choices from the individual's horizon, which results in the reduction of the choices available.[109] Even on this level, however, compelling counterarguments can be lodged, which put many relevant concerns to rest and thus cannot be overlooked in a fair evaluation of the nudge theory[110]:

Foremost among them, default options cannot, by definition, be absolutely neutral. Especially in the transaction realm, they must be formed one way or another, pointing in one direction or another; the existence of a certain *choice architecture*, or a frame of 'navigability,' will be in many cases *inevitable (non-neutrality thesis: there is no neutral design)*. Even the weather can be deemed

107 See Glaeser, 29 *Regulation* (2006), 32 ff.; Lichtenberg, Paternalism, Manipulation, Freedom, and the Good, pp. 495–496; Kalliris, *Autonomy, Well-Being and the Law, passim*, pp. 55 ff., 133, 137 ff., 170 ff., esp. 173–174, 195 ff., esp. 198–199; Rizzo/Whitman, 2009 *B.Y.U.L.Rev.* (2009), 905 ff. *passim*; Rebonato, 37 *J.Consum.Policy* (2014), 368–369; more extensively Bubb/Pildes, 127 *Harv.L.R.* (2014), 1596 ff., esp. 1605 (: "Soft paternalist measures run the risk of being less visible than more traditional regulations and mandates"), who advance the position that in many cases the establishment of *direct/explicit mandates* would be more preferable; in a similar vein, see Hausman/Welch, 18 *J.Polit.Philos.* (2010), 130 ff., esp. 134 ff., and Leggett, 42 *Policy Polit.* (2014), 3 ff.; *cf.* further Conly, *Against Autonomy...*, who advocates *coercive paternalism*.

108 Lichtenberg, Paternalism, Manipulation, Freedom, and the Good, pp. 495–496.

109 See, indicatively, once again Kalliris, *Autonomy, Well-Being and the Law*, pp. 50 ff., esp. 55 ff., 143 ff., 170 ff., 195 ff., and 8 *Jurisprudence* (2017), 23 ff. *passim*; Conly, *Against Autonomy...*, *passim*; further Raz, *The Morality of Freedom*, pp. 377–378, 420–421.

110 For a recent extensive reply to the objections raised against libertarian paternalism, see Sunstein, *Nudging and Choice Architecture...*, pp. 1 ff., esp. 19 ff., *Fifty Shades of Manipulation*, pp. 1 ff., as well as 122 *Yale L.J.* (2013), 1881 ff., 1890 ff.; cf. further Kahneman, *Thinking, Fast and Slow*, pp. 412 ff.

to present a choice architecture; nature itself nudges us, and therefore, as the argument goes, ***human beings cannot wish choice architecture away.***[111]

On the other hand, the individual is still able to opt out of the choice architecture of the social planner and reclaim her autonomous space. In this respect, the default option operates under the ***potestative condition*** of the individual's opting out of inertia and choosing a different, autonomous path, even though the process of opting out may sometimes entail cost and effort, possibly along with stress, which the individual might not wish to undertake.[112] In most cases, though, opting out of a default rule entails low or even totally negligible, transaction costs. (For example, when by default a bank ATM does not provide a printed transaction receipt for environmental reasons, there is a crystal-clear, transparent nudging default that the individual can easily override with the press of a button.) This critical trait justifies, in principle, the characterization of this kind of nudging paternalism as ***mild***; at the same time it shows that individuals who wish to opt out of the default option do not need to give up their autonomy.[113] To me, this is a significant response to the manipulation objection to the Sunstein and Thaler–style libertarian or mild paternalism.

Recently, though, Sunstein himself concedes that "at least some degree of manipulation may be involved whenever a choice architect is targeting emotions or seeking a formulation that will be effective because of how it interacts with people's intuitive or automatic thinking."[114] In the same vein, Sunstein further

111 For the above, see Thaler/Sunstein, *Nudge…*, *passim*, esp. pp. 10–11 (: "… In many situations, some organization or agent *must* make a choice that will affect the behavior of some other people. […] …governments […] have to provide starting points of one or another kind. This is not avoidable."), 74, 83, 86, 237 (: "In many cases, some kind of nudge is inevitable, and so it is pointless to ask government simply to stand aside. Choice architects, whether private or public, must do *something*"), and 252–253; the same, 70 *U.Chi.L.Rev.* (2003), 1164 ff., esp. 1166, 1174–1175, 1177, 1182–1183, 1184, 1190; Sunstein, *Misconceptions about Nudges*, 4 (: "… a great deal of nudging is inevitable. […] If the law establishes contract, property, and tort law, it will be nudging, if only because it will set out default rules, which establish what happens if people do nothing. […] As Hayek well understood, a state that protects private property and that enforces contracts has to establish a set of prohibitions and permissions, including a set of default entitlements, establishing who has what before bargaining begins. For that reason, it is literally pointless to exclaim, "do not nudge!"—at least if one does not embrace anarchy."); the same, *Nudging and Choice Architecture…*, pp. 1 ff. *passim*, esp. 10 ff., 44 and 49–50; the same, 122 *Yale L.J.* (2013), 1834, 1836 ff., 1879 ff.; the same, *Choosing Not to Choose…*, *passim*, esp. pp. 5–6, 15 ff., 51–52; the same, The Ethics of Nudging, pp. v ff.; Thaler, 108 *Am.Econ. Rev.* (2018), 1285; Thaler/Sunstein/Balz, Choice Architecture, pp. 430–431; Lichtenberg, Paternalism, Manipulation, Freedom, and the Good, pp. 495, 496–497 (where reference to the '*nonneutrality thesis*'); Leggett, 42 *Policy Polit.* (2014), 15; Saint-Paul, *The Tyranny of Utility…*, p. 84; Neumann, *Libertärer Paternalismus…*, pp. 39 ff.; even Waldron, It's All for Your Own Good, chapter 1 (: "There is no getting away from this: choices are always going to be structured in some manner…"). However, *cf.* also the objections raised in this context by Wright/Ginsburg, 106 *Nw.U.L.R.* (2012), 1062–1063, and Mitchell, 99 *Nw.U.L.R.* (2005), 1250 ff.

112 See also Johnson/Goldstein, 302 *Science* (2003), 1338–1339.

113 See, indicatively, also DellaVigna, 47 *JEL* (2009), 323, 324, 365.

114 Sunstein, The Ethics of Nudging, p. xv.

openly acknowledges that "some (certainly not all) nudges can be considered as manipulative within an ordinary understanding of that term. But when nudges fall within the periphery of the concept, when they have legitimate purposes, when they would be effective, and when they do not diverge from the kinds of influences that are common and unobjectionable in ordinary life, the burden of justification can often be met."[115]

Apart from the above general remarks, let us now turn to the field of *contracts* in particular and see the practical usefulness of default rules. Let's think, for example, about a transactors pair ready to conclude a lease contract. If the transactors 'enjoy' the possibility of (absolute) active choosing, they will have to decide among a plethora of available regulatory options with regard to the lease terms, which might not be a particularly enjoyable situation. Instead of such disturbing abundance, the transactors should have the benefit of a set of default rules, on which they may rely for their contractual relationship, without having to attend to every contractual detail. In this way they can focus their attention on determining the so-called *essentialia negotii* (e.g., the object of the contract, the price to be paid). And, indeed, every modern legal system resorts to setting detailed default rules, especially in the field of contracts, in view of the very real possibility that the parties have left unaddressed some critical parameters of their contractual relationship (such as the time or place of performance). Therefore, realistically, the issue to be dealt with is not whether the legislator must act or not, but how she may form those unavoidable default rules in the best way possible.[116]

The default rules contained in the various contract law systems relieve us of the negotiations-generated cost and effort that would occur if the parties had to review every aspect of a contractual relationship. Default rules greatly reduce transaction costs (the more so the closer they are to the will of the contracting parties).[117] (By the way, the same holds true for *General Contract Terms* as well.[118]) The parties are thus allowed to focus on the main issues of the transaction:

115 Sunstein, The Ethics of Nudging, p. xv.

116 *Cf.* also Sunstein, 73 *U.Chi.L.Rev.* (2006), 258 ff.

117 See Kronman, 92 *Yale L.J.* (1983), 766–767; Ayres, 73 *U.Chi.L.Rev.* (2006), 13–14; Ayres/Gertner, 99 *Yale L.J.* (1989), 93, 111–112; the same, 101 *Yale L.J.* (1992), 731; Cooter/Ulen, *Law & Economics*[6], p. 293; Unberath, Long-Term Contracts and the DCFR..., pp. 96–97 (who, at the same time, rightly points out that if the default is inefficient the parties will attempt to contract out of it: "[c]ontract law then increases transaction costs"); Trebilcock, *The Limits of Freedom of Contract*, p. 16; Cserne, *Freedom of Contract...*, p. 58; Sunstein, *Choosing Not to Choose...*, *passim*, esp. p. 18; Kähler, *Begriff und Rechtfertigung...*, pp. 96, 141–142, esp. 163 ff.; Möslein, *Dispositives Recht...*, pp. 33–34, 280–281; Ringe, 213 *AcP* (2013), 101, 107, 110–111, 117 ff. *passim*; Unberath/Cziupka, 209 *AcP* (2009), 43–44, 49–50; Schäfer/Ott, *Lehrbuch der ökonomischen Analyse des Zivilrechts*[4], p. 426; Drexl, *Die wirtschaftliche Selbstbestimmung...*, pp. 306, 308, 311; Grigoleit, Zwingendes Recht..., p. 1823; Bachmann, *Private Ordnung...*, p. 122.

118 See Schäfer/Ott, *Lehrbuch der ökonomischen Analyse des Zivilrechts*[4], pp. 426–427; Kötz, *JuS* (2003), 211 ff.; Kähler, *Begriff und Rechtfertigung...*, pp. 203–204; Kittner, *Schuldrecht*[2], no. 821.

specific nature of performance and price.[119] In this way default rules release resources—primarily time—for more productive or pleasant activities (such as leisure activities). They thus contribute to individual and social welfare, to the enhancement of our autonomy, and at the end of the day, to a better quality of life; and this is probably the most significant contribution of contract law default rules, which is, however, sometimes disregarded in the relevant discourse.[120]

In addition, especially in the field of contract law, default rules are not often suitable as manipulative tools. Often enough, they are characterized by a degree of transparency, not only when they affect the field of transactions but also when they are still being formed by the legislator, since normally such formation comes after public consultation and scrutiny. Thus the contractual default rule is not *usually* hidden or lurking (behind a manipulative choice architecture) but is visible to the transactors, who still possess the power to opt out of its regulatory framework.[121]

And in all cases, how realistic is it to see the setting of such default rules as an act that lies at the core of the notion of manipulation? In general, manipulation is multi-faceted and has various shades.[122] The setting of contract law default rules could be thought of as possibly touching only upon the periphery of the notion. Even more so if manipulation is defined as an act that "attempts to influence people subconsciously or unconsciously, in a way that does not respect their capacity for conscious choice."[123]

Moreover, is it indeed a morally reproachable 'manipulation' when the person is nudged to make a decision that she would also reach had she acquired adequate knowledge and information on the issue to be decided? When the default option is in alignment with the hypothetical will of an adequately informed person, should it really be dropped on moral grounds for being 'manipulative'?[124]

Especially in the field of contract law the default rules crystallize, in an abstract-typical way, long-standing transaction practice and thus the typical interests of the majority of the transactors.[125] As a matter of fact, this approach

119 Unberath, Long-Term Contracts and the DCFR..., pp. 96–97.

120 *Cf.*, though, Sunstein, 162 *U.Penn.L.R.* (2013), 8–9, 46–47, 53, 57; further Sneddon, 33 *CRITICA* (2001), 109–110.

121 See Sunstein, *Nudging: A Very Short Guide*, p. 2, and *Choosing Not to Choose...*, pp. 51–52, 193; for more detail, the same, *Nudging and Choice Architecture...*, pp. 19, 34 ff., esp. 42 and 45 ff., as well as 122 *Yale L.J.* (2013), 1890 ff.; *cf.* also Hausman/Welch, 18 *J.Polit.Philos.* (2010), 130 ff. *passim*, esp. 134; Goodwin, 32 *Politics* (2012), 87 ff., esp. 90–91; Leggett, 42 *Policy Polit.* (2014), 16.

122 On these various shades, see Sunstein, *Fifty Shades of Manipulation*, pp. 1 ff., *passim*.

123 Sunstein, The Ethics of Nudging, pp. xiii–xiv; the same, *Nudging and Choice Architecture...*, pp. 34 ff., esp. 35, 40 and 49; *cf.* also the same, *Fifty Shades of Manipulation*, pp. 6 ff.

124 *Cf.* also Elster, *Ulysses and the Sirens...*, pp. 81 and 83.

125 See, indicatively, Grigoleit, Zwingendes Recht..., p. 1823; Unberath/Cziupka, 209 *AcP* (2009), 41, 48 ff. *passim*; Cserne, *Freedom of Contract...*, p. 58; *cf.* further Ayres/Gertner, 99 *Yale L.J.* (1989), 87 ff., esp. 90 ff.; Porat/Strahilevitz, 112 *Mich.L.Rev.* (2014), 1423 ff., esp. 1425 ff.; Charny, 89 *Mich.L.Rev.* (1991), 1823 ff.; Sunstein/Bar-Gill, *Regulation As Delegation*, p. 5; Schäfer/Ott, *Lehrbuch der ökonomischen Analyse des Zivilrechts*[4], pp. 427–428.

reflects the so-called '*majoritarian default-rules theory*,' the most widely accepted theory among law-and-economics theorists on the matter: this theory demands, namely, that "a default rule should mimic the term that the majority of the parties to whom it applies would have agreed on had they considered it as an option when making their contract."[126] In the same vein, it is rightly suggested that contract law default rules reflect the contractual content that most parties would choose if they acted *in a state of adequate information (the informed-chooser default)*.[127] This approach to the content of contract law default rules is also closely related to the pertinent classical doctrine of German law (going back to the great legal scholars Windscheid and Savigny), according to which default rules reflect the hypothetical or presumed will of the parties (in German: *Simulation des Parteiwillens*); they set out the rules on which the parties would have agreed after relevant negotiations.[128]

Notwithstanding the above, in practice, instances of nontransparent and thus problematic defaults in the realm of contract law may still come up. This might occur especially when there is a large divergence of the default rule from the presumed will. It may, namely, be the case that the default scheme leads the transactors to accept (by default) rules that they are ignorant of—or that are not easily accessible to them—and that they would have not chosen if they had known of their existence at the time of the conclusion of the contract. The failure of a default due to lack of transparency is epitomized by the *United Nations Convention on Contracts for the International Sale of Goods* (CISG, Vienna 1980), which, pursuant to its Article 6,[129] constitutes *in toto* an opt-out regulatory instrument. However, the parties to an international sale of goods, which falls within the scope of the CISG, may often not be aware of its existence—or its application by default. Thus, afterward, they may be confronted with the unpleasant surprise of having to abide by its rules, even though they might have explicitly substituted an applicable national law, though without clarifying whether it should be the national sales law or the specific national law ratifying the CISG. In such a case, the problem lies with the fact that on the one hand there is *no explicit exclusion* of the application of the CISG (i.e., no explicit opt-out, as Article 6 demands), and on the other hand, the applicable national substantive law embraces the CISG as well, so the latter is in principle applicable, although the parties might

126 Porat/Strahilevitz, 112 *Mich.L.Rev.* (2014), 1425 (: "The logic behind the majoritarian default-rules theory is simple: since default rules aim to decrease transaction costs, they should fit the parties' preferences as closely as possible"), who, however, cast doubt on the efficiency of this model, pointing at the (practical) difficulty in predicting most parties' preferences (*ibidem*, pp. 1425 ff.); see also Unberath, Long-Term Contracts and the DCFR..., p. 97, where further references to pertinent literature.

127 See Sunstein, 162 *U.Penn.L.R.* (2013), 31 ff., and *Choosing Not to Choose*..., pp. 72 ff.; Wagner, Zwingendes Vertragsrecht, p. 16; *cf.* also Cooter/Ulen, *Law & Economics*[6], pp. 293–294.

128 See, indicatively, in detail Kähler, *Begriff und Rechtfertigung*..., pp. 96 ff.; Möslein, *Dispositives Recht*..., pp. 89 ff., 281; also Ringe, 213 *AcP* (2013), 110–111, 118–119.

129 "The parties may exclude the application of this Convention or, subject to article 12, derogate from or vary the effect of any of its provisions."

actually have intended to apply a national sales law (e.g., the relevant sales law provisions of the German Civil Code), with which they were familiar and more comfortable. In light of this problematic situation and, in particular, in light of the widely acknowledged reduced attractiveness of the CISG as a regulatory tool for international sales of movable goods, in recent decades national case law and theory tend to infer the exclusion of the CISG in cases where the parties have explicitly chosen a national law as applicable substantive law (*implicit exclusion* of the CISG); an additional condition is that the parties must have known, at the time of the conclusion of their contract, the existence of the CISG. Moreover, some authors have gone one step further, suggesting that the CISG, contrary to the clear wording of Article 6 and the intention of the CISG's drafters, may be perceived as an *opt-in* regulatory framework.[130] In any event, an eventual 'implicit' inference of the CISG's exclusion will depend upon a proper interpretation of the contractual clause regulating the applicable substantive law.[131]

The aforementioned example seems to reinforce the view that, in general, default rules sometimes come close to functioning as mandatory rules *(implicit mandates)*,[132] mostly owing to the low rates of opting out, which advance the purposes of mild or libertarian paternalism; *but this does not mean that default rules should be largely replaced by mandatory rules*[133] for there is still a crucial difference between the two types of rules—namely, *the freedom to opt out.* And in a legal system that really values private autonomy, it is vital that any individual who wishes to opt out is free to do so. Libertarian paternalism essentially promotes an *assisted choice* mechanism; within this mechanism, and in contrast to *mandatory prohibitive* or *imperative rules* (e.g., the requirement to wear a seat belt when driving a car, or the compulsory 'participation' in a pension program),[134] the freedom of choice, as a fundamental constituent of personal autonomy, human

130 On all the above, see MünchKomm(BGB)/Westermann, Article 6 CISG no. 1 ff., esp. 5 ff.; Ferrari, 4 *ZEuP* (2002), 737 ff., esp. 741–742; Stürner, *BB* (2006), 2029 ff.; Möslein, *Dispositives Recht* ..., pp. 369–370; Graffi, 4 *Eur.L.For.* (2000–2001), 241; Ringe, 213 *AcP* (2013), 103.

131 *Cf.* also the practitioner's viewpoint, which precisely points to the problems discussed above: Larionova/Monroe, *CISG: To Include or Exclude – That is the Question*, where, *inter alia*, the following thoughts are articulated: "... Although I agree with the many commentators on the CISG that the CISG is beneficial because it increases the predictability of outcomes in international trade, I almost always exclude the CISG. / To answer the question of whether to include or exclude the CISG, the answer remains, it depends. However, and most importantly, is to be aware of the CISG's potential application and then to analyze whether or not it should apply to the contract to avoid having the CISG apply by default because the issue was not addressed in a written contract. Typically the CISG exclusion clause is included in the governing law clause as follows: 'The provisions of the United Nations Convention on the International Sale of Goods shall not apply to this Agreement.'"

132 On the *quasi* or *de facto mandatory force* of contractual default rules see pp. 27–28 above, with references to the pertinent literature.

133 This is, however, the suggestion of Bubb/Pildes, 127 *Harv.L.R.* (2014), 1596 ff.

134 For this useful notional distinction (in German: *Wahlhilfe, Wahlverbot, Wahlgebot*), see van Aaken, Begrenzte Rationalität..., pp. 124 ff., and Schmolke, *Grenzen der Selbstbindung*..., pp. 30 ff., 69–70, esp. 226 ff., 256 ff., 839 ff., 870 ff., 926 ff.

dignity, and economic freedom, is regularly preserved: the individual is called upon to freely choose whether she wishes to stick with the default rule or to opt out.[135] For this reason, at least in the realm of contract law, the configuration of a certain choice architecture, through default rules, does not typically appear to deprive the individual of an *adequate range of options*, which is, according to Raz, indispensable for preserving the fundamental principle of self-authorship.[136]

Last but not least, the 'manipulation objection' is considerably weakened in light of critical empirical evidence on contract law default rules, which shows that the default rule is easily overridden when the transactors hold strong opposite *antecedent preferences.* Such preferences are not bent by the default rule and thus survive in a contest with the latter, especially when the default rule is so extreme as to cause a *reactance* on the transactors' part; in such a case the default rule *backfires.*[137] For instance, if the default contribution to a pension program is set at 30% of an employee's wage, most employees will opt out of the program and search for another pension scheme because they have a certain resistance (or *reactance*) point, which the (extreme) default option cannot bend.[138] Strong antecedent preferences can be observed in the similar but more compelling case of spouses' surnames after marrying. In countries where the law provides that, in principle, spouses maintain their surnames after their marriage (see, for instance, Article 1388 of the Greek Civil Code), despite said provision, and probably because of the sexist history of name-changing conventions, wives often choose to use the surname of their husband (alone or along with their own surname), either unofficially in their social activities or officially after having submitted a time-consuming declaration to the registry office (in this case it might be statutorily permissible only for the wife to add her husband's surname to hers but not to take it as her only surname).[139] In such instances, transactors exercise their freedom of choice with a view to reversing the default option. Thus the argument that default rules necessarily restrict private autonomy proves to be false, at least in the absolute manner in which it is sometimes articulated.

In general, rules that are strongly opposed by individuals and induce the reactance phenomenon are already known in the legal literature; they constitute a particular category of default rules, which, especially in the field of contract law, are called *penalty default rules (Ayres/Gertner).* In contrast with the usual

135 See, indicatively,Thaler/Sunstein, *Nudge...*, passim, esp. pp. 5; the same, 70 *U.Chi.L.Rev.* (2003), 1173, 1182; van Aaken, Begrenzte Rationalität..., pp. 125, 135, 138; also Schmolke, *Grenzen der Selbstbindung..., passim*, esp. pp. 256 ff. and 921 ff.

136 See, once again, Raz, *The Morality of Freedom*, esp. pp. 204–205 and 371.

137 On the so-called *reactance or backlash effect*, see Sunstein, 64 *Duke L.J.* (2014), 9–10 (esp. fn. 24), 162 *U.Penn.L.R.* (2013), 16–17, 26 ff., 122 *Yale L.J.* (2013), 1894, and more recently *Choosing Not to Choose..., passim*, esp. pp. 27–28, 118, 132 ff.; *cf.* further Pavey/Sparks, 33 *Motiv.Emot.* (2009), 277 ff.; Mols/Haslam/Jetten/Steffens, 54 *EJPR* (2015), 86.

138 See also Sunstein, 162 *U.Penn.L.R.* (2013), 26–27, where reference to the relevant research, which precisely proves the above assumption.

139 For detail on this thorny topic, Porat/Strahilevitz, 112 *Mich.L.Rev.* (2014), 1463 ff.; Sunstein, 162 *U.Penn.L.R.* (2013), 25–26, 34; Emens, 74 *U.Chi.L.Rev.* (2007), 761 ff.

default rules that purport to crystallize long-standing transaction practice or to mimic the parties' hypothetical will, penalty (or '*minoritarian*') default rules are designed to give at least one contracting party the incentive to opt out and thus to make both parties formulate an autonomous contractual provision—insofar as, of course, the relevant transaction costs are not prohibitive for such contracting around. In other words, penalty default rules intentionally incorporate provisions that *the parties would not want*, in order to make them take into their own hands the fate of the contractual content and engage in negotiations in which *they will be practically forced to exchange or reveal crucial information* about the contractual object that has to be regulated, or even reveal their actual transactional purposes. Such rules incentivize the party possessing specific information to reveal it to the other party, thus paving the way to the conclusion of an efficient contract *(information-forcing defaults)*. In essence, penalty default rules operate as nudges. They are intended primarily to mitigate *information asymmetries* that come up in transactions. For instance, an employment contract might include default rules so exceptionally favorable to the employee and unfavorable to the employer that the latter, who is the well informed party, is forced to disclose significant information about the contractual object or her actual intentions with respect to the protection to be granted to the employee; such a disclosure could result in some employee rights being replaced by a higher wage, which might be more desirable to the employee than keeping in force other terms or provisions that are in her favor.[140]

Notwithstanding the above, a significant caveat must be entered here: since the default option is set by the legislator, individuals may often consider it to be *de facto* binding upon them; that is, they may feel compelled to follow its direction, even though it is a default (not mandatory) rule and the costs of contracting away might be low. Thus individuals may succumb to the power of the *dictum* of the legislative authority, due to *authority bias*,[141] which is accompanied by an *endowment effect* that individuals might develop in relation to the statutory default.[142] In essence, both biases amount to a significant *status quo*

140 For the above, see Ayres/Gertner, 99 *Yale L.J.* (1989), 91 ff., esp. 95 ff., wherein they characteristically underscore (pp. 106–107) that "when individual parties have private incentives to withhold information, it may be desirable for the law to give them a nudge"; see also Porat/Strahilevitz, 112 *Mich.L.Rev.* (2014), 1428 ff.; Trebilcock, *The Limits of Freedom of Contract*, pp. 122 ff.; Issacharoff, 74 *Tex.L.Rev.* (1996), 1792 ff.; Sunstein, 162 *U.Penn.L.R.* (2013), 35; the same, *Choosing Not to Choose...*, pp. 80–81; Unberath, Long-Term Contracts and the DCFR..., pp. 98–99; extensively Bechtold, *Die Grenzen zwingenden Vertragsrechts...*, pp. 216 ff. (: "*informationsinduzierende dispositive Regelungen*," "*informationsinduzierende Funktion dispositiven Vertragsrechts*"), 256–257, 260, 295–296, 297; Kähler, *Begriff und Rechtfertigung...*, pp. 143–144, 149 ff., 183; Unberath/Cziupka, 209 *AcP* (2009), 63 ff.

141 See esp. Tscherner, 1 *ALJ* (2014), 147, and Kähler, *Begriff und Rechtfertigung...*, pp. 182. More generally, with respect to *authority bias*, see Sunstein, 162 *U.Penn.L.R.* (2013), 23–24; the same, *Choosing Not to Choose...*, pp. 41, 51; the same, *Fifty Shades of Manipulation*, pp. 16–17; Hinnosaar/Hinnosaar, *Authority Bias.*

142 For the possibility of an instant endowment effect in relation to legal provisions, see p. 29 above.

bias in relation to the default rule, which, as already discussed above, makes the transacting parties stick with the latter despite its eventual inefficiency. In other words, even if the default does not appear attractive or satisfying—but also not totally repellent—the individual's (internal) inclination to follow the command of the legislative authority will always reduce the rates of opting out (especially in situations where the cost of doing so is not negligible). It may therefore sometimes be risky to set penalty (i.e., sub-optimal) default rules, for it is possible that the parties will not opt out of them and thus such rules will prevail in practice, even though the parties would significantly benefit from opting out.[143]

bb Personal autonomy in need of a rethink?

Apart from the above, there is nowadays a more general, fundamental claim with respect to personal autonomy and its role in modern societies. In particular, it has been rightly suggested that we sometimes stretch its importance too much, while at the same time we tend to neglect the practical demands of everyday life.[144] As Alemanno and Sibony have recently eloquently argued, "individual autonomy is in need of rethink" for, although it certainly is a fundamental value, "its operationalisation in an age characterized by a rapid increase in cognitively-intensive tasks requires more nuanced views as to what individual decisions deserve protection from interference by government. As a matter of fact, not all decisions are equally deliberative. Normatively, it is not equally important that all individual decisions be taken more reflectively. [...] Autonomy, if it is to remain a meaningful value, should not require conscious, active and deliberative choice all the time."[145] Alemanno and Sibony go on and correctly

143 In this regard, see Unberath, Long-Term Contracts and the DCFR..., pp. 98–99, who rightly remarks that "[s]etting default rules deliberately at an inefficient level is [...] presumably greatly inefficient [...]: Empirical studies plausibly demonstrate that even where transaction costs are low, actors tend to go with the default rule despite its inefficiency. In addition to this significant "status quo bias" one must consider the various legal and factual hurdles to replace statutory or judicial defaults..."; also Unberath/Cziupka, 209 *AcP* (2009), 68; Kähler, *Begriff und Rechtfertigung*..., pp. 182–183. For extensive criticism of this concept of penalty default rules in the American literature, see E.Posner, 33 *Fla.St.U.L.Rev.* (2006), 563 ff., according to whom Ayres and Gertner do not provide any persuasive examples of such rules and thus their concept is a theoretical curiosity that has no existence in contract doctrine.

144 Besides the fact that "[t]he meaning of 'autonomy,' after all, remains the locus of substantial controversy"—so Gardner, 9 *Oxf.J.Leg.Stud.* (1989), 21.

145 Alemanno/Sibony, Epilogue ..., p. 333. See also Hacker, 2 *ERPL* (2016), 309–310, who, *inter alia*, points out, "Alberto Alemanno and Anne-Lise Sibony [...] convincingly advocate a more contextualized, procedural concept of autonomy that does not require more deliberative capacity from individuals than can be expected in concrete instances. [...] In contemporary societies [...] our decisions will always be subjected to a significant degree of external input. Therefore, what seems crucial is that these influences be made explicit so that the subject can take a critical stance toward them. This is why transparent, i.e., factually visible, nudges in fact do generally respect autonomy." In a similar vein, Arvanitis/Kalliris, 30 *Philos.Psychol.* (2017), 773: "... no one exhibits autonomous motivation and self-authorship all the time [...]. Autonomous motivation will also vary with the activity or the action that is under

put emphasis on the need to "consider the distinct imperative to respect the balance between those decisions we want to take deliberately and those that we prefer to take automatically."[146] And in our everyday lives the latter decisions are plenty. Under this realistic prism, Alemanno and Sibony aptly conclude that "[a]s we cannot realistically decide everything in life in a deliberative manner, deliberation cannot be the touchstone of what we value and protect in individual decisions under the name of autonomy. Instead, the focus should shift to when and how we accept to be assisted or influenced in our decision-making, either by private or public intervention."[147] And it is true that especially as consumers we do not have unlimited processing power nor unlimited time at our disposal; hence, it helps when somebody else assists us in our decision-making (by doing some of the data or info crunching for us, and so forth).

Alemanno and Sibony offer a convincing, revised perspective on autonomy, which, in my opinion, should be taken seriously into consideration in the relevant debate. It certainly diminishes the value of the objection relating to the undermining of personal autonomy through the nudge theory but, on the other hand, "does not legitimize all behavioural interventions."[148]

In addition to the above, we also cannot fail to notice that there is nowadays a widely held scientific view, according to which free will and human freedom—which embrace, of course, freedom of choice as well—are actually an *illusion*, or of limited importance to our "drifting through life,"[149] which is thought to be determined, in large part, by electrochemical brain processes falling beyond our sphere of influence—these processes are either deterministic or random or a combination of both. In essence, under this view, determinism and randomness leave hardly any room for free will. This view is mainly based on recent findings of neuroscientists who explore the electrochemical brain processes with the help of fMRI scanners. Even if such approaches sometimes seem to exaggerate the impact of recent scientific findings and may be in need of sounder evidence, it is, in all events, rather certain that the tenor of the debate over autonomy is now shifting; neuroscience has much to offer to this philosophical debate and its findings cannot be henceforth overlooked.[150]

---

question. Some activities may be self-authored and some may not, depending on the level of internalization or the existence of intrinsic motivation."

146 Alemanno/Sibony, Epilogue..., p. 333.

147 Alemanno/Sibony, Epilogue..., p. 333.

148 Alemanno/Sibony, Epilogue..., p. 333, wherein further: "... we invite lawyers and philosophers to look into what could be called a procedural conception of autonomy — where the term does not refer to legal procedures but to decision-making procedures. Future research should aim at identifying more precisely what restricts autonomy in a world in which autonomous decisions cannot realistically be equated with decisions taken in a fully deliberative manner."

149 Raz, *The Morality of Freedom*, p. 371.

150 See, indicatively, Harari, *Homo Deus*..., pp. 327 ff., who succinctly summarizes the relevant findings as follows (pp. 328–329): "The electrochemical brain processes that result in murder are either deterministic or random or a combination of both—but they are never free. For example, when a neuron fires an electric charge, this may be either a deterministic reaction

c. *The separate issue of informational nudging and the specific dangers associated with it*

As already discussed above, before the individual proceeds to a harmful activity (e.g., smoking) or transaction (e.g., excessive borrowing), she may be provided with relevant information. Such information provision may be considered an *informational nudge*. Informational nudges do not typically undermine personal autonomy or infringe on human dignity.[151] To the contrary, the provision or dispersal of information, especially by public authorities, in order to enhance individuals' freedom of choice or deter their engagement in harmful activities, does not normally count as paternalistic interference.[152] If the information provided is accurate and not misleading or deceptive,[153] it is solely *autonomy supportive*.[154]

Even John Stuart Mill would have embraced this approach. Specifically, on the one hand, he would have generally objected to the external guidance of individuals toward a life or choice path that would be deemed beneficial to them,[155] declaring that it is not a proper mission of the society to interfere with the personal preferences or interests of individuals.[156] On the other hand, though, he would probably not have objected to a benevolent guiding paternalism intended to benefit individuals who suffer from behavioral weaknesses when deciding on an action, since he argued that the provision of advice or guidance and the

---

to external stimuli, or perhaps the outcome of a random event such as the spontaneous decomposition of a radioactive atom. Neither option leaves any room for free will. Decisions reached through a chain reaction of biochemical events, each determined by a previous event, are certainly not free. Decisions resulting from random subatomic accidents aren't free either; they are just random. And when random accidents combine with deterministic processes, we get probabilistic outcomes, but this too doesn't amount to freedom. [...] To the best of our scientific understanding, determinism and randomness have divided the entire cake between them, leaving not even a crumb for 'freedom'"; see also *ibidem*, pp. 354–355. In a similar vein, *cf.* further the relevant thoughts articulated in the entertaining book by Gray, *The Soul of the Marionette...*, who likens human freedom to the freedom of a marionette, whose "movements are directed by the will of another" and who "has no choice in how it lives" (p. 1); this position follows the understanding of scientific materialism, which relies on the belief that "human beings *are* marionettes: puppets on genetic strings, which by an accident of evolution have become self-aware" (pp. 9–10); the illusionary character of human freedom necessarily entails the lack of control over our own lives: "We think we have some kind of privileged access to our motives and intentions. In fact we have no clear insight into what moves us to live as we do" (*ibidem*, p. 137).

151 This is the counterargument against Waldron from Sunstein (in: Nudges: Good and Bad ...).

152 Also rightly so Hausman/Welch, 18 *J.Polit.Philos.* (2010), 127, 130 and 136, wherein *inter alia* (127): "... Informing workers of hazards or warning people to drink water in hot weather is [...] not paternalistic."

153 *Cf.* also Akerlof/Shiller, *Phishing for Phools...*, pp. 7 ff.

154 On this specific form of assistance, see Moller/Ryan/Deci, 25 *JPP&M* (2006), 109 ff.; of course Sunstein, 122 *Yale L.J.* (2013), 1887 ff., 1898–1899.

155 Mill, On Liberty, esp. chapter III, p. 66: "It is possible that he might be guided in some good path, and kept out of harm's way ... But what will be his comparative worth as a human being?"

156 Mill, *op.cit.*, esp. chapter III, p. 95: "... with the personal tastes and self-regarding concerns of individuals the public has no business to interfere."

use of persuasion might be acceptable forms of steering behavior in a proper direction.[157] This line of thought is a fundamental assumption of the nudge theory as well. Even more important, however, is the fact that Mill does not, in principle, rule out state intervention aimed at discouraging people from engaging in harmful (to themselves) activities[158] by setting relevant *indirect* limits[159] under the basic but rather self-explanatory condition that such interventions do not demean adult citizens to children (or primitive humans) constantly being under custody.

Alas, the aforementioned initial reservation about the possibly misleading or deceptive character of a piece of information, even if it comes from a public authority, should not be underestimated. The informational nudge might sometimes trespass on private autonomy, especially when public or private entities *tamper with public information* with a view to bringing about a behavioral change that they say the citizens would have chosen anyway if they had carefully and rationally processed the accurate information (though they may believe that those citizens are not, in fact, capable of processing the information).[160] Despite the noble motives that informational nudges might serve, they are by their very nature susceptible to manipulation, or even deception, of citizens[161]; therefore legislative and public authorities should take great caution in using them.

The figures that public authorities may release on smoking and its relation to lung cancer offer a telling example about the way in which a critical piece of information should be presented.[162] Let's assume that a scientific paper shows that 20%–25% of longtime smokers die from lung cancer. If the authorities really wish to discourage people from smoking, they should not publicize those figures since some smokers, thinking *overoptimistically*, would deem it reasonable to believe they would be among the 75%–80% of smokers who do not die from lung cancer. Therefore, the authorities should simply say (as they often actually do) that smoking considerably increases one's chances of developing lung cancer, which is true and not misleading. Such an announcement should *nudge* many people in the right direction, even though it avoids using (or distorting) a specific fact about the actual dangers of smoking.[163]

157 Mill, *op.cit.*, chapter V, p. 104.

158 Mill, *op.cit.*, chapter V, pp. 111 ff.

159 For instance, with respect to alcohol consumption, Mill suggested a prohibition of sale to people prone to abusive consumption or the setting of certain hours of operation for liquor stores so that the authorities could exercise proper control over their operation and, if necessary, revoke their license.

160 See Waldron, It's All for Your Own Good, chapter 4; Sunstein, *Nudging and Choice Architecture...*, pp. 36–37; cf. also Levitt/Dubner, *Freakonomics...*, pp. 86 ff.

161 In this regard, see also Waldron, It's All for Your Own Good, chapter 4.

162 See Waldron, It's All for Your Own Good, chapter 4.

163 It seems, indeed, that the public campaign against smoking has been successful (i.e., it has reduced smoking), at least in the United States; see Glaeser, 29 *Regulation* (2006), 35–36, 37–38; Korobkin/Ulen, 88 *Cal.L.R.* (2000), 1132–1133; Schelling, 60 *Publ.Int.* (1980), 110 ff., esp. 118.

Hence, how a piece of information is presented or 'clothed,' or the specific framing of a decision-making situation, greatly affects our preferences and final decisions. Context matters. In the behavioral sciences this effect is called *framing (or wording) effect*: its exploitation enables public or private entities (mainly companies, sellers, and so on) to guide our behavior or decisions in certain directions, alter our preferences, muddy informative messages, and thus influence our decision-making process.[164] The considerable impact that the framing effect may have on us is also evinced in the specific way that some default rules are formed by the legislative authorities[165]: their design alone already constitutes the shaping of a special decision framing or 'environment.'[166] In the field of consumer protection, default rules are usually meant to be consumer friendly.

The practice of *nudging through framing* in the field of public regulation raises, undoubtedly, serious concerns. On the other hand, though, when private organizations nudge by framing the decision-making situation, they are typically covered by the *freedom of (commercial) speech*[167]—as long as they do not deceive consumers.

164 See Sunstein/Thaler, 70 *U.Chi.L.Rev.* (2003), 1161, 1179–1180, 1182–1183; Jolls/Sunstein/Thaler, 50 *Stan.L.Rev.* (1998), 1534 ff.; Sunstein, 1 *Am.L.&Econ.Rev.* (1999), 123, 129, 134–135, 135–136, 139, 149; the same, *On Preferring A to B...*, 1 ff. *passim* (with special emphasis on the differing effects of separate evaluation and joint evaluation of choices or options and the relevant tactics that may be employed by the sellers to manipulate consumers' behavior); the same, *The Cost-Benefit Revolution*, pp. 34 ff.; Thaler, *Misbehaving...*, pp. 335 ff.; Kahneman, 93 *Am.Econ.Rev.* (2003), 1458 ff.; Tversky/Kahneman, 211 *Science* (1981), 453 ff.; Korobkin/Ulen, 88 *Cal.L.R.* (2000), 1105 ff.; Camerer/Issacharoff/Loewenstein/O'Donoghue/Rabin, 151 *U.Penn.L.R.* (2003), 1230 ff.; Kelman/Rottenstreich/Tversky, Context-Dependence..., pp. 61 ff.; Noll/Krier, Some Implications of Cognitive Psychology..., pp. 330–331, 343–344; Arrow, 20 *Econ.Inq.* (1982), 6–7; Dolan, Influencing the financial behavior of individuals..., pp. 196 ff. *passim*; Dawnay/Shah, *Behavioural Economics...*, pp. 10, 11; van Aaken, Begrenzte Rationalität..., pp. 115 ff., 131–132, 138–139; the same, Das deliberative Element juristischer Verfahren..., pp. 193 ff.; Altmann/Falk/Marklein, Eingeschränkt rationales Verhalten..., pp. 71 ff.; Neumann, *Libertärer Paternalismus...*, pp. 45 ff.; Tscherner, 1 *ALJ* (2014), 149–150. However, Rachlinski [73 *U.Chi.L.Rev.* (2006), 210 ff.] casts doubts on the reliability of the experiments supporting the ascertainment of the aforementioned behavioral phenomenon.

165 See, indicatively, Ayres, 73 *U.Chi.L.Rev.* (2006), 3 ff., esp. 9 ff.; also Ringe, 213 *AcP* (2013), 125.

166 See also Altmann/Falk/Marklein, Eingeschränkt rationales Verhalten..., p. 77. It is worth mentioning that the framing effect has already been traced to Plato; see Romeo, *Platonically Irrational*, who eloquently remarks: "Plato's work on 'framing' appears in many dialogues, both as formal analysis and dramatic depiction. In the *Theaetetus*, he observes that the same number of dice—six—can appear greater or smaller if juxtaposed to either four or 12 dice. [...] This is a basic point about arithmetic but a profound one about psychology and perception. Saying that a new soft drink has only half the calories of a Coke sounds much more attractive than saying that a new soft drink has 18 times the calories of a carrot." In general, on the close affinity between Plato's thought and behavioral economics, see fn. 47, Chapter 1, above.

167 In detail on this touchy issue of freedom of commercial speech, see Willis, 80 *U.Chi.L.Rev.* (2013), 1161: "... regulation would need to control firm-framing manipulations, a task severely circumscribed by the protections afforded commercial speech under the First Amendment"; *ibidem*, pp. 1220 ff., esp. 1220–1221: "... controls on firm marketing are likely to run afoul of

In all events, it is rightly suggested that the framing effect undermines a fundamental assumption of *rational choice theory*: namely, that our preferences or decisions between various alternatives are formed exclusively on the basis of their substantive content, that is, they are not influenced by other factors, such as the way in which the alternatives are presented (wording, context), and thus, they remain stable over time (and transitive) irrespective of their framing (*frame independence, principle of invariance*). In other words, according to rational choice theory, the various ways in which a choice situation may be presented must elicit the same preference, not various divergent preferences—*quod non* in reality, though, as we have seen above.[168]

3. *Negative externalities*

It is evident by now that the establishment of default rules or options, at least in the field of contract law, is not in principle objectionable. It is, in fact, widely unavoidable as well as usually visible to the transactors; problematic cases cannot, of course, be *a priori* ruled out, as the abovementioned example of the CISG suggests.

However, this in principle positive stance on default rules should be dropped if the legislative default engenders severe *negative externalities* for third parties. Simply put, the regulatory default rule should avoid imposing costs on parties who are not the addressees of the protective interference.[169] Yet this

---

First Amendment doctrine. Under that doctrine, any governmental restriction on commercial speech must (1) 'directly advance' a substantial governmental interest and (2) be 'narrowly tailored' to serve that interest. To meet the first part of this test, the government must demonstrate that such speech causes harm and that the regulation's restriction on speech will alleviate the harm 'to a material degree.' To meet the second part, the restriction must not burden substantially more speech than necessary to alleviate the harm. [...] / Rather than prohibiting firm speech that manipulates biases, *regulators might instead attempt to require firms to engage in more speech, speech that would pivot biases back towards the policy default.* Unless the regulation chills protected speech or is unduly burdensome, compelled commercial speech needs only to be 'reasonably related' to the government interest advanced. But developing warnings, disclaimers, or other language to counter every framing manipulation used by firms would be a never-ending regulatory project. [...] Requiring firms to add content to their marketing that goes beyond warnings or factual information, such as the Food and Drug Administration is currently attempting to do with graphic reminders of health dangers on tobacco product packaging — while potentially much more effective than dry text— is likely to be found unconstitutional."

168 See Schäfer/Ott, *Lehrbuch der ökonomischen Analyse des Zivilrechts*[4], p. 66; Altmann/Falk/Marklein, Eingeschränkt rationales Verhalten..., p. 71; Neumann, *Libertärer Paternalismus...*, p. 29; Schmolke, *Grenzen der Selbstbindung...*, pp. 111–112, 123, 216–217; DellaVigna, 47 *JEL* (2009), 315; Tversky/Kahneman, Advances in Prospect Theory..., p. 45; Kahneman, New Challenges to the Rationality Assumption, pp. 759–760, 762; in more detail, Tversky/Kahneman, Rational Choice and the Framing of Decisions, pp. 209 ff., esp. 211, 212 ff.; cf. also Saint-Paul, *The Tyranny of Utility...*, p. 21. On the basic content of *rational choice theory*, see the authors referenced in fn. 1, Chapter 1 above.

169 *Cf.* also Schweizer, Nudging and the Principle of Proportionality..., pp. 102 ff. In general, on *negative externalities*, see Cooter/Ulen, *Law & Economics*[6], pp. 39–40, 166 ff.; Wittman,

may occur, for instance, when the owner of a supermarket is statutorily forced to display products in a way that promotes a healthy diet (e.g., by placing the more healthful foods at eye level)[170] but harms her own profits.[171] It is true that "people's choices can be highly influenced by features like accessibility, salience, colors, information, and ordering of items," further that "[s]ubtle aspects of choice architecture can have significant effects on public health; if bottles of soda are easily accessible and highly salient (e.g., located at the checkout counter rather than the middle of a supermarket aisle), people are more likely to choose them."[172] Nevertheless, the need to protect the economic freedom of the businessperson may conflict with a nudging intervention that aims to protect consumers' health; indeed, the businessperson would naturally feel that where the products are placed in supermarkets or other food stores should be sovereignly decided by herself, using yardsticks that she deems appropriate to secure or increase her profits.[173]

The supermarket example demonstrates that mild paternalism aimed at protecting consumers may often adversely affect the businessperson by forcing her

---

Economic Foundations of Law..., chapter 13 (pp. 114 ff.), chapter 14 (pp. 122 ff.); Trebilcock, *The Limits of Freedom of Contract*, pp. 58 ff.; Dahlman, 22 *J.L.&Econ.* (1979), 141 ff.; Rebonato, 37 *J.Consum.Policy* (2014), 362–363; Eidenmüller, *Effizienz als Rechtsprinzip*[3], pp. 144 ff.

170 See Thaler/Sunstein/Balz, Choice Architecture, pp. 428 ff.; Thaler/Sunstein, *Nudge...*, pp. 1 ff.; Thorndike/Sunstein, 107 *Am.J. Public Health* (2017), 1582–1583; G.Dworkin, Paternalism, chapter 3.

171 This course of action reflects the pattern of *indirect paternalism*; see Kalliris, *Autonomy, Well-Being and the Law*, pp. 148–149, 153; also G.Dworkin, 56 *The Monist* (1972), 67–68; Pope, 20 *Ga.St.U.L.Rev.* (2004), 699 ff.

172 Thorndike/Sunstein, 107 *Am.J. Public Health* (2017), 1582.

173 Thorndike/Sunstein [107 *Am.J.Publ. Health* (2017), 1582–1583] still disagree on this point, relying on the following argumentation: "Ideally, of course, supermarkets would change the choice architecture on their own, and some have taken steps to do so. But evidence about retailer practices makes it reasonable to assume that most supermarkets are unlikely to move in the direction of healthier choice architecture without being required to change. We believe that a SNAP [*scil.* Supplemental Nutrition Assistance Program] choice architecture policy should be implemented that would restrict placement of certain accessory food items, such as SSBs [*scil.* sugar-sweetened beverages], desserts, candy, and salty snacks, from endcap, free-standing, and checkout counter displays in stores participating in the program. Although these items would remain available for purchase in the store aisles, they would be out of view from the highest traffic areas; thus both adults and children would see them less, leading to fewer unplanned purchases. [...] A choice architecture policy might lead some stores to not participate in SNAP because the anticipated loss of profit from SSBs and other foods would be greater than would the loss of SNAP customers. To reduce this risk, particularly for smaller stores, the US Department of Agriculture might consider a minimum choice architecture requirement—such as for SSBs and candy—and provide financial incentives to encourage stores to participate in other categories. Larger supermarket chains and superstores could—and should—find creative ways to promote healthy choices while maintaining profits. / Some opponents of SNAP choice architecture might claim that the policy represents government intrusion on personal freedom and puts undue burdens on supermarkets and other food stores. However, use of choice architecture would not regulate the attributes of the food or beverage items; it would preserve people's ability to purchase the products that they like."

to behave in a way she has not chosen to.[174] The same also holds, for example, for the 14 day cooling-off period that allows withdrawing from any contract entered into online; this period, which is accompanied by a withdrawal right—extensively on this right, Chapter 4 below—"may be a nudge from the consumers' perspective, but it is certainly coercive on the vendors that have to accept it."[175] Use of nudging regulatory tools should thus be very carefully, and *ad hoc*, balanced, by considering all factors and circumstances of the specific situation that the social planner wants to address, primarily the need to avoid harming important interests or goods of third parties—that is, the need to avoid inflicting severe negative externalities.[176]

In a nutshell, nudging in order to promote a healthier way of life by means of product placement is in principle objectionable for it strikes at the heart of the businessperson's economic freedom. However, Sunstein and Thaler themselves seem to have acknowledged this problem, suggesting that the aforementioned interference should better be restricted to sellers or retailers that *enjoy a monopolistic position* in a certain market and are not exposed to competition (e.g., owners of schools' or universities' cafes), for whom profit maximization is not the principal purpose.[177]

VI. Toward an acceptable application of the nudge theory mainly on the basis of the principle of proportionality

As may be apparent from the preceding analysis, whether a nudge, mainly a default rule, is acceptable has to be judged *ad hoc*.[178] Before using a nudge to eliminate or limit a systematic bias or a rationality deficit of individuals, an

174 The same danger is pointed out by Waldron, It's All for Your Own Good, chapter 2 *in fine*: "Soft paternalism for the consumer might [...] presuppose hard regulation for the retailer." More recently, Schweizer, Nudging and the Principle of Proportionality..., pp. 93 ff., *passim*, esp. 114: "... the implementation of nudges will often involve coercive measures against persons other than the decision maker, and therefore trigger constitutional scrutiny as they interfere with the personal freedom of those forced to implement the nudge." *Cf.* further Sunstein, *Nudging and Choice Architecture...*, pp. 14–15.

175 So Schweizer, Nudging and the Principle of Proportionality..., p. 102, who also rightly doubts if the statutory provision of the aforementioned withdrawal right can be called a 'nudge' at all.

176 *Cf.* also Schweizer, Nudging and the Principle of Proportionality..., pp. 102 ff. For possible 'negative externalities' *affecting the person meant to be protected herself cf.*, further, Ghisellini/Chang, *Behavioral Economics...*, p. 212: "... even nudges with the right core content may impact adversely on other interests pursued by individuals. Nudges increasing savings can lead, for example, to a cut of cultural consumption (books, concerts, etc.), so the net effect can turn negative."

177 See Sunstein/Thaler, 70 *U.Chi.L.Rev.* (2003), 1165.

178 See also Eidenmüller, *JZ* (2011), 818, and Waldron, It's All for Your Own Good, chapter 4. In the same vein, see Sunstein, *Nudging and Choice Architecture...*, *passim*, esp. pp. 32 ff. ("... any action by government, including nudging, must meet a burden of justification," p. 40—see also p. 42).

acceptability test should be applied. In my opinion, this acceptability test should be based on the following criteria:

a *The severity of the behavioral bias* that the social planner seeks to address: On the one hand, this criterion means that the old Roman law rule '*de minimis non curat praetor*' holds in this case as well; that is, the concern of the planners (i.e., mostly the legislative authorities) must lie only with severe cases of behavioral biases. On the other hand, it also means that there must be adequate evidence of the existence and severe impact of each bias, *and that evidence must be substantiated*, not just *hypothesized (need for evidence-based intervention)*. There must be, namely, adequate convincing evidence showing the existence of a severe, persistent behavioral bias in a specific life or transactional situation (such as *hyperbolic discounting* leading to excessive borrowing in order to purchase a house).[179] On that basis, a subsequent paternalistic intervention may draw people's attention to the danger they are about to encounter and thus attempt to deter them from proceeding to the harmful activity (e.g., by providing the borrower with easily digestible information about the possible hazards of an adjustable-rate mortgage).

 It should not go unnoted that not all findings or outcomes of behavioral or psychological research and experiments are sound or unassailable, and therefore all such findings must be approached with caution, especially with respect to their interpretation and practical exploitation.[180] Nevertheless, it is true that, in general, "[p]olicy-making takes place unavoidably under the circumstances of uncertainty and on the basis of revisable theories."[181] And even if empirical findings or laboratory experiments may never provide definitive results, "incomplete evidence is arguably better than no evidence."[182]

179 *Cf.* also van Aaken, Judge the Nudge..., p. 107: "... nudges need to show their effectiveness, based on sound empirical evidence"; Tomer, *Advanced Introduction to Behavioral Economics*, pp. 88–89. Even Richard T. Ely (1854–1943), a leading interventionist economist of his era, rightly—and early on—underscored the need "to rely on strong evidence rather than intuition when proposing any intervention in the economy" [Campbell, 106 *Am.Econ.Rev* (2016), 2].

180 In this regard, see also Faure/Luth, 34 *J.Consum.Policy* (2011), *passim*, esp. 354: "Using behavioural insights for policy should in our view be done quite cautiously for the simple reason that although there now is an impressive body of behavioural literature, the discipline is still relatively young and much more research may be needed to come to firm conclusions"; Cserne, Making Sense of Nudge-Scepticism..., pp. 284 ff., who also expresses his skepticism about the generalization of the relevant empirical findings, mainly focusing on the lack of adequate robustness (*ibidem*, p. 286); Camerer/Issacharoff/Loewenstein/O'Donoghue/Rabin, 151 *U.Penn.L.R.* (2003), 1211 ff. *passim*, esp. 1212, 1214, 1251; Issacharoff, 51 *Vand.L.Rev.* (1998), 1734 ff.; Feldman/Lobel, Behavioural Trade-Offs..., pp. 301 ff.; Alemanno/Sibony, Epilogue..., pp. 338 ff.

181 Cserne, Making Sense of Nudge-Scepticism..., p. 286.

182 Cserne, Making Sense of Nudge-Scepticism..., p. 286, who further claims (*ibidem*, p. 290) that "empirical findings of behavioural research *alone* do not determine how the law should 'model' its subjects and regulate their behaviour."

b *The intensity of the particular means of paternalistic interference with private autonomy*, which should be *as mild as possible*.
c *The easy –and cheap– reversibility of the default rule (or opting-out of it)*. This requirement implies that the process of opting out should not be burdensome or time-consuming.[183]
d *The transparency of the nudging tool to be used*: As discussed above, the nudging tool must not develop its force in a covert way or deceive or mislead the individuals it is intended to protect. In contrast, it must, in principle, be visible, transparent, for visible nudges generally respect individual autonomy,[184] whereas "invisible nudges (manipulation) are not choice-enhancing but restrict choice invisibly."[185] Thus, the available options must be clearly stated or openly communicated.[186] This also means that none of the available options should be emphasized over the others, by exploiting the aforementioned *framing effect* (for example, by printing 'yes' in boldface type and 'no' in regular type).[187]
e *The clear possibility of causing severe negative externalities to third parties* who are not the individuals meant to be protected by the paternalistic intervention. If there is such a possibility, then the intervention is not acceptable (e.g., compulsory product placement in supermarkets on the basis of the marketing idea that "*eye level is buy level*"—see further pp. 59 ff. above).[188]

Now, if the above criteria are considered and a nudging intervention passes their test, the intervention is in principle justified. On the other hand, from the same viewpoint, interventions that *fly below the radar of rational scrutiny* by the individuals and entail severe negative externalities for third parties (such as the aforementioned compulsory product placement) should not be accepted.[189]

The above criteria specify, in essence, the commands of the fundamental *principle of proportionality*. This principle requires a careful balancing each time the social planner examines the possibility of enacting a nudging intervention.[190] More particularly, as is widely agreed, the principle of propor-

183 This parameter is highlighted by Thaler/Sunstein, *Nudge…*, *passim*, esp. p. 6 (: "To count as a mere nudge, the intervention must be easy and cheap to avoid"), 237 (: "… our own libertarian condition, requiring low-cost opt-out rights, reduces the steepness of the ostensibly slippery slope"), 248–249; Sunstein, 122 *Yale L.J.* (2013), 1893–1894; Thaler, The Power of Nudges…; also Bechtold, *Die Grenzen zwingenden Vertragsrechts…*, pp. 254 ff. *Cf.*, however, also the relevant objections of Rebonato, 37 *J.Consum.Policy* (2014), 357 ff. *passim*, esp. 383–384.

184 See Hacker, 2 *ERPL* (2016), 310, 316–317.

185 van Aaken, Judge the Nudge…, p. 110.

186 *Cf.* van Aaken, Judge the Nudge…, p. 110.

187 See, indicatively, Thaler, The Power of Nudges…; *cf.* also Rebonato, 37 *J.Consum.Policy* (2014), 357 ff. *passim*, esp. 391 ff.

188 *Cf.* also Schweizer, Nudging and the Principle of Proportionality…, pp. 102 ff.

189 On this flaw in Sunstein and Thaler's approach, see Rebonato, 37 *J.Consum.Policy* (2014), 357 ff. *passim*, esp. 366, 368–369, 392; also Mols/Haslam/Jetten/Steffens, 54 *EJPR* (2015), 87–88, 94–95.

190 *Cf.* Schweizer, Nudging and the Principle of Proportionality…, pp. 93 ff., esp. 106 ff. and 110; van Aaken, Judge the Nudge…, pp. 88 ff. and 106 ff.; Stürner, *Der Grundsatz der*

tionality functions as ***a limit to the limiting*** of individual rights or liberties, it thus ***restricts the restrictions*** (in German: *Schranken-Schranke*)[191]; in the particular case examined here it may be viewed as a limit to the limit set on private autonomy by means of the nudging intervention.[192] Therefore, a crucial three-prong test should also be employed here to examine whether the regulatory intervention is (a) ***necessary*** (for the accomplishment of the aim sought), (b) ***suitable and appropriate*** (that is, it can effectively lead to the accomplishment of the aim sought), and (c) ***milder*** than other (possibly) available means.[193]

The most important limit to the regulatory intervention, in this context, is contained in the fundamental command of European constitutional law that ***forbids the regulatory authority (legislative or administrative) to exceed a reasonable limit when it interferes with individual rights or liberties*** (in German: *Übermaßverbot*) and, in the same vein, in the need to choose ***the mildest possible means of interference*** (in German: *Gebot des schondendsten Eingriffs*).[194] According to that demand, when there are multiple available means of interference, the regulatory authority should choose the one that does not go further than necessary in limiting the individual's freedom. In the words of van Aaken, the typical assisted-choice scheme (in German: *Wahlhilfe*) that is promoted through the nudge theory, chiefly by means of default rules and the provision of information (disclosure rules), will regularly be milder than the mandatory rules that forbid or exclude choices (in German: *Wahlverbote*) or impose choices (in German: *Wahlgebote*).[195] Assisted choice is therefore,

---

Verhältnismäßigkeit..., *passim*, esp. pp. 285 ff., 318 ff., 444 ff. Generally, though, for a critical approach on the principle of proportionality, see Tsakyrakis, 7 *I•Con* (2009), 468 ff., and 8 *I•Con* (2010), 307 ff., who argues that "proportionality constitutes a misguided quest for precision and objectivity in the resolution of human rights disputes," and suggests that "courts should focus, instead, on the real moral issues underlying such disputes"; *cf.* also the same, Disproportionate Individualism, pp. 237 ff.

191 See also Schweizer, Nudging and the Principle of Proportionality..., p. 97.

192 *Ad hoc* Schmolke, *Grenzen der Selbstbindung...*, *passim*, esp. pp. 268–269; van Aaken, Begrenzte Rationalität..., pp. 124 ff., esp. 133 ff., 139–140; Schweizer, Nudging and the Principle of Proportionality..., p. 97.

193 *Cf.* also Schweizer, Nudging and the Principle of Proportionality..., pp. 93 ff., *passim*, esp. 106 ff.; Englerth, Vom Wert des Rauchens..., p. 239. In general, the principle of proportionality consists of three sub-principles, namely, the principles of suitability, necessity, and proportionality in the narrow sense, which are practically translated into "a three-prong test that assesses (a) whether a measure that interferes with a right is suitable for achieving its objective, (b) whether it is necessary for that purpose, and (c) whether it burdens the individual excessively compared with the benefits it aims to secure"; so Tsakyrakis, 7 *I•Con* (2009), 474 ff.; see also Alexy, 16 *Ratio Juris* (2003), 135.

194 See Zippelius, *Juristische Methodenlehre*^{10}, § 10 III c (p. 55) and V (pp. 60–61), § 17 b (pp. 103–104); Röhl/Röhl, *Allgemeine Rechtslehre*^{3}, p. 656; Engel, *JZ* (2005), 582; Adomeit, *NJW* (1994), 2467.

195 See van Aaken, Begrenzte Rationalität..., pp. 124 ff.; also Schmolke, *Grenzen der Selbstbindung...*, pp. 30 ff., 69–70, esp. 226 ff., 256 ff., 839 ff., 870 ff., 926 ff.

in principle, to be given priority, unless there are other compelling reasons to favor a coercive option.[196]

It is worth noting that at EU level the above approach is in accordance with the demands of the proportionality principle as entrenched in Article 52(1) of the EU Charter of Fundamental Rights, which states: "Any limitation on the exercise of the rights and freedoms recognised by this Charter must be provided for by law and respect the essence of those rights and freedoms. Subject to the principle of proportionality, limitations may be made only if they are necessary and genuinely meet objectives of general interest recognised by the Union or the need to protect the rights and freedoms of others."[197]

Notwithstanding the above, where there is *doubt* about whether the suggested means of intervention is proportionate to the purpose sought, the social planner will have to follow the (libertarian) presumption in favor of liberty—that is, "*in dubio pro libertate*"[198] (and not the presumption "*in dubio pro tutela*")—and refrain from intervening.[199]

Last but not least, in alignment with the above, in the German literature it has been suggested[200] that a paternalistic intervention, even in the form of a nudge, may not be justified in principle unless it concerns individual decisions that (a) are difficult to make, (b) will have long-run consequences, or (c) are

196 This is also the basic thesis of van Aaken, Begrenzte Rationalität..., pp. 124 ff., esp. 133 ff., 139–140, who elaborates on the *principle of the mildest paternalistic means (Prinzip des schonendsten Paternalismus)*, advancing precisely the need to choose the mildest means of interference for restoring or limiting people's preferential disorders—and the mildest means will be the *assisted choice* (*Wahlhilfe*); in a similar vein, see Schmolke, *Grenzen der Selbstbindung...*, pp. 30 ff., 69–70, esp. 226 ff., 256 ff., 839 ff., 870 ff., 926 ff.; Schweizer, Nudging and the Principle of Proportionality..., pp. 106 ff., who rightly concludes that "[a] nudge will generally be less restrictive than a coercive measure" (*ibidem*, p. 107), and that "nudges should generally fare well under the balancing test" (*ibidem*, p. 115). Also moving in more of less the same direction: Cserne, *Freedom of Contract...*, pp. 65, 66 (: "... the maxim of minimal intrusiveness seems not only compatible with libertarian paternalism but may directly support it. This maxim requires that other things being equal, *the least intrusive regulatory instrument should be preferred*. For instance, information provision should be preferred to prohibition ..."); Sunstein, 122 *Yale L.J.* (2013), 1835, 1859 ff. *passim*; Drexl, *Die wirtschaftliche Selbstbestimmung...*, pp. 210, 449 ff., 544–545; Bechtold, *Die Grenzen zwingenden Vertragsrechts...*, pp. 264, 265, 294 ff., 318, 334 ff., esp. 339; Schön, in: *FS Canaris*, pp. 1204 ff.; Kähler, *Begriff und Rechtfertigung...*, pp. 363 ff., esp. 366 and 367. *Cf.* further Englerth, Behavioral Law and Economics..., pp. 121; Möslein, *Dispositives Recht...*, pp. 384, 396–397; G.Dworkin, 56 *The Monist* (1972), 84; Kalliris, *Autonomy, Well-Being and the Law*, *passim*, esp. pp. 115–116, 119–120, 154, 165, 166, 179–180.

197 *Cf.* van Aaken, Judge the Nudge..., pp. 106 ff. *Cf.* further Article 6 of the Treaty on European Union.

198 See Hesse, *Grundzüge des Verfassungsrechts*[20], no. 72 (*Ausgangsvermutung zugunsten der Freiheit*); also Röhl/Röhl, *Allgemeine Rechtslehre*[3], p. 656.

199 See also Schmolke, *Grenzen der Selbstbindung...*, p. 270 (: "Dabei gilt die verfassungsrechtlich verankerte Zweifelsregel „in dubio pro libertate," die auch vor dem Hintergrund der durch die Verhaltensökonomik aufgedeckten systematischen Rationalitätsdefizite menschlicher Entscheider nicht in ein „in dubio pro tutela" verkehrt werden darf und soll."); Schön, in: *FS Canaris*, p. 1205.

200 Eidenmüller, *JZ* (2011), 818.

made rarely in the course of a lifetime, provided that in all three of these cases the decision-maker does not have adequate information or any information at all at her disposal.[201] More specifically, (a) the more difficult the decision to be made, the greater the risk that rationality deficits will arise and lead the individual astray, that is, to a wrong decision; (b) decisions giving rise to consequences manifested after a considerable period of time often fail owing to our *over-optimism bias*—or unrealistic optimism or cock-of-the-walk confidence—along with *hyperbolic discounting* (such as our decision to give in to excessive borrowing); and (c) decisions we make rarely or just once in a lifetime do not offer us the chance to benefit from the *learning effect (experience)*—that is, to learn from our mistakes and not repeat them in the future (e.g., once again, our decision to expose ourselves to excessive borrowing).[202] At any rate, the aforesaid decision situations must also be accompanied by a severe information deficit on the part of the deciding individual, which reinforces the need for regulatory protection.

VII. Default rules or freedom of active choosing?

Now, a critical question must be asked: what would a good, liberal legislator optimally do? Should she, namely, abstain from setting default rules and instead recognize individuals' *absolute freedom of active choosing*? In this scenario there would be no state interference with individual choices—even in areas where a more drastic intervention by means of mandatory rules is today considered necessary. In a lease contract, for example, this would mean that the parties to it would have to determine themselves all the specific issues nowadays addressed in the default rules of contract law. Such issues have already been discussed above—especially in the context of fleshing out the positive effects of default rules—but now it is time to consider the regulatory picture in broader and more systematic terms, this time juxtaposing the default rules with the absolute freedom of active choosing.

First and foremost, it should be noted that in general the existence of choices in our lives is typically a *blessing*, a kind of gift; it can, however, also be a *curse* if the choices place a heavy burden on the shoulders of the individual.[203] The freedom of choice may, as Mill eloquently argues, resemble a muscle that has to be exercised in order not to atrophy.[204] But, often enough, the very same muscle

201 Sunstein and Thaler make a similar point, that the nudging interference is necessary especially when we are concerned with decisions that are *difficult, complex, or seldom*, and in relation to which the deciding individuals do not have direct access to relevant information or have no experience (*Nudge*..., pp. 72, 75, 76–77, 247, 250–251).

202 See the authors referenced in fn. 59, chapter 1, above.

203 In detail Sunstein, 64 *Duke L.J.* (2014), 1 ff. *passim*, esp. 51; the same, *Choosing Not to Choose*..., *passim*, esp. pp. 157 ff.; the same, *Forcing People To Choose Is Paternalistic*, 21–22; also DellaVigna, 47 *JEL* (2009), 355.

204 See Mill, On Liberty, chapter III, pp. 65 ff., esp. 65: "The human faculties of perception, judgement, discriminative feeling, mental activity, and even moral preference, *are exercised only in*

also risks becoming tired or sore if it is over-exercised. According to Sunstein and Thaler, too many choice situations might create a state of *hypertrophy*. The setting of default rules or options aims to avoid such an unpleasant state by releasing us from the burden of constant decision-making that the path of *active choosing* would impose upon us.[205] In other words, the default rules purport to relax our spiritual muscles and create a necessary breathing space, sparing us from dealing every day with a plethora of choice situations of all types, big and small, which would certainly lead to plenty of mistakes.

Viewed more systematically, default rules seem to entail a series of decisive advantages over the absolute freedom of active choosing. These advantages indicate that default rules have a clear lead against the absolute freedom of active choosing. This lead can be observed in the many modern private law codifications—especially in the field of contract law—that favor exhaustive default rules (consider, for instance, the provisions on breach of contract, seller's or contractor's liability for defects, and lease contracts).[206] The advantages of default rules can be summarized as follows[207]:

a In the context of active choosing, individuals do not receive any kind of assistance. This ***puts a sometimes heavy burden on the choice-making individuals*** that may be time-consuming and expensive.[208] We all know that the ordinary consumer does not waste too much time thinking about how to make her day-to-day transactional decisions; thoroughly thinking

---

making a choice. He who does anything because it is the custom, makes no choice. He gains no practice either in discerning or in desiring what is best. ***The mental and moral, like the muscular powers, are improved only by being used***" (emphasis added). See also Wright/Ginsburg, 106 *Nw.U.L.R.* (2012), 1068–1069, 1072; Sunstein, *Nudging and Choice Architecture...*, p. 43; the same, *Choosing Not to Choose...*, pp. 103–104, 208; the same, The Ethics of Nudging, p. xvi; Rebonato, 37 *J.Consum.Policy* (2014), 384 ff., esp. 389. *Cf.* further, once more, Raz, *The Morality of Freedom*, *passim*, esp. p. 371: "... autonomy [...] contrasts with a life of no choices, or of drifting through life without ever exercising one's capacity to choose."

205 See Sunstein, 64 *Duke L.J.* (2014), 31 ff., esp. 32, and Sunstein/Thaler, 70 *U.Chi.L.Rev.* (2003), 1173 ff. *passim*. It suffices to ponder how much we are relieved, for example, by the use of navigation machines (GPS), which nudge us in the right direction and remove from us the burden of actively choosing—a removal that we gladly accept; in this respect, see Sunstein, *Nudging and Choice Architecture...*, pp. 7, 16, 27–28, 32; the same, 122 *Yale L.J.* (2013), 1855, 1874, 1883–1884; Thaler/Tucker, 91 *Harv.Bus.R.* (2013), 4 ff. It is a different issue whether certain parts of our brain may possibly atrophy with the extended use of such devices; such issues may better be left to neuroscientists—see Sunstein, 64 *Duke L.J.* (2014), 31, and *Choosing Not to Choose...*, p. 104; Rebonato, 37 *J.Consum.Policy* (2014), 387, 388–389.

206 See, indicatively, Drexl, *Die wirtschaftliche Selbstbestimmung...*, pp. 305 ff., esp. 311–312.

207 For the following analysis, see Sunstein, 64 *Duke L.J.* (2014), 1 ff. *passim*, esp. 39 ff.; the same, 162 *U.Penn.L.R.* (2013), 1 ff. *passim*, esp. 8 ff. and 46 ff.; the same, *Choosing Not to Choose...*, *passim*, esp. pp. 138 ff., 145 ff.; the same, 122 *Yale L.J.* (2013), 1883 ff.; the same, *Nudging and Choice Architecture...*, pp. 29 ff.; the same, *Forcing People To Choose Is Paternalistic*, 1 ff., esp. 6 ff.; Sunstein/Thaler, 70 *U.Chi.L.Rev.* (2003), 1173 ff. *passim* and *Nudge...*, *passim*, esp. pp. 10 ff., 76 ff., 91 ff., 145 ff.; Dawnay/Shah, *Behavioural Economics...*, pp. 12 ff.

208 See also Johnson/Goldstein, 302 *Science* (2003), 1338–1339.

through every aspect of every transactional decision would be a mission impossible.[209] Especially in the field of contract law, it is a comfort to have detailed default rules on our side on which we may explicitly or tacitly rely. As already pointed out, these default rules save us the cost and effort that a negotiation over every aspect of a contractual relationship would demand. Such rules considerably reduce transaction costs. They allow resources and primarily time to be diverted to more productive or pleasant activities, thus enhancing individual and general welfare. They also reduce the risk of error.

b In the same vein, if the decision-makers were forced to actively choose on every issue associated with daily life, the kaleidoscopic variety of choices and amount of information would be so daunting as to lead to wrong or *sub-optimal* decisions, or to a state of paralysis or helplessness, leaving the decision-makers unable to reach any decision at all.[210] Let us consider, for instance, the case of a doctor who, in the context of the 'informed-consent model' in health treatment, explains to a patient all of the possible therapies for a particular disease, without making clear which is the most effective or suitable for that patient. The patient will probably be confused, spend time trying to process the specialized information, spend money investigating the suggested treatments, and finally, possibly end up rejecting that doctor, who placed such a heavy informational burden on her.[211] Such a detailed, meticulous information may sometimes entail a transfer of responsibility. In particular, the person with specialized knowledge of the subject matter, the doctor, transfers the decision-making responsibility to a person without any relevant knowledge, the patient, for whom making an appropriate decision is practically impossible. In other words, there is here "a shifting of the burden and the responsibility for decision-making from somebody who knows something — namely, the doctor — to somebody who knows nothing and is almost certainly sick and thus, not in the best shape to be making decisions — namely, the patient."[212]

But aren't we supposed to adhere to the maxim that more choices are always preferable to fewer? In general, *prima facie* and according to traditional economic thinking, the maximal provision of choices is always beneficial, since an additional choice always reflects an additional *utility unit*, provided that the decision-making costs are not thus rendered prohibitively high.[213] Com-

209 See also Wagner, Zwingendes Vertragsrecht, p. 16.

210 See Rachlinski, 70 *S.Cal.L.R.* (1996), 118; Korobkin, 70 *U.Chi.L.Rev.* (2003), 1227; Ayres, 73 *U.Chi.L.Rev.* (2006), 13–14; Ringe, 213 *AcP* (2013), 125–126; *cf.* also G.Dworkin, 7 *Midwest Stud.Philos.* (1982), 50, 55–56.

211 See also Sunstein, *Behaviorally Informed Health Policy?...*, pp. 1 ff. *passim*. In particular, on the issue of how much information should doctors provide to patients in their attempt to gain informed consent, see Siegal/Bonnie/Appelbaum, 40 *J.L.Med.&Ethics* (2012), 359 ff.

212 Schwartz, *The Paradox of Choice*, TEDGlobal 2005, 03:20–04:42; see also the same, *The Paradox of Choice—Why More is Less*, *passim*.

213 See, indicatively, Thaler, 1 *J.Econ.Behav.Organ.* (1980), 55; in detail G.Dworkin, 7 *Midwest Stud.Philos.* (1982), 48–49.

mon experience, though, shows that, independently of the decision-making costs, we reach better decisions when we focus on a limited set of choices than when we are confronted with abundant choices or, similarly, too much information.[214] This is called the ***paradox of choice***. This paradox refers to the fact that being forced to choose among different alternatives "(which implies devoting time to read and to understand the implications of each choice) is in itself a painful and frustrating experience."[215] This phenomenon is also known as ***choice overload***: namely, when faced with an increased set of available options, "many people defer making a decision or feel less satisfied with the decision they make."[216]

More particularly, it has been attested that we can lose control, feel overwhelmed, or become paralyzed when faced with an amount of information that exceeds our capacity to properly process it. This is called ***information overload or overkill***. In effect, once we are in possession of a certain amount of information, the marginal utility from an additional piece of information turns negative because we are no longer in a position to master it. As a result, our ability to make good decisions deteriorates. More specifically, this phenomenon is described as the law of ***diminishing marginal utility of information***.[217] In other words, after a certain point, the value of any additional piece of information ***is diminished in relation to the cost of its acquisition and processing***.[218]

Especially with respect to the abundant mandatory disclosure rules allegedly meant to strengthen the protection of consumers,[219] theory correctly

214 See also Moller/Ryan/Deci, 25 *JPP&M* (2006), 106, 107.

215 Ghisellini/Chang, *Behavioral Economics...*, p. 210. See also, in detail, Schwartz, *The Paradox of Choice – Why More is Less*, whose basic tenet is that *too much choice undermines happiness* and that eliminating consumer choices can greatly reduce anxiety for shoppers.

216 Cartwright, *Behavioral Economics*^{2}, p. 487.

217 On the significant danger of ***information overload or overkill*** (in German: *Informationsüberforderung*) in the field of consumer protection law and the relevant *law of diminishing marginal utility of information provision*, see Eidenmüller, *JZ* (2005), 218, 221; the same, *JZ* (2011), 816, 818; Eidenmüller/Jansen/Kieninger/Wagner/Zimmermann, *JZ* (2012), 276–277; Schmolke, *Grenzen der Selbstbindung...*, pp. 262–263, 821, 840 ff., 874; Bechtold, *Die Grenzen zwingenden Vertragsrechts...*, pp. 57 ff.; Haupt, 4 *Ger.Law J.* (2003), 1142 ff.; Tscherner, 1 *ALJ* (2014), 148, 149; Grundmann, *JZ* (2013), 57; Grigoleit, *NJW* (2002), 1155; Wiedemann/Wank, *JZ* (2013), 345; Herresthal, Consumer Law in the DCFR..., p. 201; von Bar/Clive/Schulte-Nölke et al., *Principles, Definitions and Model Rules...*, p. 368; further Malhotra, 8 *J.Cons.Res.* (1982), 420 ff.; Paredes, 81 *Wash.U.L.Q.* (2003), 441 ff.; Persson, 2 *BBP* (2018); Becher, 68 *La.L.Rev.* (2007), 169 ff. In general, on the *law of diminishing marginal utility (of wealth: the more money you have, the less another dollar/euro is worth to you)*, *cf.* R.Posner, *Economic Analysis of Law*^{6}, pp. 10–11, 78, 228 (fn. 3), 470 ff., 618; Cooter/Ulen, *Law & Economics*^{6}, pp. 22 ff., 44 ff.; Schäfer/Ott, *Lehrbuch der ökonomischen Analyse des Zivilrechts*^{4}, pp. 72 ff.; Julius, *Prospect Theory...*; Becker, *The Economic Approach to Human Behavior, passim*, esp. pp. 6, 239–240; Thaler, *Misbehaving...*, pp. 28–29.

218 *Cf.* Engel/Stark, Buttons, Boxes, Ticks, and Trust..., pp. 108, 111.

219 One very characteristic example of informational overreach is the disclosure provision of Article 6 para. 1 of the Consumer Rights Directive 2011/83/EU, which lists 20 items (along with

points out that the value of the information provided to consumers is inversely proportional to its quantity. That is to say that a great amount of information can have less utility for consumer-protection purposes than a lesser amount; in this respect, "*less can be better*."[220] Therefore, it can be concluded that *the maximum quantity of information that can be provided to the consumer is not to be equated with the optimal amount*, since an increase in the amount of information may, after a certain point, adversely affect the quality of the consumer's decision.[221]

c Further, active choosing would entail the imposition of a heavy burden on businesses or providers of goods (products or services): their transaction costs—specifically *contract drafting and administrative costs*—would skyrocket if they had to take into account the preferences of each consumer with respect to each aspect of a good and adjust the goods and the relevant contractual terms accordingly. In such a case the costs to businesses and providers would be totally prohibitive, or, in any event, the latter would have

---

various sub-items) to be disclosed for any distance or off-premises sale of a consumer good. *Cf.* Hacker, 3 *ERPL* (2017), 667.

220 Smith, Economics in the Laboratory, pp. 340–341; see also Sah/Cain/Loewenstein, Confessing One's Sins but Still Committing Them..., pp. 148 ff. *passim*, esp. 157: "Much of the research [...] concludes that having more information does not necessarily mean better decisions. [...] if the person who receives the disclosure is overwhelmed by information with no way to discern what information is important, then disclosure will have little positive effect"; Porat/Strahilevitz, 112 *Mich.L.Rev.* (2014), 1422, 1470 ff.; Engel/Stark, Buttons, Boxes, Ticks, and Trust..., pp. 108, 111, 113; Hacker, 3 *ERPL* (2017), 666–667. More generally, on the, nowadays, growing criticism of the efficacy of the abundant disclosure rules, see, indicatively, Sah/Cain/Loewenstein, *op.cit.*, pp. 148 ff., who maintain that "disclosure is not a panacea," for "it often fails to serve its intended functions and may sometimes backfire, hurting the interests of those it was intended to protect" (p. 148). For further arguments against the usefulness of disclosure rules, see Ben-Shahar/Schneider, 159 *U.Pa.L.Rev.* (2011), 647 ff., esp. 684 ff., who suggest that disclosure to consumers rarely achieves what it is meant to achieve, for the disclosures get so lengthy and cumbersome that consumers are not in a position to read and process them in their entirety; more recently, the same, More Than You Wanted to Know: The Failure of Mandated Disclosure (2014). *Cf.* further Sibony/Helleringer, EU Consumer Protection and Behavioural Sciences ..., pp. 219 ff., who do agree with Ben-Shahar and Schneider that "information requirements, as they now exist in EU law, are largely ineffective," but in the absence of available data are uncertain "if they are harmful as the two authors claim" (*ibidem*, p. 219); in any event, Sibony and Helleringer rightly clarify that they do not dispute that "compliance costs are passed on to consumers but wonder whether these costs are very large, notably because it is cheap to provide information online..." (*ibidem*, p. 219 fn. 48).

221 See also Haupt, 4 *Ger. Law J.* (2003), 1142 ff., esp. 1143: "... with a rising quantity of information the quality of consumers' decisions cannot be improved proportionally, so that, therefore, *the marginal utility of information is decreasing*. If too much and too detailed information is offered, consumers are often not able to take up, to understand and process the data. Therefore it is important *to find the optimal, instead of the maximal, amount of information* that has to be disclosed" (emphasis added); in the same vein, Fleischer, *Informartionsasymmetrie...*, pp. 115–116, 176; for more detail, De Palma/Myers/Papageorgiou, 84 *Am.Econ.Rev.* (1994), 419 ff., and Becher, 68 *La.L.Rev.* (2007), 170 ff.; *cf.* also G.Dworkin, 7 *Midwest Stud.Philos.* (1982), 50, 55–56; Conlisk, 34 *JEL* (1996), 686 ff.

no other option but to pass them on, to a significant degree, to the consumers in the final price of their goods. In this way, active choosing would end up harming consumers' interests.[222] Thus another considerable advantage of the use of default rules is the avoidance, or at least the restriction, of such costs (which initially appear to affect only businesses and providers).[223]

Notwithstanding the above, the priority given in principle to default rules must be combined with allowing enough room for absolute freedom of choice. Absolute freedom of choice must be granted, especially in cases where the disadvantages of active choosing are absent, for example, when active choosing is relatively simple and does not demand a great deal of effort, or when people's preferences change rapidly and thus a default rule is not, objectively, in a position to accommodate them.[224] And it is of no avail to say that in all events our decision to enter a market or into a specific transaction must normally be absolutely free, in the sense that we freely and autonomously formulate our transactional choices. We choose the products or services that we deem will best meet our expectations or needs (e.g., a smartphone or a car). For this reason, at this initial stage, there can be, in principle, no default rules or options (e.g., we should not be 'navigated' to buy a smartphone or a car because of an existing default rule); we are usually confronted with such rules or options when we have narrowed down our transactional choices—that is, when we are already focused on a specific product or service.[225]

VIII. The recent trend toward personalizing private law

The last suggestion, though, does not fully reflect the modern transactional reality, whereby the large internet retailers (such as Amazon) are indeed in a position to create ***personalized default options*** governing our initial transactional choices by processing ***big data***. These data are collected chiefly from our previous transactions. Retailers' processing of our personal information enables them to predict, with a high degree of accuracy, our future transactional choices and decisions and thus to lead us into a frame of ***predictive shopping***. This holds especially for products and services that consumers do not often change their preferences about over time (such as regular goods of household consumption).[226]

To the extent that a passive stance or silence on the consumer's part alone does not have any legal consequence—that is, it does not generate any contractual undertaking, for example, by being perceived as tacit consent—or the relevant information provided by the retailer is not misleading, deceptive,

222 See also Sunstein, *Choosing Not to Choose* ..., p. 147.
223 Also Thaler, 1 *J.Econ.Behav.Organ.* (1980), 58–59.
224 *Cf.* also Sunstein, 64 *Duke L.J.* (2014), 41–42.
225 In the same vein, Sunstein, 64 *Duke L.J.* (2014), 45 ff.
226 So Sunstein, 64 *Duke L.J.* (2014), 45 ff., and 162 *U.Penn.L.R.* (2013), 48 ff.; for more detail, recently, the same, *Choosing Not to Choose* ..., *passim*, esp. pp. 157 ff., 175 ff.

disturbing, or untimely, it would seem that, in principle, significant objections to such commercial practices cannot be raised. In fact, such practices make our daily life simpler, and what is more important, they create free time for us to channel into other activities (either productive and profitable or not, such as leisure activities).[227] On the other hand, though, there are paramount concerns about the way big data are gathered and processed; such concerns mainly call for an efficient, enhanced protection of our rights to privacy and to actual consent. In this 'brave new world' the legal systems are called upon to protect privacy and also to secure the individual's freedom of choice. A continuous, suffocating pursuit of consumers through the use of 'personalized defaults' that cover a wide spectrum of daily transactional decisions can severely undermine autonomous choice.

Aside from the concept of ***predictive shopping***, there is nowadays the further idea of ***personalizing legal default rules.***[228] This idea was recently picked up and extensively elaborated by Porat and Strahilevitz, who offer a comprehensive theory of personalized default rules with the aid of big data processing.[229] They advocate, more particularly, a personalized default-rule regime implementable in many fields—that is, consumer contracts, medical malpractice, organ donation, inheritance (wills), landlord-tenant relations, and labor law; thus, for example, they support default rules tailored to the personal characteristics of specific contracting parties. Porat and Strahilevitz[230] somehow downplay the data privacy issues relating to their proposal, although they acknowledge that in the EU, "where regulators have generally taken a more aggressive approach to data privacy than their American counterparts, such restrictions could well thwart the development of personalized default rules."[231] They posit that "[m]aking consumers aware of the potential benefits from personalized defaults and personalized disclosure may, in the long-run, prompt fewer consumers to try to thwart tracking. After all, most consumers bring strongly pragmatic perspectives to privacy trade-offs, and they are increasingly willing to share information about themselves when the benefits from sharing are increased and the threats from sharing are diminished."[232] Hence, Porat and Strahilevitz's belief is that in the long run "the benefits of personalized default rules will prompt more consumers to surrender private information, a development that is positive in

227 See also Sunstein, *Choosing Not to Choose ...*, *passim*, esp. pp. 157 ff.

228 Cf. the remarks of Sunstein, 162 *U.Penn.L.R.* (2013), 57: "In many domains, personalized default rules are the wave of the future. We should expect to see a significant increase in personalization as greater information becomes available about the informed choice of diverse people. The coming wave, very much in progress, will create serious risks, but it also promises to make our lives not only easier and simpler ..."; further the same, 122 *Yale L.J.* (2013), 1870–1871, and *Choosing Not to Choose...*, *passim*, esp. pp. 16–17, 19–20.

229 Porat/Strahilevitz, 112 *Mich.L.Rev.* (2014), 1417 ff.

230 Porat/Strahilevitz, 112 *Mich.L.Rev.* (2014), 1467 ff.

231 Porat/Strahilevitz, 112 *Mich.L.Rev.* (2014), 1467.

232 Porat/Strahilevitz, 112 *Mich.L.Rev.* (2014), 1468.

efficiency terms but problematic to theorists who argue that privacy produces positive externalities."[233]

In the same vein, Porat and Strahilevitz further propose[234] "a regime of 'personalized disclosure' whereby data about individual preferences, characteristics, and predilections would be employed to improve the signal-to-noise ratio of disclosures concerning products and services"[235]; such a personalization strategy, based on the proliferation of big data, would make the disclosures "each consumer sees shorter and more relevant".[236]

Recently, Ben-Shahar and Porat[237] also advocate an idea for ***personalizing mandatory rules***, which rests on the following main line of reasoning: "Instead of one-size-fits-all protective mandates, the law would tailor the protection to the personal attributes of each protected party. Similar to the method through which other services like insurance, education, medicine, and marketing are personalized—firms using Big Data to tailor their product to the predicted personal needs of each client—the service of legal protection could be personalized to correspond to the predicted protective needs of contracting parties."[238] Ben-Shahar and Porat further argue that "if done properly, personalization could increase the benefits and reduce the unintended costs of mandatory law. Protective needs would be better addressed, and more consumers would be served."[239] On this thought-provoking proposal, though, I will elaborate at a later point—see Chapter 4 below.

Admittedly, there is nowadays a general trend toward ***personalizing private law***—also affecting European academia, which mainly draws on the abovementioned work of Ben-Shahar, Porat, and Strahilevitz. Namely, Philipp Hacker, who recently pushes hard this idea, claims that private law stands much to gain from tailoring its regulatory apparatus to the needs of individual legal subjects, "according to their revealed and often easily accessible behaviour."[240] On the basis of the findings of behavioral economics and big data analytics we should attempt, as the argument goes, to personalize EU private law across different regulatory tools such as disclosures, nudges, and mandates. In this respect private

233 Porat/Strahilevitz, 112 *Mich.L.Rev.* (2014), 1469. On the concept of ***personalized default rules*** of Porat and Strahilevitz, see also Feldman/Lobel, Behavioural Trade-Offs..., pp. 321–322.

234 Porat/Strahilevitz, 112 *Mich.L.Rev.* (2014), 1422, 1470 ff.

235 Porat/Strahilevitz, 112 *Mich.L.Rev.* (2014), 1422.

236 Porat/Strahilevitz, 112 *Mich.L.Rev.* (2014), 1472. Also in favor of a ***personalized mandated disclosure scheme***, very recently Ben-Shahar/Porat, 86 *U.Chi.L.Rev.* (2019), 274. Furthermore, on an attempt to personalize ***negligence law*** as well, once again with the aid of big data, see Ben-Shahar/Porat, 91 *N.Y.U.L.Rev.* (2016), 627 ff., whose basic tenet is that "negligence law should give much of its objectivity by allowing courts to 'subjectify' the standard of care—that is, to tailor it to the specific injurer's tendency to create risks and her abilities to reduce them" (***ibidem***, p. 627).

237 Ben-Shahar/Porat, 86 *U.Chi.L.Rev.* (2019), 255 ff.

238 Ben-Shahar/Porat, 86 *U.Chi.L.Rev.* (2019), 256.

239 Ben-Shahar/Porat, 86 *U.Chi.L.Rev.* (2019), 256.

240 Hacker, 3 *ERPL* (2017), 651, 654.

law "should embrace and actively harness Big Data and digital technologies, wherever possible, as a source of social good in order to solve legal problems in novel ways."[241] In a nutshell, under this approach, the overwhelming power of big data may take behavioral interventions to "an entirely new level."[242]

The possible benefits from such a regulatory shift toward personalization are deemed to be manifold.[243] Its primary benefit is that it may minimize regulatory errors generated in the current practice of private law. Indeed, there are many such—long-attested—errors in the current practice.[244] They mostly relate to the—sometimes unconsidered—abstract differentiations drawn by the European legislator between different groups of persons: for example, there are different rules for consumers and sellers/traders, or for professional and retail investors. These distinctions are not always successful in practice. As Hacker rightly points out, "[t]hese categories [...] are often simultaneously over- and underinclusive. For example, partners of major law firms are considered consumers when

241 Hacker, 3 *ERPL* (2017), 654.

242 Hacker, 2 *ERPL* (2016), 297. More specifically, Hacker (3 *ERPL* (2017), 651 ff.) believes that "[t]he time seems ripe for lawmakers to use digital technologies in order to take European market regulation one step further. By harnessing Big Data techniques, laws can be tailored to individual characteristics of addressees; the relevant parameters could then be stored and updated in a 'legal blockchain.' Through the use of different metrics and pseudonymization, the right to privacy, a key feature of European law in the digital age, can ultimately be respected" (*ibidem*, p. 651). Thus Hacker "introduces the instrument of a 'legal blockchain' to operationalize personalized law in different settings" (*ibidem*, p. 654). See also, once again, the same, 2 *ERPL* (2016), 321–322, wherein *inter alia*: "In the arena of lawmaking, the next methodological frontier will most likely follow from an audacious combination of behavioural studies and data science. The predictive power of such types of big data analysis will allow for a quantum leap in the design of regulation: personalized law. [...] This procedure involves two basic steps: First, individual actors are classified according to their personality traits by big data analysis. Second, certain specific legal rules attach to these personality categories; the features of these norms can be designed in order to specifically adapt to the particularities of the respective category." Apart from Hacker, *cf.* also Casey/Niblett, 92 *Ind.L.J.* (2017), 1401 ff., who suggest that advances in technology (such as big data and artificial intelligence) will give rise to 'microdirectives,' that is, 'context-specific laws' (or rules), which will be tailored to each and every context and will be able to adapt to any situation; as this larger trend toward context-specific laws continues, "the fundamental cost trade-off between rules and standards will disappear, changing the way society structures and thinks about law" (*ibidem*, p. 1401). This new form of lawmaking, which generates context-specific rules—that is, 'microdirectives'—is "the future of law" (*ibidem*, p. 1402). Casey and Niblett's long-run prediction is "that microdirectives will become the dominant form of law, culminating in the death of rules and standards. But even if that full evolution does not happen, microdirectives are certain to become a viable alternative for many laws" (*ibidem*, p. 1404). Cf. further Willis, 82 *U.Chi.L.Rev.* (2015), 1309 ff., who advocates a 'performance-based consumer law,' which can be developed with the help of big data and the prevalence of technological devices: this new form of consumer law "recognizes that with new empirical techniques, the law need not rely on regulatory and judicial models or myths about the 'reasonable,' 'average,' or even 'vulnerable' consumer. Instead, we can measure what actual consumers know and do so as to ground the law in a more objective measure of what is reasonable" (*ibidem*, p. 1407).

243 See Hacker, 3 *ERPL* (2017), 658 ff.

244 Hacker, 3 *ERPL* (2017), 658–659.

buying a house for themselves, while owners of small pet shops in their business dealings are not, despite the fact that the former certainly have more business experience and expertise than the latter. A central problem for the contemporary theory of private law, therefore, is the staggering degree of *heterogeneity* within the groups the law traditionally distinguishes between—be it differences in experience, rationality, willpower, economic resources, or else."[245] With the help of personalization—that is, by taking into account factors such as the degree of rationality or willpower, the income or wealth of each actor—the legal categories could be rendered more precise, granular and refined in order to match reality as closely as possible[246]; moreover, different legal consequences could be attached to each category.[247] For example, disclosures, default rules, or mandatory rules for people who are prone to underestimate their future consumption could be designed differently from those that govern the behavior of rational actors or "economically better calibrated individuals"[248]—that is, individuals who, above all, do not succumb to *hyperbolic discounting*.

Thus personalization may indeed be used to address the problem of *heterogeneity*. Such a personalization may be seen as furthering *equality before the law*, since equal treatment—also according to the relevant CJEU case law—asks us, *inter alia*, to treat different situations differently: "similarly situated subjects are treated similarly, and differently situated ones—differently".[249]

At the same time, this approach does not overlook the privacy and data protection concerns that arise through a holistic attempt to personalize private law[250] for this attempt presupposes that a plethora of personal data is collected, stored, or otherwise processed.[251] This raises more concerns in the EU—than in the United States—which, as is widely known, adheres to a strict regime of data protection by virtue of the General Data Protection Regulation (GDPR); the scope of this regime encompasses a wide terrain of privacy breaches both by private parties and by the state.[252] Within this framework, a series of specific measures

245 Hacker, 3 *ERPL* (2017), 658 and 674 ff. *Cf.* the same, 11 *ERCL* (2015), 311 ff.; also Casey/Niblett, 92 *Ind.L.J.* (2017), 1405: "Rules will no longer be over- and underinclusive"; further Willis, 82 *U.Chi.L.Rev.* (2015), 1309 ff. *passim*. On the above critical issue of *heterogeneity*, see also Bar-Gill/Ben-Shahar, 50 *CML Rev.* (2013), 113–114.

246 Hacker, 3 *ERPL* (2017), 658 ff., 676.

247 Hacker, 3 *ERPL* (2017), 659 and 676.

248 Hacker, 2 *ERPL* (2016), 321.

249 Hacker, 3 *ERPL* (2017), 659–660 and 677.

250 *Cf.* also Casey/Niblett, 92 *Ind.L.J.* (2017), 1441–1442, where further references to the relevant—already vast—literature (*ibidem*, fn. 177).

251 See Hacker, 3 *ERPL* (2017), 664.

252 See Hacker, 3 *ERPL* (2017), 664, who rightly concludes that "[c]oncerns about an increase in the processing of personal data, which personalized law would potentially imply, [...] have to be treated with the utmost seriousness in the context of European law." In contrast, the United States is viewed as ill-equipped in matters of privacy and data protection; see, indicatively, Pro-Market (The blog of the Stigler Center at the University of Chicago Booth School of Business), *How to Address the Privacy and Security Challenges Posed by Big Tech*, which, *inter alia*, underscores the fact that "[t]he idiosyncracies of the American approach also impede efforts to

should be taken, which would enhance privacy and data protection. It is suggested that first and foremost it should be necessary to enact a law sanctioning the collection and processing of data for the purpose of personalization (cf. recital 46, Article 6 para. 3, and Article 22 para. 2 sect. b of GDPR).[253] On the other hand, it is maintained that the aim of tailoring legal rules to individual data subjects does ensure that the data is collected for specified, explicit and legitimate purposes (Article 5 para. 1 sect. b of GDPR).[254] Nonetheless, the issues to be dealt with are a lot and seem to impose serious constraints to a broad personalization project; data abuse by governments or companies cannot, of course, be ruled out.[255] And such concerns may not be easily alleviated.[256]

It is evident that with the advance of algorithmic processing of big data and the general proliferation of artificial intelligence, personalized disclosures, defaults, or mandates will become another hotbed of legal scholarship in the near future. In the preceding analysis I have only flagged the areas where great caution is needed. Self-evidently, I cannot explore here the far-reaching effects of this new personalization trend on the general structure of law and, specifically, our right to privacy.[257] The question I will now ponder on is whether there might be other regulatory tools available, which go beyond defaults, opt-out or opt-in systems.

harmonize global privacy law, threatening the free flow of data in international e-commerce." ProMarket basically proposes the widespread introduction of default provisions that enhance the privacy and security of Facebook, Google, Amazon, and other platforms; such provisions are called "consumertarian default rules": those are, namely, legal defaults used in privacy and security settings and preferred or expected by a majority of consumers. In the context of this interesting proposal for consumertarian default rules, it is further rightly—and in line with my own general approach (see Chapters 3, 4, and 5)—suggested that "waivers of protections granted to consumers by default would be valid if the waiver was narrow (aimed at waiving one right rather than a large aggregation of rights), knowing, and secured in a non-manipulative manner" (ProMarket, *ibidem*).

253 Hacker, 3 *ERPL* (2017), 664.

254 Hacker, 3 *ERPL* (2017), 664.

255 Hacker himself (3 *ERPL* (2017), 664–665) seems to acknowledge the great difficulties that have to be encountered, concluding that "EU data protection law does not categorically rule out the individual tailoring of laws; but it should be treated as a yardstick against which the degree of invasiveness of every collection of data in the name of personalization, and the risk it poses for the personal integrity of the data subject, must necessarily be measured. [...] Personalized law must aim at minimal invasiveness into privacy and maximum scrutiny of the validity of data, which makes trade-offs necessary" (*ibidem*, p. 665).

256 See also Casey/Niblett, 92 *Ind.L.J.* (2017), 1442.

257 See also Casey/Niblett, 92 *Ind.L.J.* (2017), 1401 ff., esp. 1405 ff., who in general believe that the coming technological revolution will have a "momentous effect" on law (*ibidem*, p. 1406).

3 Beyond defaults, opt-out or opt-in systems

The recourse to the visible hand of the mandated-choice model

As already discussed in the previous chapter, the admissibility of some defaults or opt-out systems raises concerns. In particular, the pre-conditions under which they may be acceptable can be highly controversial.

Consider once again the opt-out system in (post-mortal) organ donation. According to that regulatory model, every person is presumed to be an organ donor unless she expresses an explicit objection. This form of nudging may be acceptable, however, insofar as every citizen (a) is informed of this default option in an overt and explicit manner,[1] and (b) is not obliged to pay a high 'bureaucracy tax,' that is, waste considerable time and energy before a public authority in order to reverse the default option (***easy and cheap reversibility***; e.g., a citizen could be asked to express her objection by simply ticking a box when electronically submitting her tax declaration, since such an act entails trivial effort cost).[2]

The Greek legislator recently dealt with this issue. It serves our discussion to see which path it decided to follow. EU Directive no. 2010/53 was initially transposed into the Greek legal order by Law no. 3984/2011. Subsequently twice amended, the law today basically incorporates an opt-out system, subject to the consent of the presumed donor's family (Article 9 para. 2 of Law no. 3984/2011 as currently in force). Thus, the Greek legislator tied the opt-out system to the consent of the family, without which it is often difficult for physicians to proceed with organ removal.[3] So, still, the family is asked for their permission before

1 *Cf.* also van Aaken, Judge the Nudge..., pp. 94–95: "If [...] individuals do not know whether their country has an opt-in or an opt-out system of organ donation, they are unaware of their choice. This should not be permissible."

2 For the great importance of the latter pre-condition, see Thaler/Sunstein, *Nudge*..., pp. 177–178.

3 *Cf.* Berger, Singapore's compulsory organ transplants. Against the need for consent on the part of the family—whose refusal to allow organ donation is practically seen as an unnecessary barrier—Thaler/Sunstein, *Nudge*..., p. 176. *Cf.* also Klassen/Klassen, 125 *Ann.Intern.Med.* (1996), 70 ff., who, ***inter alia***, rightly though underline that "research has shown that communication and consensus between caregivers and the family are critical, even in situations in which advance directives exist" (***ibidem***, p. 71).

organ donation takes place.[4] Yet this hybrid opt-out system seems to suffer from two severe flaws: (a) because Greek citizens are not officially—that is, through a wide public information campaign—informed of their (presumed) status as organ donors, the vast majority are ignorant of this fact; and as a matter of principle, a default option must be visible. (b) The objection declaration entails high effort tax—that is, it is a costly bureaucratic process that requires one to file a declaration with the National Organization for Transplantation that must then be verified by a public authority. Recently, though, a relevant decision of the Ministry of Health gives the possibility to file this declaration electronically through the national online tax declaration system of the Ministry of Finance.

Arguably, the Greek legislator could have directly opted for a more transparent and cost-effective system, such as allowing citizens to express their objection when submitting their yearly tax declaration online; if such a solution were adopted, citizens would also automatically be informed of their presumed status as organ donors for ***consent by stealth*** cannot be permissible in a free, liberal society. Or as Benjamin Cardozo has eloquently put it, "[e]very human being of adult years and sound mind has a right to determine what shall be done with his own body."[5]

In my opinion, a different, third path, would be preferable to the legislator. Lying between the opt-out and the opt-in system, this path has been suggested over the past two decades by many scholars, as well as medical experts and professional associations (mainly the American Medical Association), and its scope might not be restricted to the thorny topic of organ donation. Namely, the legislator could avoid predetermining citizens' initial position (for or against organ donation) by ***compelling them*** to take a position on the matter—for example, by ***requiring*** them to tick yes or no when submitting their tax declaration (or tax return) or applying for or renewing their vehicle driver's license. Under this scenario, the tax declaration could not be submitted without ticking the relevant box; the same would hold, ***mutatis mutandis***, for the driver's license, though the solution there would lack inclusivity, since not all members of the population possess a driver's license.[6]

4 This is also the solution recently adopted in the UK, see www.organdonation.nhs.uk/helping-you-to-decide/about-organ-donation/faq/what-is-opt-out/.

5 Cardozo, in: *Schloendorff v. Society of New York Hospital*, 211 N.Y. 125, 105 N.E. 92 (1914). By the way, in the United States, there is still an opt-in system for organ donation, see Becker/Elias, Cash for Kidneys ... (see also, though, fn. 7 below).

6 For more detail as to how individuals are to be compelled to choose, see Chouhan/Draper, 29 *J. Med. Ethics* (2003), 158: "... questions about organ donation could form part of tax returns, vehicle driver's licence application forms, state benefit claims, and so forth. It would be a requirement that before returns/applications/claims are processed, questions about organ donation are answered, so that individuals ***who fail to decide*** would be penalised by not being able to drive, claim benefits, or would be subject to the penalties for failure to complete their tax forms properly. The system of registration must be ***as inclusive as possible*** to reach all the members of the population. So, for instance, tax forms alone would not suffice, as this would be unfair on those who do not earn enough to complete a tax return. Likewise, not all of the population drive cars or claim benefits" (emphasis added).

This is the so-called ***mandated (or forced-, prompted-, required-) -choice system*** (in German: *zwingendes Optionsmodell*).[7]

Under this system, citizens would feel that their freedom of choice is being respected, having been asked directly if they wish to become organ donors (and even to specify which organs they would like to donate). They would become donors only after explicitly consenting. Furthermore, individuals could be provided with the additional option to let their relatives have the final say.[8] Such a system would need to be accompanied by extensive, openly *prodonation* public education and the provision of information—that is, public information campaign—about the social benefits as well as the implications of organ donation. Individuals would also be informed of their right *to easily revoke their previous decision at any time*, be it for or against organ donation; the option to revoke should be *online* available at any time. Thus their choice would be, in many aspects, an informed one.[9]

7 As already mentioned above, in the field of organ donation the idea is, of course, not new: see Chouhan/Draper, 29 *J.Med.Ethics* (2003), 157 ff., who ardently defend the idea as the best way to increase the number of cadaveric organs available for transplantation, while at the same time honoring personal autonomy, freedom of choice, and self-ownership; said authors also refer to the significant prehistory of the idea (*ibidem*, p. 158): "Mandated choice has been widely debated in the USA. It was first proposed by Veatch, but Spital is perhaps its most ardent proponent. He conducted a survey in a population of young adults in the USA that indicated that an overwhelming ninety per cent would support mandated choice, while only sixty per cent approved of presumed consent. It is the preferred option of the AMA [*scil.* American Medical Association] and the United Network for Organ Sharing (UNOS) but was rejected out of hand by the BMA [*scil.* British Medical Association] in its report." See also Siegal/Bonnie, 34 *J.L.Med.&Ethics* (2006), 415: "Among the ideas that have been proposed to increase prospective donations, 'mandated choice', endorsed in principle by the AMA in 1994, would require people to state their preferences regarding organ donation when performing state-mandated tasks, such as renewing driver's licenses or filing tax returns. This approach would leave the current donation-based system in place while trying to overcome impediments that prevent people who are inclined to be donors from recording their desire to do so and that tend to dissuade their families from authorizing organ removal upon death. However, a decade later, no state currently uses this approach, and its critics have argued that it could be counterproductive if ambivalent or even distrustful people are forced to make a decision on the record"; Klassen/Klassen, 125 *Ann.Intern.Med.* (1996), 70 ff., where there is reference to some U.S. states that have introduced the mandated-choice system on organ donation; van Aaken, Judge the Nudge..., p. 98, who also favors mandated choice in the case of organ donation (or pension plans): "... People can be asked to choose explicitly. In other words, it is mandated that individuals actively choose one option. This means that people must decide at some point of time (e.g., when turning 18, renewing passports, or applying for a driving license)"; Lichtenberg, Paternalism, Manipulation, Freedom, and the Good, p. 496; Cartwright, *Behavioral Economics*[2], p. 531.

8 See Chouhan/Draper, 29 *J.Med. Ethics* (2003), 158.

9 See Chouhan/Draper, 29 *J.Med. Ethics* (2003), 158: "A move to mandated choice would also have to be accompanied by extensive public education so that when making their choices, people are sufficiently informed about both the need for choice and the implications of their decision. Finally, choices, though binding, would also be revocable: indeed, people could change their minds as often as they wished, and the most recent choice would prevail. In addition to granting individuals the opportunity to be proactive in revising their decisions, a system could also facilitate periodic but regular review." Also *ibidem*, p. 161: "... a system of mandated choice where

In all events, the individuals' express and active decision to be an organ donor would be easier to respect for their family and relatives. The express and clear will of a person who actively accepts the role of organ donor, who affirmatively says "yes," is more likely to be respected by her family and relatives than the passive failure to express her objection to a (default) position of which she was possibly ignorant.[10] This would be a great benefit from reaching out for ***the visible hand of the mandated-choice system.***

Practically speaking, it is possible that the adoption of such a system could produce fewer organ donors than the opt-out system.[11] Even if this were the result, the will of the citizens would be expressed and would need to be respected: ***hoc volunt, sic jubent, sit pro ratione voluntas.***[12]

In light of the above features, it comes as no surprise that nowadays also German MPs are backing the adoption of the mandated-choice model in their country, stressing, ***inter alia***, the need to preserve freedom of choice and self-determination, as well as to keep people always informed about the choice they have to be organ donors or not.[13]

The mandated-choice model may indeed be crucial for very important decisions in our lives such as organ donation or pension plans.[14] But it is not just that. As already alluded to above, this system may have a broader scope of application in the area of private law, especially in the field of consumer protection provisions,

---

the accompanying public education and information is similarly prodonation. [...] all public information and educational material that accompanies a move to mandated choice should be biased in favour of donation."

10 This position is, effectively, also shared by Thaler/Sunstein, *Nudge*..., pp. 180, Thaler/Sunstein/Balz, Choice Architecture..., p. 431, and recently Thaler, *Misbehaving*..., pp. 328–329. See also, once again, Chouhan/Draper, 29 *J.Med. Ethics* (2003), 159, 160: "If [...] a person decides not to donate, at least her survivors will be aware of her wish, will be spared the uncomfortable situation which might arise when hospital staff approach them about donation and they refuse. And furthermore, they may be comforted in knowing that the deceased's wishes are being honoured."

11 However, in an online experiment carried out in the past by Johnson/Goldstein [78 *Transplantation* (2004), 1714–1715, and 302 *Science* (2003), 1338–1339; see also the same, Decisions by Default, p. 423, as well as Lichtenberg, Paternalism, Manipulation, Freedom, and the Good, p. 496], the findings showed that ***the opt-out condition does not differ significantly from the "neutral condition," which requires a choice without a default option*** (namely, 79% of participants who must decide choose to be organ donors, 82% in the opt-out default remain as donors, and only 42% in the opt-in condition agree to become donors). *Cf.* further, though, Klassen/Klassen, 125 *Ann.Intern.Med.* (1996), 72–73, who in general are critical of the mandated-choice system on organ donation.

12 *Cf.* Chouhan/Draper, 29 *J.Med. Ethics* (2003), 160, 161: "... the process of actively deciding against donation in the face of literature etc attempting to persuade one to do the opposite, is an active expression of autonomy and therefore worthy of respect..." *Cf.* further Hausman/Welch, 18 *J.Polit.Philos.* (2010), 135.

13 See, indicatively, www.bundesgesundheitsministerium.de/fileadmin/Dateien/3_Downloads/O/Organspende/Gesetzentwurf_zur_Sta__rkung_der_Entscheidungsbereitschaft_bei_der_Organspende.pdf.

14 *Cf.* van Aaken, Judge the Nudge..., p. 98.

which currently take the form of *mandatory law*, although they could have been drafted *in a less coercive manner*.[15] Under a more flexible mandated-choice regime, private autonomy and freedom of contract would be left *with more breathing space*. Consumers themselves would benefit. They could, namely, acquire some goods (products or services) at a lower price, if they had the option to waive, at their own discretion, the special consumer law protections, which are today conferred on them as mandatory law. For instance, under EU mandatory law (which has been transposed into the national laws of the member states) a person who buys a used car cannot waive her rights deriving from an eventual defectiveness of the car (repair, substitution, rescission, or damages); in other words, she cannot buy the car '*as is where is*' in order to pay a lower price. Yet this was an option in the past before the enactment of EC Directive no. 1999/44. In Germany, for example, many young people—mainly students—would buy a car to drive just for the winter season (so-called *Winterautos*). Under a mandated-choice scheme, the buyer of a used car would have the right to choose between a contract with consumer protection at a higher price—that is, an *insurance premium*—and a contract without such protection at a lower price. This possibility would enhance the buyer's freedom of choice, advance the interests of lower-income consumers, and eliminate the socially unjust phenomenon of *cross-subsidization*, whereby lower-income consumers are forced to subsidize the greater protection that higher-income consumers enjoy.[16]

In sum, the mandated-choice model promotes autonomy because, in principle, as Gerald Dworkin points out, having choices increases the probability of satisfying our wants and gives us greater control over our lives.[17] Under that model, though, there is no abundance of choices, which would lead to the aforementioned *paradox of choice*; the choices presented to the individual are restricted to a few—normally two. Especially in the realm of organ donation, mandated choice recognizes the individual's legitimate interest in maintaining control over her own body, even after death.[18] Thus, it enhances autonomy and preserves *self-ownership*—although whether the dead can still be thought to own their bodies is, admittedly, a controversial issue.[19] The mandated-choice system in the case of organ donation admittedly rests on a coerced choice "to the extent that one is forced to choose if one wants to obtain other goods that one desires (like consideration of one's tax returns, a driver's licence or state benefits)."[20] This system is, however, acceptable, in the end, also in terms of moral philosophy, "because substantial benefit can be gained and harm prevented by the small

15 In general, for a justified open criticism of the European mandatory contract law aiming to protect the consumer, see, indicatively, Bar-Gill/Ben-Shahar, 50 *CML Rev.* (2013), 109 ff.

16 For more detail, see Chapter 4 below, with references to pertinent literature.

17 Dworkin, *The theory and practice of autonomy*, p. 8. *Cf.* also Lichtenberg, Paternalism, Manipulation, Freedom, and the Good, p. 496.

18 See Chouhan/Draper, 29 *J.Med. Ethics* (2003), 159.

19 See Chouhan/Draper, 29 *J.Med. Ethics* (2003), 159.

20 Chouhan/Draper, 29 *J.Med. Ethics* (2003), 159.

restriction of liberty that mandating causes."[21] Truth be told, nonetheless, such balancing raises broader philosophical issues that cannot be addressed in this book.

In the following Part B, I examine whether the mandated-choice model may indeed have a broader scope of application in the area of private law, especially in the field of consumer protection provisions, which currently take the form of mandatory law. The particular case-studies, which will concern me, are (a) the withdrawal right in distance contracts, (b) the sale "*as is where is*," and (c) the strict product liability. All these cases will be examined mainly through the lens of BEAL. I will now begin by first exploring the possibility of applying the mandated-choice model to the withdrawal right in distance contracts.

21 Once again, Chouhan/Draper, 29 *J.Med. Ethics* (2003), 159, and 160, wherein *inter alia*: "If someone decides to donate, her organ(s) can confer huge benefits on the recipient(s), and unless she has a religious or ethical objection against transplantation, contributing is a very easy thing to do in terms of time, effort, and effects on other responsibilities"—also *ibidem*, p. 161.

Part B

EU private law and possible scope of application of the mandated-choice model under a Behavioral Economic Analysis of Law (BEAL) approach

In the following Part B, I explore whether the mandated-choice model may have a broader scope of application in the area of private law, especially in the field of consumer protection provisions, which currently take the form of mandatory law. The particular case-studies, which will concern me, are (a) the withdrawal right in distance contracts, (b) the sale '*as is where is*,' and (c) the strict product liability. All these cases are examined mainly through the lens of BEAL. I begin by first exploring the possibility of applying the mandated-choice model to the withdrawal right in distance contracts provided for in Directive 2011/83/EU on Consumer Rights. The conclusion drawn here from the behavioral approach is that the mandated-choice model would be a more preferable, more efficient regulatory option than the existing mandatory law protection. It would be, namely, better if in distance contracts the law obligatorily provided the consumer with the possibility to choose between a contract without a withdrawal right and a contract with a withdrawal right and a higher price. This mandated-choice path currently finds considerable resonance in German theory and is advanced by eminent legal scholars. It has also been endorsed by me in my Greek monograph under the title "Private Autonomy and Consumer Protection – A Contribution to Behavioral Economic Analysis of Law" (2016).

4 The withdrawal right pursuant to Directive 2011/83/EU and the application of the mandated-choice model

I. Directive 2011/83/EU on Consumer Rights[1]

Directive 2011/83/EU on Consumers' Rights (hereinafter: ***DCR***) replaced Directives 85/577/EEC on *off-premises contracts* and 97/7/EC on *distance selling*, seeking to simplify and modernize the pertinent legal framework. It establishes, *inter alia*, a withdrawal right (in German: *Widerrufsrecht*; in French: *droit de rétractation*) in off-premises and distance contracts, which provides for a *cooling-off period* (or *period for sober reflection; spatium deliberandi*) in favor of the consumer. The DCR is one of the most significant recent EU legislative reforms in the field of contract law.[2] The European Commission itself has attached great importance to the DCR and its effects on improving consumer protection and harmonizing the internal market. This is clearly manifested in the *DG Justice Guidance Document* of the European Commission, issued in June 2014, which reflects an authentic interpretation of the provisions of the DCR.[3]

It is noted that there has recently been published a *Proposal for a Directive* aiming to amend four existing Directives, *inter alia* the DCR.[4] This new Directive

1 Directive 2011/83/EU of the European Parliament and of the Council of 25 October 2011 on consumer rights, amending Council Directive 93/13/EEC and Directive 1999/44/EC of the European Parliament and of the Council and repealing Council Directive 85/577/EEC and Directive 97/7/EC of the European Parliament and of the Council (O.J. L. 304). See, indicatively, Grundmann, *JZ* (2013), 53 ff.; Wendehorst, *NJW* (2014), 577 ff.; the same, in: *FS Griss*, pp. 717 ff.; Jud/Wendehorst, 6 *GPR* (2009), 68 ff.; Zöchnling-Jud, 212 *AcP* (2012), 550 ff.; Wipperfürth, *Die Verbraucherrechte-Richtlinie*..., *passim*, esp. pp. 26 ff.; Förster, *JA* (2014), 721 ff., and 801 ff.; Meier, *JuS* (2014), 777 ff.; Micklitz/Reich, *EuZW* (2009), 279 ff.; Tonner/Tamm, *JZ* (2009), 277 ff.; Zypries, 2 *ZEuP* (2009), 225 ff.; Weatherill, *EU Consumer Law*..., pp. 108, 110 ff., 132 ff.; Loos, Rights of Withdrawal, pp. 1 ff.

2 Also Grundmann, *JZ* (2013), 53 and 65.

3 See https://ec.europa.eu/info/sites/info/files/crd_guidance_en_0.pdf.

4 *Proposal for a Directive of the European Parliament and of the Council amending Council Directive 93/13/EE of 5 April 1993, Directive 98/6/EC of the European Parliament and of the Council, Directive 2005/29/EC of the European Parliament and of the Council and Directive 2011/83/EU of the European Parliament and of the Council as regards better enforcement and modernisation of EU consumer protection rules* [COM(2018) 185 final, 11.04.2018]—see https://eur-lex.europa.eu/legal-content/EN/TXT/?uri=COM%3A2018%3A185%3AFIN. On the more recent European Parliament legislative resolution and position of 17 April 2019 on the Proposal, suggesting extensive amendments to it, see www.europarl.europa.eu/doceo/document/TA-8-2019-0399_EN.html. **More recently, on 18.10.2019, the text of the new Directive has been finalized (PE-CONS 83/19).**

seeks, in general, to further modernize EU consumer protection rules, mainly by providing for (a) additional information requirements for contracts concluded on 'online marketplaces' and (b) an extension of the withdrawal right to digital services for which consumers do not pay a price but provide personal data (such as cloud storage, social media, and e-mail accounts). The following analysis, though, rests on the, currently still in force, legal framework of the DCR.

II. The withdrawal right[5]

1. The withdrawal right justified by virtue of BEAL

In recent decades, the withdrawal right has been recognized by the European legislator as a fundamental pillar of consumer protection policy—the other two, equally fundamental pillars are the EU mandatory disclosure rules and the control of General Contract Terms (especially with respect to their possible abusive character).[6] The European legislator espouses the general concept that the consumer must be able to rescind, or withdraw from, a contract within a *cooling-off period (spatium deliberandi)*, especially in off-premises and distance contracts. The cooling-off period is 14 days.[7] This approach is also in line with similar considerations offered in the *Draft Common Frame of Reference* (see Articles II.-5:101–106, II.-5:201–202).

The consumer exercises the withdrawal right without having to justify her withdrawal. This right resembles the so-called *repentance right* (in German: *Reurecht*), which is an old idea going back to the end of the 19th century

5 In general, on the withdrawal right as provided for in the DCR, see, indicatively, Schärtl, *JuS* (2014), 577 ff.; Ernst, *NJW* (2014), 817 ff.; Förster, *JA* (2014), 728 ff., 801 ff.; Weatherill, *EU Consumer Law*..., pp. 113 ff.; Loos, Rights of Withdrawal, pp. 2 ff.; Eidenmüller, Widerrufsrechte, pp. 109 ff.; the same, 7 *ERCL* (2011), 1 ff.; Kroll-Ludwigs, 18 *ZEuP* (2010), 509 ff.; Wipperfürth, *Die Verbraucherrechte-Richtlinie*..., pp. 59 ff.; Grundmann, *JZ* (2013), 59; Karampatzos, Rechtspaternalismus im Europäischen Verbraucherschutzrecht..., pp. 213 ff.; *cf.* also Paparseniou, *Griechisches Verbrauchervertragsrecht*..., pp. 118 ff., 185 ff.; Schäfer, Widerrufsrechte..., pp. 189 ff.; Schwab, Widerrufsrechte..., pp. 149 ff.; Bechtold, *Die Grenzen zwingenden Vertragsrechts*..., pp. 93 ff.; Reiner, 203 *AcP* (2003), 1 ff.; Lettl, *JA* (2011), 9 ff.; Zimmermann, Rückabwicklung nach Widerruf, pp. 167 ff.; Fischer, *DB* (2002), 253 ff.; Heyers, *NJW* (2014), 2619 ff.; Fuchs, 196 *AcP* (1996), 313 ff.; Gernhuber, *WM* (1998), 1797 ff.; Rekaiti/van den Bergh, 23 *J.Consum.Policy* (2000), 371 ff.; Cserne, *Freedom of Contract*..., pp. 111 ff.

6 See Eidenmüller, Widerrufsrechte, pp. 109 ff., 160 ff., 162, 165; Zimmermann, Rückabwicklung nach Widerruf, pp. 167 ff.; Schmolke, *Grenzen der Selbstbindung*..., *passim*, esp. pp. 861–862; Riesenhuber, Wandlungen oder Erosion der Privatautonomie?, pp. 5 ff.; Tscherner, 1 *ALJ* (2014), 146 ff., esp. 148 ff.; Wipperfürth, *Die Verbraucherrechte-Richtlinie*..., pp. 59, 60; Paparseniou, *Griechisches Verbrauchervertragsrecht*..., *passim*, esp. pp. 151, 226; Kittner, *Schuldrecht*[2], nos. 877, 881; Martinek, *NJW* (1998), 207; Gernhuber, *WM* (1998), 1797; see also, extensively, Kroll-Ludwigs, 18 *ZEuP* (2010), 509 ff., 514 ff., 523 ff.

7 See, indicatively, Wiedemann/Wank, *JZ* (2013), 341; Medicus/Lorenz, *Schuldr I – AT*[18], no. 585; Schwab, Widerrufsrechte..., pp. 149, 150–151.

when the noted German legal scholar Philipp Heck conceived it. He suggested that it was particularly useful in the context of 'credit sales' (in German: *Abzahlungskäufe*).[8] Heck pointed out that customers often purchase products they do not really need and that exceed their financial means. This phenomenon, Heck argued, is easily explained in psychological terms: people are inclined to downplay the future repercussions of a commitment if it provides instant pleasure in the present.[9] This is a key factor shaping consumers' contractual decisions: in this respect Heck, already at the end of the 19th century, was alluding to the phenomenon of *hyperbolic discounting*.

By and large the same *rationale* backs the modern withdrawal right. This right gives the consumer the chance to reconsider her initial contractual decision by granting her *additional time for (sober) reflection*[10] (in German: *zweite Reflexionschance*[11]). During this period the consumer can consider whether said decision was justified or just an impulse; if not justified, the decision need not be binding. The consumer may exercise the withdrawal right without any financial burden or penalty, at least in principle. Sober reflection is an indispensable part of the decision-making process justified by the fact that the consumer, primarily in off-premises and distance transactions, often makes decisions in a state of *bounded rationality* and especially *bounded self-control*.[12]

It is evident, then, that *from the viewpoint of BEAL*, the social usefulness of the withdrawal right resides in its prevention of the fulfillment of contracts concluded as a result of a rationality deficit or preferential disorder on the part of the consumer which distorts her ability to make a rational decision. Contracts associated with severe rationality deficits are considered *inefficient* because they bring about an *inefficient allocation of resources*, which is in general undesirable.

On the other hand, the social usefulness of the withdrawal right must always be weighed against the *social cost* related to its statutory provision and actual exercise. This cost *mainly* lies here in the uncertainty caused by the provision of such a right. For 14 days the bindingness of off-premises and distance contracts is not definite, causing contingency. This means that, from the viewpoint

8 Heck, Wie ist den Missbräuchen…, pp. 131, 180 ff.; see also Eidenmüller, Widerrufsrechte, pp. 110, 114, and Loos, Rights of Withdrawal, p. 2; *cf.* further Reich, *JZ* (1975), 550 ff., esp. 551 ff.; Mankowski, *Beseitigungsrechte…*, pp. 3 ff.

9 Heck, Wie ist den Missbräuchen…, p. 148: ("… psychologisch erklärlich, da eine erst in Zukunft zu erfüllende Verbindlichkeit im Austausch gegen einen augenblicklichen Genuss meist unterschätzt [werde]").

10 von Bar/Clive/Schulte-Nölke et al., *Principles, Definitions and Model Rules…*, pp. 346, 354, 356.

11 See Eidenmüller, Widerrufsrechte, pp. 149–150; the same, 210 *AcP* (2010), 91; Wolf/Neuner, *AT des BürgR*[10], § 43 no. 1; also Riesenhuber, Wandlungen oder Erosion der Privatautonomie?, p. 7.

12 See Sunstein/Thaler, 70 *U.Chi.L.Rev.* (2003), 1187–1188, 1191; Camerer/Issacharoff/Loewenstein/O'Donoghue/Rabin, 151 *U.Penn.L.R.* (2003), 1238 ff., esp. 1240 ff.; Schürnbrand, *JZ* (2009), 135.

of BEAL, not clashing in this case with the *conventional* economic analysis of law,[13] the withdrawal right is justified only in transactional situations where the relevant cost-benefit analysis shows that its introduction has a clear surplus value: that is, the social usefulness clearly outweighs the costs relating to the statutory provision and the actual exercise of the right.[14]

Let us now take a closer look at the exercise of the withdrawal right. As has already merged, to exercise the withdrawal right the consumer need not provide any kind of justification. *Mere repentance suffices.*[15] The consumer may, then, exercise the right because she attests that the good she acquired does not meet her needs or expectations, because in the meantime she found a more attractive alternative offer for a similar good, or because she has used the good for the purpose she initially sought and now no longer needs it and wants a refund. The last two reasons present the possibility of a serious *moral hazard* at work here; the consumer may be engaging in *opportunistic conduct*, which in a wide variety of transactions could undermine the binding force of a contract and, more generally, the safety of transactions.[16]

In light of the above, it is evident that the various withdrawal rights provided by *mandatory law* in relation to certain types of consumer contracts constitute a severe interference with private autonomy. They give individuals the right to break promises, thus deviating from the rule *pacta sunt servanda*. They provide an easy way out of contracts, based merely on the repentance or remorse of one contracting party, the consumer. For these reasons, the introduction of withdrawal rights into law should always be backed by concrete and well-founded reasoning.[17] By the same token, any provision of withdrawal rights must be in accordance with the demands of the proportionality principle.[18] Therefore, withdrawal rights must not be introduced unless deemed necessary and appropriate, because of the drastic interference with private autonomy that they entail.

13 In general, on this poignant terminological distinction between *conventional* and *behavioral* economic analysis of law, see Jolls/Sunstein/Thaler, 50 *Stan.L.Rev.* (1998), 1473 ff. *passim*; Sunstein, 1 *Am.L.&Econ.Rev.* (1999), 147 ff. *passim*; Arlen, 52 *Vand.L.Rev.* (1998), 1765 ff. *passim*.

14 See Eidenmüller, Widerrufsrechte, pp. 126 ff., 163; also Kroll-Ludwigs, 18 *ZEuP* (2010), 520; Schmolke, *Grenzen der Selbstbindung...*, pp. 864, 880 ff.

15 *Cf.* also article II.-5:102(1) of the DCFR: "A right to withdraw is exercised by notice to the other party. *No reasons need to be given*"; von Bar/Clive/Schulte-Nölke et al., *Principles, Definitions and Model Rules...*, pp. 346–347, 350–351. *Cf.* further Mankowski, Widerrufsrecht, p. 1793; Möllers, *JZ* (2002), 130; Wiedemann/Wank, *JZ* (2013), 341; Rekaiti/van den Bergh, 23 *J.Consum.Policy* (2000), 375–376 ("*regret contingency*"), 383.

16 See also Bechtold, *Die Grenzen zwingenden Vertragsrechts...*, pp. 97 ff.; Loos, Rights of Withdrawal, pp. 15 ff.; Haupt, 4 *Ger. Law J.* (2003), 1149, 1150; Rekaiti/van den Bergh, 23 *J.Consum. Policy* (2000), 381. *Cf.*, though, also Mankowski, *Beseitigungsrechte...*, pp. 1146 ff.

17 See also Fuchs, 196 *AcP* (1996), 327; Canaris, 200 *AcP* (2000), 345; Camerer/Issacharoff/Loewenstein/O'Donoghue/Rabin, 151 *U.Penn.L.R.* (2003), 1239–1240; Loos, Rights of Withdrawal, pp. 3–4.

18 See Wolf/Neuner, *AT des BürgR*[10], § 43 no. 1. See also Chapter 2, pp. 62 ff. above.

But there is a further reason to favor a reluctance to intervene. The conclusion and execution of a single inefficient contract that is detrimental to the consumer may, over time, have desirable consequences. The consumer may become more careful and 'transactionally wiser' in the future, so that she does not repeat the same transaction or a similar one. This is the *learning effect* (see Chapter 1, pp. 17 ff. above), which is lost when the consumer is allowed to break her contractual promise by exercising her withdrawal right.[19] This is also true in more general terms: the learning effect is lost whenever the legislature or the judiciary intervenes in order to redress rationality deficits, when every 'wrong' transactional decision is subsequently reversed by virtue of a protective intervention. Within such a paternalistic bubble the moral hazard is grave and it may greatly undermine the safety of transactions.

However, some resistance to this view may be well justified. The idea (see, once again, Chapter 1, pp. 17 ff. above) that a previous bad transactional experience (: the conclusion of an inefficient, detrimental contract) might have a positive future effect holds as long as the bad decision does not lead to devastating consequences for the consumer, especially for her economic interests (such as excessive borrowing). In other words, if the consumer is life-long disabled due to a bad transactional decision, she will not be able to engage in the same transaction again. In such a case the learning effect is meaningless. In general, *the life we live is neither a rehearsal nor a game that can be repeated; it is a one-shot game.*

After these initial remarks, in the following paragraphs I outline the practical usefulness of the withdrawal right, at least in *distance contracts.*

2. *The rationale behind the withdrawal right in distance contracts*

Let us now turn to distance contracts (mainly online) and the specific rationale justifying the introduction of the withdrawal right. As is widely argued, this rationale lies with (a) the need to protect the consumer against aggressive sales methods by the seller or provider who is not in the presence of the consumer, and (b) the *information asymmetry* present at the conclusion of such contracts, where almost all goods (or services) being provided are *experience goods (or services).* Experience goods are goods whose quality and other features may only be ascertained or revealed after the purchaser has received and experienced or used them. This means that when a distance contract is concluded the consumer is not yet in a position to inspect the good, ascertain its quality, or discuss it with the seller. These circumstances hold, however, for one-time purchases, not for repeated transactions related to the purchase of a particular good (or service) by the same consumer. In repeated transactions, the consumer will have acquired

19 See Eidenmüller, Widerrufsrechte, p. 128.

relevant previous experience with the good (or service) and thus no information asymmetry will exist.[20]

In economic theory, experience goods (or services) are juxtaposed to the so-called *search goods (or services)*, the quality of which can be checked before the conclusion of a contract. Fruit for sale in an open-air market or a grocery store is a good example. In these instances there is no information asymmetry issue. There are also the so-called *credence goods (or services)*, which the consumer is not in a position to physically check either before or shortly after the conclusion of a contract. As a result, information asymmetry remains after the conclusion of the contract, and the negative effects resulting from the use or consumption of the good or service may be revealed only after a considerable lapse of time, or they may be detected only with specialized technical assistance. In the latter case the consumer is normally *de facto* forced to place trust in the representations or assurances of the seller or provider with respect to the properties or quality of the good or service they offer. Medical and legal services, investment and insurance products, and car repair services are good examples of credence goods or services. An information deficit on the part of the consumer in relation to the quality of the good or service remains after the conclusion of the contract and even after its full execution.[21]

Of the two justifications for the provision of a withdrawal right in distance contracts—that is, (a) the need to protect the consumer against aggressive sales methods and (b) the need to restore the information deficit of the consumer[22]—clear priority is rightly given to the latter. This is because in distance contracts the goods provided typically qualify as *experience goods*, indeed. The need to protect the consumer against aggressive sales methods does not provide a similarly strong argument for the introduction of a withdrawal right because such methods and tactics are regularly not the case in distance (mainly online) contracts.[23] Specifically:

20 For the above, see Nelson, 78 *J.Polit.Econ.* (1970), 311 ff.; Mankowski, *WM* (2001), 796–797; the same, Widerrufsrecht, pp. 1791, 1792; Haupt, 4 *Ger. Law J.* (2003), 1148, 1150; Wolf/Neuner, *AT des BürgR*[10], § 43 no. 15; Medicus/Lorenz, *Schuldr I – AT*[18], no. 592; Wagner, Mandatory Contract Law…, pp. 25–26; Ernst, *NJW* (2014), 817, 820; Reiner, 203 *AcP* (2003), 10; Adams, *BB* (1989), 784, esp. fn. 30; Kroll-Ludwigs, 18 *ZEuP* (2010), 511; Loos, Rights of Withdrawal, pp. 7–8; Borges/Irlenbusch, 163 *J.Inst.Theor.Econ.* (2007), 85; Rekaiti/van den Bergh, 23 *J.Consum.Policy* (2000), 379–380, 386; von Bar/Clive/Schulte-Nölke et al., *Principles, Definitions and Model Rules..*, pp. 347, 356, esp. 389 and 394; also Riesenhuber, *System und Prinzipien des Europäischen Vertragsrechts*, pp. 327–328; Paparseniou, *Griechisches Verbrauchervertragsrecht…*, pp. 149 ff., 169.

21 For the above, see Nelson, 78 *J.Polit.Econ.* (1970), 312 ff.; Haupt, 4 *Ger.Law J.* (2003), 1148, 1150; Eidenmüller, Widerrufsrechte, pp. 129–130, 138; Parisi, The Harmonization of Legal Warranties…, pp. 22–23; Mankowski, *WM* (2001), 796–797; Darby/Karni, 16 *J.L.&Econ.* (1973), 67 ff.; Rekaiti/van den Bergh, 23 *J.Consum.Policy* (2000), 379–380, 386; Faure/Luth, 34 *J.Consum.Policy* (2011), 340–341; Landes/Posner, 14 *J.Leg.Stud.* (1985), 547–548.

22 See *Reiner*, 203 *AcP* (2003), 9 ff., 19 ff., 29 (*informationelle Schwäche des Verbrauchers*).

23 So aptly Schäfer, Widerrufsrechte…, pp. 193–194; also Bechtold, *Die Grenzen zwingenden Vertragsrechts…*, pp. 96 ff.; Becher, 68 *La.L.Rev.* (2007), 161 ff.; Purnhagen, Why Do We Need Responsive Regulation…, p. 62.

In e-commerce we have to, in principle, exclude the possibility of the consumer being taken by surprise or pressured to engage in a transaction. When concluding a contract over the internet, the consumer is usually sitting at a computer at home or in an office. She is therefore under no pressure to proceed with the purchase; to the contrary, she is in a position to soberly and carefully compare and reflect on her transactional choices, to reject a product she does not like, or to revisit a product whenever she wishes to.[24] As a consequence, in distance selling the rationale for the withdrawal right is the assumption that at the time the contract is concluded the consumer has no physical contact with the good (or service) offered by the seller that would allow her to inspect and examine it closely and thus conclude whether it suits her needs or expectations. This rationale is also endorsed in the Preamble to the DCR,[25] ***though, admittedly, the practical reasons a consumer will exercise the right to withdraw from a distance contract may vary.***

These practical reasons are important not to overlook. As alluded to above, the consumer may exercise the right because: (a) after delivery, she realizes, during an *ex post quality assessment*,[26] that she does not like the good because it does not meet her needs or expectations (for quality, performance, size, color, and so on); (b) *her preferences* changed and she decides to purchase a similar or different good from another provider; (c) her intention from the beginning (i.e., from the conclusion of the contract) was to 'borrow' the good (without paying for it) to use on one occasion (e.g., a dress for a wedding), or to enjoy the entire value of the good (e.g., by watching a movie on DVD or downloading a television series to her own device). Such consumers, who purchase with the intent to first use and then return the goods, have been called '*returnaholics*.'[27] This behavior falls, clearly, into the category of ***abusive-opportunistic consumer conduct.***[28]

Notwithstanding the above, by establishing a withdrawal right, the European legislator sought to strengthen consumers' trust in distance transactions and in e-commerce.[29] The goal of the EU policy has been two-pronged: (a) to integrate

24 See also Wagner, Mandatory Contract Law..., p. 25; *cf.* further Becher, 68 *La.L.Rev.* (2007), 161 ff.

25 Recital 37: "Since in the case of distance sales, the consumer is not able to see the goods before concluding the contract, he should have a right of withdrawal. For the same reason, the consumer should be allowed to test and inspect the goods he has bought to the extent necessary to establish the nature, characteristics and the functioning of the goods. Concerning off-premises contracts, the consumer should have the right of withdrawal because of the potential surprise element and/or psychological pressure. Withdrawal from the contract should terminate the obligation of the contracting parties to perform the contract."

26 See Loos, Rights of Withdrawal, p. 7.

27 Ben-Shahar/Porat, 86 *U.Chi.L.Rev.* (2019), 257.

28 See also Rockenbach, 163 *J.Inst.Theor.Econ.* (2007), 106, 107; Ben-Shahar/Posner, 40 *J.Leg. Stud.* (2011), 115, 116, 137; Bechtold, *Die Grenzen zwingenden Vertragsrechts...*, pp. 97 ff.; Schwab/Hromek, *JZ* (2015), 279 ff.

29 Generally, on how contracting online has changed commercial practice and especially the tectonic shifts it caused to the contracting behavior of younger consumers—mainly of

the internal market by making cross-border commerce easier, and (b) to reduce cross-border transaction costs through the harmonization of legal provisions, especially in the field of contract law. The commercial hurdle addressed here concerns consumers' reluctance to engage in distance transactions because they have no opportunity to inspect the good or service. This reluctance may lead consumers to prefer products provided by a 'next-door merchant' over those from an internet provider.[30] The withdrawal right serves precisely the purpose of fighting off this reluctance.

In more general terms, it seems that the CDR has, by and large, met the above expectations. As the European Commission has recently attested, "Directive 2011/83/EU has contributed significantly to the functioning of the internal market and ensured a high common level of consumer protection by removing differences between national laws relating to business-to-consumer contracts. It has increased legal certainty for traders and consumers, especially those engaged in cross-border trade. In particular, consumer trust has increased significantly in recent years in the growing market of cross-border ecommerce."[31] To the same end, and after prolonged consultation, the EU has recently published two Directives: namely, (a) *the Directive (EU) 2019/770 of 20 May 2019 on certain aspects concerning contracts for the supply of digital content and digital services (OJ 2019 L 136/1)* and (b) *the Directive (EU) 2019/771 of 20 May 2019 on certain aspects concerning contracts for the sale of goods, amending Regulation (EU) 2017/2394 and Directive 2009/22/EC, and repealing Directive 1999/44/EC (OJ 2019 L 136/28)*. Both Directives—which will apply from 1 January 2022 and are *maximum harmonization* Directives—aim to ensure that "all market participants enjoy smooth access to cross-border

---

millenials—*cf.* Hoffman, 91 *N.Y.U.L.Rev.* (2016), 1595 ff., whose experimental research shows, in particular, that millennials (a) are internet-friendly contract formalists, that is, they are more likely to think that contracts are written documents, which, in online transactions, happen digitally; (b) think contract law is unforgiving, that is, those who have breached are viewed as losers, to whom the law provides no excuse; and (c) are not averse to contracts and the commitment stemming therefrom.

30 See Loos, Rights of Withdrawal, pp. 7 ff., who in the end, though, suggests that the aforementioned argument from removing barriers to transborder commerce cannot in itself, in principle, justify the establishment or preservation of such a drastic right as the withdrawal right; also Howells/Wilhelmsson, *EC Consumer Law*, p. 176: "The European Commission also has an interest in promoting confidence in distant selling. In addition to the consumer protection objectives included in the Treaty of European Union, distant selling is a tool by which the market can be integrated"; Paparseniou, *Griechisches Verbrauchervertragsrecht...*, pp. 150 ff., 226; Martinek, *NJW* (1998), 207, 208; Rockenbach, 163 *J.Inst.Theor.Econ.* (2007), 106; Purnhagen, Why Do We Need Responsive Regulation..., p. 62; Eidenmüller/Engel, *Against False Settlement...*, chapter B I; *cf.* further Eidenmüller, in: *FS Stürner*, pp. 1026 ff.; Eidenmüller/Jansen/Kieninger/Wagner/Zimmermann, *JZ* (2012), 269 ff., 286, 288; Cherednychenko, 10 *ERCL* (2014), 394; Rekaiti/van den Bergh, 23 *J.Consum. Policy* (2000), 380.

31 See https://eur-lex.europa.eu/legal-content/EN/TXT/?uri=COM%3A2018%3A185%3AFIN, Explanatory Memorandum to the Proposal, point 2 (p. 8).

sales of goods including in e-commerce transactions"[32] as well as to digital content or services.[33]

3. *A third way: the mandated-choice model as a means of reinforcing private autonomy and efficiently protecting consumers*

a. The need to steer a middle course between mandatory and default rules

According to Akerlof's *theory on the market for lemons*,[34] the information asymmetries that arise in many market situations may lead to *a race to the bottom (a downward spiral)* in the quality of the products or services offered. Without good information, people make poor decisions and the sophisticated or informed party may take advantage of them. Information asymmetries may ultimately lead to market failures. In such cases, the state must intervene and chiefly introduce mandatory legal rules in order to set aside the information asymmetry each time detected.[35] Mandatory rules play an important role in instances where significant information asymmetries exist, or where consumer preferences are

32 See the Preamble to the New Sale of Goods Directive, passim, esp. recital 4: "E-commerce is a key driver for growth within the internal market. However, its growth potential is far from being fully exploited. In order to strengthen Union competitiveness and to boost growth, the Union needs to act swiftly and encourage economic actors to unleash the full potential offered by the internal market. The full potential of the internal market can only be unleashed if all market participants enjoy smooth access to cross-border sales of goods including in e-commerce transactions. The contract law rules on the basis of which market participants conclude transactions are among the key factors shaping business decisions as to whether to offer goods cross-border. Those rules also influence consumers' willingness to embrace and trust this type of purchase." See also *ibidem*, recital 9: "While online sales of goods constitute the vast majority of cross-border sales in the Union, differences in national contract laws equally affect retailers using distance sales channels and retailers selling face-to-face and prevent them from expanding across borders. This Directive should cover all sales channels, in order to create a level playing field for all businesses selling goods to consumers. By laying down uniform rules across sales channels, this Directive should avoid any divergence that would create disproportionate burdens for the growing number of omni-channel retailers in the Union."

33 See also, indicatively, Letten, *New Directive on contracts for the sale of goods...*; www.consilium.europa.eu/en/press/press-releases/2019/04/15/eu-adopts-new-rules-on-sales-contracts-for-goods-and-digital-content/; in detail, Stabentheiner/Wendehorst/Zöchling-Jud, *Das neue europäische Gewährleistungsrecht – Zu den Richtlinien (EU) 2019/771 über den Warenkauf sowie (EU) 2019/770 über digitale Inhalte und digitale Dienstleistungen* (2019).

34 Akerlof, 84 *Quart.J.Econ.* (1970), 488 ff. See Emons, 46 *J.Econ.Theory* (1988), 16 ff.; Schelling, *Micromotives and Macrobehavior*, pp. 99 ff.; Schäfer/Ott, *Lehrbuch der ökonomischen Analyse des Zivilrechts*[4], pp. 341 ff., 513 ff.; Kirchgässner, *Homo Oeconomicus*[4], pp. 72 ff.; Grundmann, Wissen und Information..., pp. 976 ff.; Kötz, *JuS* (2003), 209, 212–213; Wagner, Mandatory Contract Law..., pp. 18, 29–30; the same, Zwingendes Vertragsrecht, p. 18; Bachmann, *JZ* (2008), 12, 13; Bechtold, *Die Grenzen zwingenden Vertragsrechts...*, pp. 33–34, 57; Bar-Gill, *Seduction by Contract...*, p. 16.

35 See also Eidenmüller, Widerrufsrechte, p. 163; Wagner, Mandatory Contract Law..., pp. 25 ff.; van Aaken, Judge the Nudge..., p. 97.

very homogenous, whereas, on the other hand, "default rules are particularly important when consumers have heterogeneous preferences."[36]

It appears, though, that in distance transactions there is no need for introducing mandatory law. In practice, most sellers already voluntarily provide consumers with a withdrawal right as a way of signaling the high quality and reliability of their products (: the withdrawal right as a *signal of quality*); they explicitly draw consumers' attention to the option to easily extract themselves from the contract without providing any reason whatsoever.[37] Therefore, in distance contracts there is, typically, no need to generally impose a withdrawal right by means of mandatory law, because the right is voluntarily provided by the online sellers themselves.[38] The voluntary provision of the withdrawal right both facilitates consumers' transactional decision-making and serves the interest of the sellers, both by signaling quality and by delicately 'exploiting' consumers' *loss aversion*: when consumers know they are free to return a purchase and have their money refunded, they are more likely to purchase the good in the first place, since they sense that the *loss* of the price paid may only be provisional.[39]

There is concrete empirical research to back up this claim.[40] It shows, in fact, that in distance commerce, companies tend, indeed, to offer the withdrawal right as a signal of the good quality of their goods or services. It is an attempt to demonstrate reliability and negotiate successfully from a distance (i.e., in the physical absence of the parties to the transaction). Thus companies use the withdrawal right to attract more customers and increase profits. In essence, that right functions in the same way that a seller's warranty or guarantee does. It seems to have equal commercial value and does not demand from the consumer to invoke and prove the existence of a defect on the product or service in order to terminate the contractual commitment (a mere change of mind on the consumer's part suffices).[41]

Additional relevant research carried out in Germany[42]—reflecting one of the many fortunate examples of interdisciplinary collaboration between law

36 See ProMarket, *How to Address the Privacy and Security Challenges Posed by Big Tech.*

37 See Wagner, Mandatory Contract Law..., pp. 26, 28; Ben-Shahar/Posner, 40 *J.Leg.Stud.* (2011), 120–121, 144–145; Rekaiti/van den Bergh, 23 *J.Consum.Policy* (2000), 381; Schäfer, Widerrufsrechte..., pp. 195–196; Kroll-Ludwigs, 18 *ZEuP* (2010), 528–529. The big retail businesses (Amazon, Walmart, and others) offer, indeed, by themselves a right to return goods, usually within 30 days after the delivery of the good; see also Ben-Shahar/Posner, *ibidem.*

38 See Eidenmüller, Widerrufsrechte, pp. 123, 125, 131 ff., 163; in the same vein, Kroll-Ludwigs, 18 *ZEuP* (2010), 528–529. *Cf.*, though, the opposite view of Mankowski, *Beseitigungsrechte...*, pp. 235 ff., 268 ff., as well as Hellgardt, 213 *AcP* (2013), 797, who considers that in this case the mandatory law provision is desirable, since it leads to equal competition terms between all distance sellers and thus sets the foundations for a competition in prices and quality between them; *cf.* further Schmolke, *Grenzen der Selbstbindung..., passim*, esp. pp. 865, 877 ff.

39 See Zamir, Law's Loss Aversion, p. 274; *cf.* also Bar-Gill, Consumer Transactions, p. 486.

40 See, once again, Eidenmüller, Widerrufsrechte, pp. 119 ff., 152 ff., 162.

41 See, indicatively, also Ben-Shahar/Posner, 40 *J.Leg.Stud.* (2011), 135.

42 See Borges/Irlenbusch, 163 *J.Inst.Theor.Econ.* (2007), 84 ff.; *cf.* also Bechtold, *Die Grenzen zwingenden Vertragsrechts...*, pp. 99 ff.

and economics[43]—shows that after the initial introduction of the withdrawal right in distance contracts into the German legal order by Directive 97/7/EC there was a considerable increase in the rate of withdrawal, even though most sellers were already voluntarily offering a withdrawal right. This finding adds to the relevant research evidence[44] which reaffirms the widespread assumption that *withdrawal rates are higher when the relevant right is statutorily provided for than when it is voluntarily offered by sellers in their contracts.* The same research, based on a carefully designed experiment,[45] found strong evidence that the voluntary provision of withdrawal rights is perceived by consumers as a generous gesture on the seller's part. Consumers, then, feel the need to *compensate* by being 'good.' 'Good behavior' is behavior that does not exploit the legal remedies that *the contract* grants to consumers. Because consumers seem to appreciate the conduct of the seller, they show reluctance to exercise the *contractually* provided withdrawal right. In other words, they tend to act in a *reciprocal and fair way* toward the seller. This tendency reflects the '*reciprocity and fairness effect*,' in BEAL terms (the effect is discussed in detail in the next paragraph). When the same right is provided, though, *through a statutory provision*, consumers do not demonstrate the same appreciation or behavior. In other words, the research reveals the tendency of the participants to distance themselves from *fairness and reciprocity considerations* and to seek instead the satisfaction of their individual interests when the withdrawal right is *statutorily* imposed.[46]

Demonstration of such behavior is telling of BEAL's commitment to deal with real-world human behavior and debunks, on an empirical basis, the neo-classical assumption that transactors need to maximize their individual benefit or utility at all costs. In particular, when consumers are voluntarily granted the withdrawal right, they appear to behave opposite to the way the addressee of the offer in the famous *ultimatum game* does (see Chapter 1, p. 12 above). They do not feel that they are being treated unfairly. Unlike in the ultimatum game, where the respondent, in a rather irrational manner, rejects low offers of the proposer,

43 *Cf.* Rockenbach, 163 *J.Inst.Theor.Econ.* (2007), 106, 107.

44 See Eidenmüller, Widerrufsrechte, pp. 119 ff., 152 ff., 162, and Roland Berger Strategy Consultants, *Aktueller Status der Retourensituation…*

45 The experiment was carried out at the internationally renowned *Laboratorium für experimentelle Wirtschaftsforschung* of the University of Cologne, with 179 participants. *Cf.*, though, also the methodological objections of Güth/von Wangenheim, 163 *J.Inst.Theor.Econ.* (2007), 102 ff., and Rockenbach, *ibidem*, p. 107.

46 See Borges/Irlenbusch, 163 *J.Inst.Theor.Econ.* (2007), 99; also Güth/von Wangenheim, *ibidem*, p. 104: "If this right is provided by law, consumer participants feel entitled to it and see no moral obligation […] to compensate their seller by behaving nicely"; in a similar vein, Rockenbach, *ibidem*, p. 106: "When the withdrawal right is not granted by law, but voluntarily offered by the seller, the buyer may interpret this as a friendly act and reciprocate by not misusing it. However, when the right is granted by law, the seller is not able to send such a signal and the buyer may be more inclined to misuse the right to his/her own benefit." For the above see further, in detail, Bechtold, *Die Grenzen zwingenden Vertragsrechts…*, pp. 100 ff., 110 ff., esp. 112–113.

feeling that she was treated unfairly by the latter and preferring to having them both getting nothing than accepting an 'unfair' offer. In our case consumers are satisfied by the seller's voluntary provision of the withdrawal right. So, it seems that when consumers feel that the seller is *treating them fairly*, they want to '*pay her back in the same coin*.'[47] In a nutshell, the example of the voluntary provision of the withdrawal right validates a crucial lesson drawn from the ultimatum game—that, especially in the transactions realm, people are interested in being treated fairly *(inequity aversion)* as well as in treating others fairly.[48]

After all, the above assumptions seem to suggest that the distance contract market should not be over-regulated through mandatory withdrawal rights. It has already moved by itself in a direction that serves consumers' interests and needs. The broad voluntary provision of the withdrawal right has had beneficial effects on the operation of the market, given that it isolates bad products and bad salespeople who are not willing to offer such a guarantee, or *signal of quality*, for their products. In terms of efficiency, this type of *market self-regulation* serves the interests of the society and the economy by throwing out 'lemons' and thus preventing a market failure.[49]

Nevertheless, it seems that self-regulation is not enough; the risk of the emergence of a 'market for lemons' due to information asymmetry, which some irrational sellers are ready to exploit, still hovers. In other words, there is always the possibility that an isolated, inexperienced, or simply naïve consumer will be exploited by a company or salesperson that sells them low-quality products without offering a withdrawal right.[50] But still this risk is apparently not widespread in the market and therefore does not by itself justify the establishment of a *mandatory* withdrawal right invariably applicable to all distance contracts.

If one rejects the option of a mandatory withdrawal right applicable to all distance contracts because it restricts autonomy and undermines the rule *pacta sunt servanda* on dubious grounds, there is also the option to establish said right as a *default*, from which the consumer may choose to opt out. This is likely to work,

47 In general terms, some emphasize here the distinction between *positive* and *negative reciprocity* (in German: *positive/negative Reziprozität*): the former gives an incentive to show cooperative conduct, the latter an incentive to punish unfair conduct by the other side; see Magen, Fairness, Eigennutz und die Rolle des Rechts..., p. 325, and Sunstein, 1 *Am.L.&Econ.Rev.* (1999), 116, 125 ff.

48 See Kahneman/Knetsch/Thaler, 59 *J.Bus.* (1986), 299; *cf.* also Etzioni, 34 *Law Soc.Rev.* (2000), 164. Further, on the unexpected "tip-phenomenon," see Korobkin/Ulen, 88 *Cal.L.R.* (2000), 1128: "... a self-interested diner should certainly not leave a tip if he never intends to visit the restaurant again. The overwhelming weight of evidence, however, suggests that (at least in the United States) almost all diners do tip, even when they are traveling far from their hometowns and are extremely unlikely ever to return to the establishment, thus creating a significant anomaly for the self-interest version of rational choice theory" (also *ibidem*, pp. 1130–1131); Jolls/Sunstein/Thaler, 50 *Stan.L.Rev.* (1998), 1492–1493; Landsburg, *The Armchair Economist...*, p. 19.

49 *Cf.* also Englerth, Vom Wert des Rauchens..., p. 249.

50 See also Güth/von Wangenheim, 163 *J.Inst.Theor.Econ.* (2007), 104–105.

as the parties to distance contracts usually favor the existence of such a right. In this respect, the default would mimic existing transactional practice, while it would further set the specific features of the right—that is, the particular way in which the right can be exercised, the length of the cooling-off period, and the legal effects resulting from the exercise of the right.

Once again, however, there lurks the risk that some sellers will take an irrational path by excluding the (default) withdrawal right through their general contract terms, whose acceptance or not is a matter to be decided by the consumer. Most consumers, though, might be unaware of the existence of the withdrawal right, and if the right is excluded by the general contract terms, they are unlikely to be informed that it was there in the first place.[51] The equally high likelihood that such a contractual exclusion would be considered by the courts as invalid pursuant to the pertinent provisions of the Directive 93/13/EEC on Unfair Terms in Consumer Contracts cannot be further discussed at this point. Nonetheless, it seems sufficient to point out that the whole issue would then be transferred to the courts, which, in the context of a *judicial review*, would have to decide, in each case, whether a relevant cost-benefit analysis would speak in favor of the provision of the withdrawal right in a distance contract—that is, whether the provision of the right would be an efficient means of consumer protection (if not, then it would rightly be excluded).[52] The courts, however, would normally lack the necessary information and time to conduct carefully and efficiently such an *ad hoc* cost-benefit analysis. Instead, they would possibly resort to a general, unconsidered consumer-friendly approach, by accepting that the deprivation of the withdrawal right amounts, in any case, to an unconscionable, unfair treatment against the consumer. This general assumption would ascribe *de facto* mandatory character to the withdrawal right.[53]

In a nutshell, the regulatory option of a default rule would rather make things highly complex. Above all, it would pass on to the courts the resolution of a

51 *Cf.* also Schmolke, *Grenzen der Selbstbindung...*, pp. 865, 868–869; Bar-Gill, Consumer Transactions, p. 484.

52 *Cf.* Eidenmüller, Widerrufsrechte, pp. 133–134; Wagner, Zwingendes Vertragsrecht, pp. 27–28; Zöchnling-Jud, 212 *AcP* (2012), 565.

53 Rightly so Eidenmüller, Widerrufsrechte, pp. 133–134. *Cf.*, though, also Wagner, Zwingendes Vertragsrecht, pp. 27–28, who is, in principle, supportive of such a judicial review, suggesting that a default rule would be an option in the present case and that the aforementioned judicial review of a relevant general contract term for eventual unfairness would be a milder means of intervention in comparison to the introduction of mandatory law. Furthermore, on the trend of the German case law to indeed ascribe *de facto* mandatory force to default rules through the judicial review of general contract terms see Kähler, *Begriff und Rechtfertigung...*, pp. 198 ff., where *inter alia* (pp. 202–203): "Abdingbare Normen wandeln sich [...] über den Umweg des AGB-Rechts zu zwingenden Normen. [...] Kommt es damit vielfach zu einer Inhaltskontrolle von Verträgen, setzt sich das abdingbare Recht indirekt als Referenzmaßstab durch. Abweichungen von ihm begründen umso eher den Vorwurf einer unangemessenen Benachteiligung, je mehr ihnen ein Gerechtigkeitsgehalt zugesprochen wird." A similar trend has been detected in American case law as well, see Ayres, 73 *U.Chi.L.Rev.* (2006), 10.

problem which would demand from them to obtain information that they are regularly not in a position to obtain. It would also demand time for the search and processing of the relevant information material that the courts, once again, regularly lack.

In all events, though, since the problem of information asymmetry is inherent in distance contracts and in some cases may stand in the way of consumers' efficient decision-making, we must find an alternative, efficient means of intervention that would entail the lowest possible burden not only for the general transaction costs but also for the private autonomy of both contracting parties (i.e., consumer and seller). Is such a regulatory tool available in the present context that would go beyond the traditional regulatory *duo* of default and mandatory rules?

b. The mandated-choice solution

In my opinion, for information asymmetry in distance contracts to be efficiently dealt with, it would suffice if the law *obligatorily* provided the consumer with the *option* to choose *between a contract without a withdrawal right and a contract with a withdrawal right and a higher price.* The adoption of a mandated-choice model provides this option. Such a model has found considerable resonance in German theory (in German: *zwingendes Optionsmodell, optionales Widerrufsrecht*) and is primarily advanced by eminent legal scholars such as Horst Eidenmüller, Gerhard Wagner, and Gregor Bachmann.[54] From this perspective, the consumer is well aware of the additional cost that she has to pay for enjoying higher legal protection by means of the withdrawal right, and therefore she is in a position to weigh the pros and cons and soberly decide whether the right *is worth the money.*[55] If the consumer opts for higher protection in a distance contract, she is expressing her willingness *to buy insurance* against the risk of a negative assessment of the good she bought, after having taken possession of it. At that point she might realize that she does not need the good, that it does not meet her expectations, or simply that its (subjective) usefulness or utility does not correspond to the price paid.[56] More specifically:

54 See Eidenmüller, Widerrufsrechte, pp. 134 ff., 163; the same, 7 *ERCL* (2011), 1 ff.; the same, in: *FS Stürner*, p. 1037; the same, *JZ* (2011), 818, 819; Eidenmüller/Jansen/Kieninger/Wagner/Zimmermann, *JZ* (2012), 278; Wagner, Mandatory Contract Law..., pp. 26 ff., 40 ff.; the same, Zwingendes Vertragsrecht, pp. 29–30; Bachmann, *JZ* (2008), 11 ff., esp. 13 ff.; Ringe, 213 *AcP* (2013), 106 ff. *passim*, esp. 107; Fleischer, 76 *RabelsZ* (2012), 237 ff. *passim*; Karampatzos, Rechtspaternalismus im Europäischen Verbraucherschutzrecht..., pp. 215 ff.; *cf.* also Schmolke, *Grenzen der Selbstbindung...*, pp. 869–870; van Aaken, Begrenzte Rationalität..., p. 127; Bechtold, *Die Grenzen zwingenden Vertragsrechts...*, *passim*, esp. pp. 120 ff., 256 ff., 264–265, 331–332.

55 See Eidenmüller, Widerrufsrechte, pp. 134, 138–139; also Wagner, Mandatory Contract Law..., pp. 26.

56 See Eidenmüller, Widerrufsrechte, p. 135.

Under the mandated-choice concept, the consumer is free to choose between *a contract without a withdrawal right and a contract with the additional insurance of the withdrawal right.* It is a choice between a *definite sale* and *a pending sale dependent* on the consumer's decision not to exercise the withdrawal right within a certain period of time (in legal terms this amounts to a *suspensive condition*). The consumer will reach this decision on the basis of her own stance on risk assumption, her knowledge and experience, as well as the amount of the *insurance premium* she must pay each time to enjoy the greater legal protection (i.e., the withdrawal right).[57]

In practical terms, in the picture I paint (which may, of course, not be the whole picture) the consumer could express her decision to accept or reject the withdrawal right by simply ticking a box on the internet site of the seller or provider; in this way, her choice is registered with little effort or cost—which is very significant in terms of economic efficiency. She may, of her own free will, activate or deactivate the withdrawal right as if she flips a light switch. This switch is visible; *the hand of the mandated-choice system is visible.*

However, neither party shall be able to amend the content of the withdrawal right, which would be *statutorily standardized.*[58] As is rather evident, the statutory standardization of the right secures the main advantages ascribed to mandatory law—that is, the reduction of transaction costs, the safety of transactions and, in particular, the foreseeability of the legal effects deriving from a contractual relationship or the eventual exercise of a right, such as the withdrawal right.[59]

In essence, by adopting the mandated-choice model we rise above the dilemma between an *opt-out* and an *opt-in* solution. The consumer is asked to check one of two boxes, one indicating a purchase *with a withdrawal right* and the other indicating a purchase *without a withdrawal right.* At the same time, the seller or provider will be obliged to inform the consumer of the content and the effects of the withdrawal right and to draw her attention to the need to choose between the two 'products.' The final price of the good or service is determined only after the box has been successfully ticked.

The mandated-choice model thus gives every consumer the right to choose one of the two options; there is no predetermined default option. The seller or provider involved in distance selling will have to offer *two different products to consumers*, one *with* a withdrawal right and another *without* such a right.

57 See Eidenmüller, Widerrufsrechte, p. 135, and Wagner, Zwingendes Vertragsrecht, p. 29; *cf.* also Haupt, 4 *Ger.Law J.* (2003), 1156.

58 See also Wagner, Mandatory Contract Law..., pp. 26 ff., esp. 40: "For a general theory of contract law, it would be highly attractive to develop a tool that *would marry the virtues of mandatory law in terms of standardisation to the obvious advantages of default rules in terms of contractual efficiency.* It would have to combine the provision of a safe haven with the flexibility of allowing the parties to use it" (emphasis added)—also *ibidem*, p. 41.

59 In general, on the comparative advantages of mandatory rules in the field of contract law, see Wagner, Mandatory Contract Law..., pp. 39–40; Grigoleit, Zwingendes Recht..., p. 1823; Bachmann, *JZ* (2008), 17.

The former will undoubtedly be more expensive than the latter, since its price will also incorporate the seller's cost of providing the withdrawal right—for example, expenses for processing and executing the withdrawals, for repairing or replacing the returned goods if damaged, and legal expenses.[60] In this respect, as already mentioned above, the consumer who chooses the withdrawal right will pay an *insurance premium*, thus securing herself against the possibility that she later (*ex post facto*) regrets purchasing the good or service.[61]

c. *Insurance premium and the issue of cross-subsidization*

Within this framework, the seller's costs for providing the withdrawal right are, by and large, included in the aforementioned insurance premium and thus are not borne by all consumers but only by those who opt for the greater protection and pay the relevant premium.[62] The consumers who are *risk takers (or lovers)* and thus do not want the protective shield of the withdrawal right do not subsidize the provision of the right to those who are more *risk-averse* or cautious consumers. In this way, we avoid the phenomenon of *intraconsumer cross-subsidization*, which typically raises serious distributional concerns, since it may lead to *economically inefficient and socially unjust reallocations of resources and income (i.e., regressive cross-subsidies).*[63]

In general, the cross-subsidization advanced by the European legislator through various mandatory protections is often inefficient because "the cost to the many is greater than the benefit to the few."[64] It also often entails, indeed, an unjust, *regressive* reallocation of resources or wealth from low-income consumers

60 In detail, Bechtold, *Die Grenzen zwingenden Vertragsrechts…*, p. 97; Bar-Gill, Consumer Transactions, p. 485; Wipperfürth, *Die Verbraucherrechte-Richtlinie…*, p. 25; Eidenmüller, Widerrufsrechte, p. 135 fn. 81.

61 See Eidenmüller, Widerrufsrechte, pp. 134 ff.

62 See also Eidenmüller, Widerrufsrechte, p. 135; Bechtold, *Die Grenzen zwingenden Vertragsrechts…*, p. 97.

63 See also Wagner, Zwingendes Vertragsrecht, pp. 29–30; Eidenmüller/Jansen/Kieninger/Wagner/Zimmermann, *JZ* (2012), 278, 289; Ben-Shahar/Posner, 40 *J.Leg.Stud.* (2011), 144–145; Zöchnling-Jud, 212 *AcP* (2012), 564; Bar-Gill, Consumer Transactions, p. 485 fn. 21. In the same direction, see also Porat/Strahilevitz, 112 *Mich.L.Rev.* (2014), 1453–1454, who in general support the introduction of a *personalized default-rule regime* (see also Chapter 2, pp. 71 ff. above), which may also be implemented in the field of consumer law and especially with respect to the right to return a good, precisely with a view to diminishing an unjust and inefficient cross-subsidization. In the same vein, see Ben-Shahar/Porat, *86 U.Chi.L.Rev.* (2019), 255 ff. *passim*, esp. 256, 357–258, 261–263, 265–266, who also seek the elimination of cross-subsidies, this time though by virtue of personalizing *mandatory* rules, which may allow for the desirable price discrimination (see further in the text below). For more detail on cross-subsidization, see the exceptional paper of Quillen, 61 *S.Cal.L.R.* (1988), 1125 ff., esp. 1229 ff.; see also Priest, 96 *Yale L.J.* (1987), 1521 ff.; Posner, *Economic Analysis of Law*[6], pp. 110, 374 ff.; Schäfer/Ott, *Lehrbuch der ökonomischen Analyse des Zivilrechts*[4], pp. 338, 339–340, 482.

64 Gill/Ben-Shahar, 50 *CML Rev.* (2013), 115.

to middle- or higher-income consumers.[65] This happens because, although all consumers of a specific good pay the same additional price for certain legal protection (under mandatory law terms), middle- or higher-income consumers are more willing to exercise their rights, since they are more sophisticated and have more legal advice, time, and money at their disposal, all of which facilitates their freedom of action in the transactions realm. In contrast, low-income consumers are less likely to possess the resources to exercise their rights (for which they paid the additional price) and might even be unable to enter a market because the enhanced legal protection provided by the European legislator might have rendered it financially inaccessible (it may be argued that this is the case, for instance, for the market in package travel).[66] In other words, under the current EU consumer protection mandatory regime, consumers "pay for protections that many of them would rather waive for a discount. This price effect is particularly disturbing when it is regressive—namely, when all consumers pay for what only the more sophisticated ones enjoy. Ironically, when the price effect is regressive, a wholesale inclusion of mandatory terms undermines rather than promotes 'social justice' concerns, which intend to protect weaker consumers and secure their access to the markets."[67]

So, in light of the above, it becomes evident that an unintended effect or, more precisely, a ***heterogony of ends*** (in German: *Heterogonie der Zwecke*)[68] might be at work here: although the EU law on consumer protection typically aims to protect financially, organizationally, or intellectually weak consumers, in practice it ends up favoring consumers who are better informed, more responsible, and aware, thus satisfying the interests of a loss-averse middle class or even elite, which enjoys rights co-financed by everyone else.[69] And in the end, this state of

65 Whereas, in general, a fair distributive policy must seek exactly the opposite—that is, the transition of wealth (or resources) from high incomes to lower incomes, chiefly by means of taxation and social allowances. See, indicatively, Jolls, Behavioral Economic Analysis..., pp. 288 ff., and Posner, *Economic Analysis of Law*[6], pp. 467 ff., esp. 472–473, 489 ff., 509 ff.

66 See also Gill/Ben-Shahar, 50 *CML Rev.* (2013), 110 and 115, wherein ***inter alia***: "To benefit from the legal protections, consumers need to be informed about these rights, to have the sophistication to insist on compliance, and to afford legal advice. The wealthier and healthier consumers are systematically more likely to invoke the protections. The poor, the elderly, the less educated—those for whom the protections are enacted in the first place—lack the information, the sophistication, and the resources. And yet, they bear an equal share of the cost. Thus, mandating such a long list of protections is likely to diminish the access to markets for those who already face the greatest barriers." In the same vein, Ben-Shahar, 112 *Mich.L.Rev.* (2014), 901.

67 Gill/Ben-Shahar, 50 *CML Rev.* (2013), 110; *cf.* also Ben-Shahar, 112 *Mich.L.Rev.* (2014), 901.

68 In purely philosophical terms, the notion of ***heterogony of ends*** goes back to the German philosopher and psychologist Wilhelm Maximilian Wundt and his treatise on *Ethik—Eine Untersuchung der Thatsachen und Gesetze des sittlichen Lebens*, pp. 230–231.

69 This critical parameter is clearly demonstrated by 4 Haupt, 4 *Ger.Law J.* (2003), 1163–1164; Micklitz, *VuR* (2003), 11; Calliess, 4 *Ger.Law J.* (2003), 337; van den Bergh, Wer schützt die europäischen Verbraucher..., p. 98. The economically inefficient and socially unjust reallocation of resources that cross-subsidization entails is also vividly illustrated by a relevant example used by Quillen, 61 *S.Cal.L.R.* (1988), 1125 ff.

things might result in the withdrawal of some categories of low-income, financially less secure, and intellectually weaker consumers, who would rather not buy a product, or even enter a market, than subsidize higher-income consumers.[70]

In a nutshell, cross-subsidization is an often underappreciated flip side of the extended EU legal paternalism. It is a hidden, negative effect of the intervention of the European legislator—by means of the establishment of a cornucopia of supposedly *progressive* mandatory protections in favor of the consumers—that leads to adverse (*regressive*) results, hitting mainly the weakest sectors of society.[71] In many instances, strong consumers are benefitting at the expense of lower-income consumers. The mandated-choice scheme may succeed in offering an efficient way out of this cross-subsidization trap.

d. Insurance premium and the issue of opportunistic consumer behavior

Notwithstanding the above, at this juncture one may reasonably wonder whether the above mandated-choice scheme might be undermined by an *opportunistic consumer behavior* relating to the insurance premium the consumer has each time to pay. Specifically:

If, for example, the good *with* a withdrawal right were offered at a price of 200€ and the good *without* a withdrawal right at the price of 150€, the following risk would arise: the consumer could first buy the good *with* the withdrawal right, test it, and if it met her requirements or needs, then exercise the withdrawal right, request a refund of the price paid (200€) and immediately repurchase the good at the considerably lower price (150€) without the withdrawal right. In practice, though, the price difference between the two products will be much smaller, as is, indeed, the transactional practice when the withdrawal right is voluntarily offered by a seller or provider[72]: in all likelihood, the price for the good *with* withdrawal right will be, for example, 160€, and for the good *without* withdrawal right 150€. In view of the actual financial burden on the seller or provider for providing the withdrawal right, this assumption about the price difference between the two goods seems realistic and would prevent the opportunistic consumer behavior described above.[73] The likelihood of opportunistic behavior might also be reduced by the *endowment effect* (see Chapter 2, pp. 27 ff. above), which causes the consumer to value the good at a higher price once it is in her possession and which may thus set aside a price difference around the

70 See Schäfer/Ott, *Lehrbuch der ökonomischen Analyse des Zivilrechts*^{4}, p. 482.

71 Respectively, very strict rules on *responsible lending* may also backfire, that is, they may deprive consumers—primarily young people, weak in terms of economic capacity—of their access to authorized banking institutions and lead them to loan sharks, who charge very high interest rates; see Cherednychenko, 10 *ERCL* (2014), 419, and Epstein, 92 *Minn.L.Rev.* (2008), 831.

72 See, indicatively, Cserne, *Freedom of Contract...*, p. 112.

73 See Eidenmüller, Widerrufsrechte, pp. 135–136; *cf.*, though, also the reluctant stance of Zöchnling-Jud, 212 *AcP* (2012), 565.

amount of 10€. In all events, the law could specifically prohibit such an opportunistic repurchase of the same product by the same seller or provider, after the exercise of the withdrawal right. Or, even better, it could leave it up to the latter themselves whether to contractually exclude such possibility or not. By virtue of private autonomy, the seller or provider would be entitled to do so in any case, that is, even in the absence of a specific legal provision allowing them to exclude such a repurchase.

Apart from the last regulatory option, it cannot be overlooked that opportunistic behavior remains possible even in the case of a small price differentiation between the two goods. In general, however, this behavior is hard to eliminate with all contracts which can be terminated by means of unjustified withdrawal, regardless of whether the right of withdrawal has the hereby described form (*mandated-choice*) or the one provided for by the European legislator with the CRD. Nothing, *prima facie*, deters the consumer from temporarily acquiring a product by, practically, borrowing it for use in the context of a specific occasion only. This is often the case with night dresses or suits, meant to be used for a specific wedding ceremony or a specific ball, or with cable television meant to be used for watching a very important game. The same phenomenon of buyer's opportunism is also encountered when, for example, a consumer acquires a DVD, copies it for future use, and then returns it to the seller.[74]

Such opportunistic behavior is the result of perfectly rational consumer decision making, at least from a short-term-benefit perspective. The opportunistic consumer choice results in a transaction inefficient to everyone but the consumer herself. The opportunistic consumer uses the product she wanted in the first place, avoiding all costs, and, then, gives it back, transferring all costs to others.[75] From a medium-long term consumer benefit perspective, however, such behavior may cause consumer harm, as soon as other consumers start mimicking it. Sooner or later the opportunistic behavior will multiply itself through everyday practice and generate a *systemic moral hazard* for transactions. The latter might lead the entire market to collapse, if suppliers gradually decide to exit.

The law needs to protect the seller and save the transactions realm from such serious moral hazards which directly undermine it. In particular, the above-mentioned opportunistic behavior can be efficiently dealt with, if *return costs*[76] combined with a *liability to pay damages for use* are imposed on the consumer. The damages will reflect the diminished value of the good resulting from its use

74 See Eidenmüller, Widerrufsrechte, p. 158, with references to relevant statistical findings from Germany; Wipperfürth, *Die Verbraucherrechte-Richtlinie...*, pp. 71–72; Ben-Shahar/Posner, 40 *J.Leg.Stud.* (2011), 116, 137–138; Borges/Irlenbusch, 163 *J.Inst.Theor.Econ.* (2007), 88; Güth/von Wangenheim, 163 *J.Inst.Theor.Econ.* (2007), 102; Rockenbach, 163 *J.Inst.Theor.Econ.* (2007), 106, 109; Schwab/Hromek, *JZ* (2015), 279 ff.

75 See also Wagner, Zwingendes Vertragsrecht, p. 29.

76 On whether it is purposeful or not to impose them on the consumer, see Loos, Rights of Withdrawal, pp. 22–23.

prior to the exercise of the right of withdrawal.[77] Under the mandated-choice model, which I hereby propose, return costs and a small price differentiation between the two products (with and without withdrawal right), would, most likely, suffice to deter opportunistic buyer behavior. In other words, it would be less rational to first buy a product with a right of withdrawal, exercise the right, return the product bearing the relevant costs, and then buy a slightly cheaper version of the same product without a right of withdrawal. As far as the liability to pay damages is concerned, such a provision is meaningful for situations similar to the scenarios described above, where consumers do not wish to come back and buy the same product again, but, quite to the contrary, prefer to acquire the product for use and then just exercise their right and return it to the seller reclaiming the price paid. The problem is quite broad and always linked to the right of withdrawal, be it of the *de lege ferenda* type proposed above or as provided for by the European legislator. The problem calls for deeper consideration. This is what I do next.

In the case of withdrawal, under EU law, the consumer is, indeed, liable to pay return costs (Article 14 para. 1 of CRD) combined with a compensation for any deminished value of the returned goods caused because of consumer use (*depreciation costs*, in German: *Nutzungsersatz*; see Article 14 para. 2 of CRD: "The consumer shall only be liable for any diminished value of the goods resulting from the handling of the goods other than what is necessary to establish the nature, characteristics and functioning of the goods."). The relevant rationale offered by the EU legislator is very enlightening (recital 47 of the Preamble to the CRD): "*Some consumers exercise their right of withdrawal after having used the goods to an extent more than necessary to establish the nature, characteristics and the functioning of the goods. In this case the consumer should not lose the right to withdraw but should be liable for any diminished value of the goods. In order to establish the nature, characteristics and functioning of the goods, the consumer should only handle and inspect them in the same manner as he would be allowed to do in a shop. For example, the consumer should only try on a garment and should not be allowed to wear it. Consequently, the consumer should handle and inspect the goods with due care during the withdrawal period. The obligations of the consumer in the event of withdrawal should not discourage the consumer from exercising his right of withdrawal.*"

77 See Eidenmüller, Widerrufsrechte, pp. 157–158. Accordingly, there are authors arguing in favor of a *rental payment* being established for using the product during the time between acquirement and the exercise of the right of withdrawal; see Rekaiti/van den Bergh, 23 *J.Consum.Policy* (2000), 387–388, 394, and Haupt, 4 *Ger.Law J.* (2003), 1150. In the summer of 2013 the online commercial portal Amazon resolved to decisively take action on the repeatedly unjust exercise of the withdrawal right by certain customers. In particular, the company started to block from its services customers with excessive rates of contractual withdrawals. This would happen immediately, with no previous warning and for an undefined period of time. Such action falls within the scope of the transactional freedom of the company and constitutes a specific demonstration of its freedom to choose whom to enter into contracts with; it is, therefore, totally legitimate. See also Wipperfürth, *Die Verbraucherrechte-Richtlinie...*, p. 72, for a further analysis of this.

The European legislator faced with the risk of opportunistic consumer behavior, decided to introduce a liability provision, instead of opting for *the absolute exclusion of the withdrawal right* in such cases, as explicitly explained in the CRD, Preamble (recital 47 as per above). The liability for any diminished value of the goods has, presumably, been considered a milder measure, as compared to the absolute exclusion of the withdrawal right.[78]

The diminished value of the good might be equal to the cleaning or repair costs (borne by the seller). At the same time, if the good, following the return, can no longer be provided for sale as brand new, according to the standards of the relevant market, the objectively justifiable loss in seller's profits should be calculated for the compensation amount, since the seller will no longer be able to avoid marketing the returned good as *used or second hand.*[79] In any case, the *burden of proof* for a claim based on the diminished value of the good lies with the seller.[80]

The value depreciation calculation is faced with great difficulties in practice (imagine, for example, clothes used for a specific social occasion); "in many if not most cases, depreciation will be impossible to estimate."[81] Besides, the depreciation amount will be, in most cases, small, while the costs of litigation will be exceeding it. Thus, it will be almost impossible or economically unreasonable for the seller to seek judicial protection.[82] This makes, in many cases, the liability to pay damages for use (i.e., *depreciation costs*) an inefficient measure for counterbalancing consumer opportunism. Such difficulties could probably argue in favor of the absolute exclusion of the withdrawal right, *at least for the cases where the consumer has obviously used the returned good.*[83] In these cases absolute exclusion of the withdrawal right seems perfectly justifiable. This would be the case for a returned good which can no longer be traded in the market, not even as used. Such a scenario might materialize either because the returned good has been seriously damaged due to consumer use or because the seller is, objectively, in no business-organizational position to circulate used goods. This is highly likely to happen with minor sellers.[84] However, this does not necessarily hold for big businesses. The latter will have a competitive advantage over minor players, under such a scenario. Minor players might even be driven

78 More on the efforts to counterbalance opportunistic consumer behavior, Loos, Rights of Withdrawal, pp. 23 ff.; Zimmermann, Rückabwicklung nach Widerruf, pp. 184 ff.; Ben-Shahar/Posner, 40 *J.Leg.Stud.* (2011), 116 ff. *passim.*

79 See DG Justice Guidance Document, June 2014, https://ec.europa.eu/info/sites/info/files/crd_guidance_en_0.pdf, p. 47.

80 See DG Justice Guidance Document, *op.cit.*, pp. 47–48, and more particularly CJEU-489/07, *Pia Messner v Firma Stefan Krüger* (2009), thought no. 27.

81 Ben-Shahar/Posner, 40 *J.Leg.Stud.* (2011), 138.

82 See Ben-Shahar/Posner, 40 *J.Leg.Stud.* (2011), 138, 144.

83 Close to this thesis, Zöchnling-Jud, 212 *AcP* (2012), 567.

84 See Ben-Shahar/Posner, 40 *J.Leg.Stud.* (2011), 121–122. For a relevant and more elaborate analysis, see Thaler, 1 *J.Econ.Behav.Organ.* (1980), 43 ff.; see also Wipperfürth, *Die Verbraucherrechte-Richtlinie...*, pp. 71–72.

out of the market. Under the same scenario, for the liability provision to make practical sense, the entire loss of profit of the seller should be recovered. This equals her entire opportunity cost, meaning the total value of the returned good which is now useless for the profit-making purposes of the seller. However, to calculate and claim a compensation amount in this way seems to fall outside the scope and, probably, even the ratio of the CRD provision on liability for diminished value.

Based on the above, there are serious reasons why the European legislator should have considered such issues further. The most important are (a) jurisprudential reasons, interlinked with the need to avoid opportunistic consumer behavior and the threatening moral hazard it gives rise to, and (b) practical reasons, based on the idea that it would quite frequently conflict with the standard of good faith to make the seller accept the returned good and, then, provide it (once more) in the market. Total exclusion of the withdrawal right seems a better solution, especially when it is easy to establish that consumers have obviously used the returned goods before withdrawal—it is no coincidence that this solution was also advanced recently in the *Proposal for a Directive* aiming to amend, *inter alia*, the DCR.[85] And once again: the above analysis holds true for the right of withdrawal in any case, that is, both under the *de lege ferenda* version proposed hereby (***mandated-choice model***) and the one already in place with the CRD.

Notwithstanding the above criticism of CRD provisions, Article 16 of CRD is well suit to contribute to the effort to reduce consumer opportunism because it includes a list of cases when the right of withdrawal is excluded.[86] The list is quite broad. As a result, the right of withdrawal is excluded in various transactions of crucial importance in practice. These are cases where providing for a right of withdrawal

85 See https://eur-lex.europa.eu/legal-content/EN/TXT/?uri=COM%3A2018%3A185%3AFIN (as per above fn. 4), Explanatory Memorandum to the Proposal, point 1.1 (p. 3): "The proposal [...] removes two specific obligations on traders about the 14-day right of withdrawal that have proven to constitute a disproportionate burden. ***The first obligation is the obligation for the trader to accept the right of withdrawal even where a consumer has used an ordered good instead of only trying it out in the same way they could have done in a brick-and-mortar shop.*** The second obligation is the obligation for the trader to reimburse the consumer even before the trader has received the returned goods back from the consumer" (emphasis added). Also *ibidem*, Article 2 (p. 20): "Article 14 of Directive 2011/83/EU dealing with the obligations of the consumer in the event of withdrawal is amended ***by removing the right of consumers to return the goods even where those have been used more than necessary to test them subject to the obligation to pay for the diminished value.*** A provision similar to the respective Digital Content Directive rule is added regarding the consumer's obligations to refrain from using the digital content or digital services after the termination of the contract" (emphasis added). **However, the above amendment was not included in the final version of the Directive dated 18.10.2019 (PE-CONS 83/19).**

86 "Exceptions from the right of withdrawal: Member States shall not provide for the right of withdrawal set out in Articles 9–15 in respect of distance and off-premises contracts as regards the following:

(a) service contracts after the service has been fully performed if the performance has begun with the consumer's prior express consent, and with the acknowledgement that he will lose his right of withdrawal once the contract has been fully performed by the trader;

would mean assigning unjustified privileges to the consumer. Therefore, the CRD excludes the right, *inter alia*, in the case of withdrawal after having, previously, reaped the full benefits of using the good, causing obvious harm to the financial interests of the seller or violating copy rights. This may be a quite frequent situation in everyday transactional practice, when, for example, the consumer makes a copy of a DVD or watches the movie she was initially interested in and then returns the good in perfect condition, having just removed the packing.

e. Juxtaposition with a scheme of personalized mandatory rules

Recently, as was shown earlier in Chapter 2 (see pp. 71 ff. above), Ben-Shahar and Porat[87] put forward a rather heretical proposal for (fully) personalizing mandatory rules, which primarily rests on the idea that *instead of one-size-fits-all protective mandates, the law should tailor the protection to the personal attributes of each protected party*. In particular, Ben-Shahar and Porat focus on mandatory rules in contract law aimed at protecting consumers, and *inter alia*, they specifically refer to the mandatory right to withdraw from a consumer

---

(b) the supply of goods or services for which the price is dependent on fluctuations in the financial market which cannot be controlled by the trader and which may occur within the withdrawal period;
(c) the supply of goods made to the consumer's specifications or clearly personalised;
(d) the supply of goods which are liable to deteriorate or expire rapidly;
(e) the supply of sealed goods which are not suitable for return due to health protection or hygiene reasons and were unsealed after delivery;
(f) the supply of goods which are, after delivery, according to their nature, inseparably mixed with other items;
(g) the supply of alcoholic beverages, the price of which has been agreed upon at the time of the conclusion of the sales contract, the delivery of which can only take place after 30 days and the actual value of which is dependent on fluctuations in the market which cannot be controlled by the trader;
(h) contracts where the consumer has specifically requested a visit from the trader for the purpose of carrying out urgent repairs or maintenance. If, on the occasion of such visit, the trader provides services in addition to those specifically requested by the consumer or goods other than replacement parts necessarily used in carrying out the maintenance or in making the repairs, the right of with drawal shall apply to those additional services or goods;
(i) the supply of sealed audio or sealed video recordings or sealed computer software which were unsealed after delivery;
(j) the supply of a newspaper, periodical or magazine with the exception of subscription contracts for the supply of such publications;
(k) contracts concluded at a public auction;
(l) the provision of accommodation other than for residential purpose, transport of goods, car rental services, catering or services related to leisure activities if the contract provides for a specific date or period of performance;
(m) the supply of digital content which is not supplied on a tangible medium if the performance has begun with the consumer's prior express consent and his acknowledgment that he thereby loses his right of withdrawal."

[The new Directive amending the DCR (see fn. 4 above) has also made significant amendments to Article 16.]

87 Ben-Shahar/Porat, 86 *U.Chi.L.Rev.* (2019), 255 ff.

contract, suggesting that its protective goal would be better served by a *personalized mandatory-rule regime* than by a uniformly applicable mandatory-rule regime. For

> [s]ome consumers need longer periods to reevaluate the deal, others can do with shorter. A 72-hour right to withdraw from a loan contract may be useless to the weakest of consumers, who are often the neediest, and are also the recipients of the most risky and complicated loan deals. They need more time to overcome the moment-of-purchase confusion. And, conversely, a two-week right to withdraw from online sales may be more than necessary for experienced internet shoppers, and surely too long for "returnaholics" who purchase with the intent to withdraw. A uniform duration may be set at the correct "average' length, but it misfires in individual cases (and [...] forces some consumers out of the market)"[88]. The authors also rightly point out that, in general, "[p]ersonalized protections also affect redistributive goals, because they eliminate cross-subsidies occurring in equal treatment pools," for "[w]hen the cross-subsidy is regressive, its elimination is desirable"[89].

In my understanding, insofar as Ben-Shahar and Porat advance a personalized mandatory-rule regime "where both the protection and the price vary across consumers"[90] and which thus links price differentiation to the degree of legal protection granted to each consumer (meaning that price differentiation goes hand in hand with personalized protection), their approach is not much different from the mandated-choice model advocated hereinabove; their thesis may be seen as a further step or refinement of this model.

However, in my opinion, this personalized mandatory-rule regime has two flaws that the mandated-choice model I endorse does not have: (a) In that regime the consumer does not have the right to choose between enhanced legal protection and no protection; that is, *she cannot waive the protection* if she rejects the personalized mandatory rule—a possibility which cannot be reasonably excluded; in other words, *forced* protection and an unwanted price increase cannot be avoided. And (b) it seems that such a regime is practically associated with very significant administrative costs for the transactions and especially for the sellers: for big data must be collected and processed, and thereafter, the sellers must supply different goods with personalized legal protection, along with a corresponding price adjusted to the specific profile of each possible customer (the case is, namely, here for an *in personam* discrimination: "a legal mandate that provides each consumer its personally optimal level of protection, and allows the seller to charge each consumer a different price"[91]). At the end of the day,

88 Ben-Shahar/Porat, 86 *U.Chi.L.Rev.* (2019), 257, also 281.
89 Ben-Shahar/Porat, 86 *U.Chi.L.Rev.* (2019), 258.
90 Ben-Shahar/Porat, 86 *U.Chi.L.Rev.* (2019), 258.
91 Ben-Shahar/Porat, 86 *U.Chi.L.Rev.* (2019), 265, also 267.

and if such a differentiation would ever be practically feasible,[92] it appears that these administrative costs would considerably affect the final purchase price; or, that only a very few big retailers (such as Amazon or Walmart) could afford them (due to economies of scale) and thus survive in the market. In addition, from a European perspective, one should once more consider the arresting data privacy issues that such a collection and processing of big data raises (see also Chapter 2, pp. 72 ff. above).

f. Concluding remarks: the middle course between mandatory and default rules, tertium datur

Where there is high information asymmetry to the detriment of the consumer—such as mainly in the case of distance contracts—the mandated-choice model is an innovative instrument of consumer protection. It reflects a reasonable and acceptable interference with private autonomy, obviously milder than a mandatory imposition of the withdrawal right without a possibility to opt out. This model is also distinguished from traditional default rules, because sellers or providers are *obliged* to offer to the consumer a choice between two products—one *with* and the other *without* a withdrawal right; in addition, they must inform her clearly and adequately about (a) the possibility to choose between two options, (b) the length of the cooling-off period, and (c) the legal consequences of the withdrawal.[93] As a matter of fact, sellers or providers offer an *insurance premium* that is paid *only by the (loss-averse) consumers who wish to enjoy greater legal protection.*[94] In this case, the costs of providing the withdrawal right are borne *only by the community of insured consumers*, not by all consumers (which would entail a Pareto inefficient transfer of resources).[95]

Consumers' private autonomy is considerably strengthened by means of the mandated-choice model.[96] The consumer is not forced to conclude a contract with a withdrawal right, but she has the option to choose between two products, one with a withdrawal right and the other without a withdrawal right. After having been specifically and adequately informed of the withdrawal right and the enhanced protection it offers, together with the more specific pre-conditions for its exercise and its legal effects—which are statutorily standardized—the consumer herself will consider it and decide for herself whether the withdrawal right is worth the money. This decision will be based on the information she has about the good (product or service), her specific

92 Ben-Shahar and Porat themselves acknowledge the problem of technical implementation of their idea, which "would require much more than to write computer code," and would demand especially the development of a very complex "personalization algorithm" (86 *U.Chi.L.Rev.* (2019), 281).

93 See also Wagner, Zwingendes Vertragsrecht, p. 28.

94 See also van Boom/Ogus, Introducing, Defining and Balancing…, p. 5.

95 See also Eidenmüller, Widerrufsrechte, p. 135, and Wagner, Zwingendes Vertragsrecht, p. 29.

96 See also, once more, Eidenmüller, Widerrufsrechte, pp. 137 ff.

needs, preferences, or concerns, as well as her general stance on transaction risks and, more particularly, her willingness to risk not being *ex post facto* satisfied by the product.[97]

This plain-vanilla mandated-choice model is situated in a middle zone between freedom of contract and mandatory law. It constitutes ***a middle course, a new type of mandatory right***, which marries the advantages of the freedom to shape the contractual content to the need to cure or limit some persistent ***cognitive or volitional*** weaknesses (or self-control problems) demonstrated by consumers in the transactions realm.[98] In essence, I endorse here a third way between dispositive and mandatory law,[99] which preserves freedom of choice and nurtures individual responsibility, both being indispensable in a free, liberal society. This third way also appears to be aligned with the general EU policy on ***consumer empowerment***, mainly by providing the consumer with more choices and information about the transactions she engages in.[100]

Airline ticket purchases are a good practical example of the mandated-choice concept. When buying a ticket, passengers are sometimes provided with a choice between a ticket with a peculiar 'withdrawal right' and a ticket without such a right. No reason is required for the passenger to exercise this 'withdrawal right,' and she is entitled to a full refund if she chooses to do so. The passenger may instead choose the ticket without a 'withdrawal right,' which is cheaper. (A similar option is also provided, e.g., by "booking.com.") Although the consumer is also able to rescind the contract after purchasing the cheaper ticket, she is required to pay a stiff penalty, considerably higher than the price difference between the above two ticket types. Hence the consumer has a strong incentive to opt for the higher-priced ticket that includes a withdrawal right, especially if she is risk-averse.[101] The decision of each consumer will ultimately depend on her individual predisposition against the specific transaction risk (that is, unexpected or unforeseen events that appear after the ticket purchase and necessitate the cancellation of the trip, or the mere change of mind on the part of the consumer): ***the bolder, risk-seeking traveler will opt***

97 *Cf.* also Wagner, Zwingendes Vertragsrecht, p. 28; Ben-Shahar/Posner, 40 *J.Leg.Stud.* (2011), 134, 144–145; Haupt, 4 *Ger.Law J.* (2003), 1156, 1158.

98 See also Bachmann, *JZ* (2008), 11, 16–17, 20.

99 *Cf.* also Wagner, Mandatory Contract Law..., p. 42; Bechtold, *Die Grenzen zwingenden Vertragsrechts...*, pp. 120 ff.

100 See, indicatively, Engel/Stark, Buttons, Boxes, Ticks, and Trust..., pp. 108 ff., Commission Staff Working Paper, ***Consumer Empowerment in the EU***, Article 2 of the ***Proposal for a Regulation of the European Parliament and of the Council on a consumer programme 2014–2020***, as well as the relevant general EU objective as described on the site of the Directorate General for Health & Consumers of the European Commission, http://ec.europa.eu/consumers/consumer_empowerment/index_en.htm, wherein the main focus is on the need of preserving the freedom of choice of the consumers: "The main objective of the EU Consumer Policy Strategy is to empower EU consumers through: Choice; Information; Awareness of consumer rights and means of redress." *Cf.* also Weatherill, *EU Consumer Law...*, pp. 310 ff.

101 See also Ben-Shahar/Posner, 40 *J.Leg.Stud.* (2011), 134.

for the cheaper ticket, whereas the more conservative, risk-averse one will choose the more expensive ticket.[102]

In general terms, the existence of such practical examples serves to refute the theoretical objection that the mandated-choice model is counterproductive and thus inefficient because it places an unjustified, heavy administrative burden on the companies, which might then opt to pass the burden on to consumers by raising prices. Transactional practice indicates that the model can indeed work in practice and that real benefits to consumers who waive their withdrawal right are in principle attainable.[103]

Behavioral economics offers, though, a further tenable objection to the mandated-choice scheme and the extension of private autonomy it entails. According to this objection, consumers tend to overestimate their capabilities and to be *overly optimistic* about the future.[104] They may, thus, often prefer to purchase the cheaper good *without* a withdrawal right, even though in some cases the opposite choice would be more appropriate for them.[105] This objection, however, does not seem plausible: *First*, as indicated above, the price difference between the two products (*with* and *without* a withdrawal right) will usually be small and thus have no deterrent effect on the consumer who feels the need for greater protection in her transactions and is risk-averse by nature.[106] *Second*, even if we assumed that the aforementioned phenomenon of making such an—

102 *Cf.* also Haupt, 4 *Ger. Law J.* (2003), 1156, 1158.

103 *Cf.*, though, the detailed criticism of the mandated-choice model by Zöchnling-Jud, 212 *AcP* (2012), 564–565.

104 In general, on *over-confidence bias* or *over-optimism* (or *unrealistic optimism*), see Korobkin/Ulen, 88 *Cal.L.R.* (2000), 1091 ff.; Jolls/Sunstein/Thaler, 50 *Stan.L.Rev.* (1998), 1501 ff., 1524–1525, 1537–1538, 1541–1542; Sunstein, 1 *Am.L.&Econ.Rev.* (1999), 136 ff.; the same, 122 *Yale L.J.* (2013), 1848 ff.; the same, Introduction, pp. 4, 8; Jolls, Behavioral Economic Analysis..., *ibidem*, pp. 291 ff.; Arlen, 52 *Vand.L.Rev.* (1998), 1773 ff., 1781 ff.; Fischhoff/Slovic/Lichtenstein, 3 *J.Exp.Psychol.-Hum.Percept.Perform.* (1977), 552 ff.; DellaVigna, 47 *JEL* (2009), 341 ff.; Weinstein, 246 *Science* (1989), 1232–1233; Ricciardi/Simon, 2 *Bus.Educ.&Tech.J.* (2000), 3–4; Rekaiti/van den Bergh, 23 *J.Consum.Policy* (2000), 375, 376–377; also van Aaken, Begrenzte Rationalität..., pp. 119, 128, 137; Englerth, Behavioral Law and Economics..., pp. 75 ff., 95–96, 115; the same, Verhaltensökonomie..., pp. 182 ff.; Schmolke, *Grenzen der Selbstbindung...*, pp. 185 ff., 229 ff.; Bechtold, *Die Grenzen zwingenden Vertragsrechts...*, pp. 71 ff. *Cf.* further the following exquisite lines of the great English poet Alexander Pope, *An Essay on Criticism*: *"Of all the Causes which conspire to blind/Man's erring Judgment, and misguide the Mind,/What the weak Head with strongest Byass rules,/Is Pride, the never-failing Vice of Fools. Whatever Nature has in Worth deny'd,/She gives in large Recruits of needful Pride."*

105 *Cf.*, more generally, Camerer/Issacharoff/Loewenstein/O'Donoghue/Rabin, 151 *U.Penn.L.R.* (2003), 1252.

106 *Cf.* Wagner, Mandatory Contract Law..., p. 41: "By offering two different kinds of contract — one including a right of withdrawal and another one excluding it — the sellers could force the buyers to separate into two different groups. One group could be labelled the 'high-cost buyers', since the frequency of withdrawal will be high, whereas the other group could be labelled the 'low-cost buyers.'" *Cf.* further Ben-Shahar/Posner, 40 *J.Leg.Stud.* (2011), 134; Haupt, 4 *Ger.Law J.* (2003), 1156.

objectively—misplaced transactional decision might indeed come up in practice, it would reflect a conscious decision by the consumer, which we should respect, since it would have been reached after the consumer had received adequate and effective information about the existence of the withdrawal right and thus, indirectly, about its practical value.

There is also a *third* counterargument, which further weakens the objection-assumption that consumers, motivated by *over-optimism*, will often prefer to purchase a cheaper good *without* a withdrawal right: Distance contracts typically refer to low-value products and services, and many consumers are regularly involved in such transactions; hence it is inevitable that such repeated transactions produce strong learning effects for the consumers. In this context, consumers may realize that in a certain transaction they should not have waived the enhanced protection offered by the withdrawal right because the protection would have provided a benefit that would have been greater than its cost; that is, the insurance premium *would be worth the money*.[107] In other words, the learning effect alone, regardless of other concurring factors, would suffice to ensure the *attractiveness* of the withdrawal right in cases where the consumer really needs it.

There is one more thing: the mandated-choice model does not constitute a real *novum* to the European legislator. Existing EU law already contains the seeds of such a regulatory approach. A shining example has been initially contained in Directive 2004/39/EU on Markets in Financial Instruments ('MiFID I'), which adopted a similar model.[108] MiFID I, namely, introduced a distinction between *retail clients* or *private individual investors* and *professional clients* of firms providing investment services; this distinction was based on the ability of each client to make investment decisions and properly identify the risks of those investments.[109] It was up to firms providing investment services to implement appropriate written internal policies and procedures to categorize clients. Pursuant to the Directive, private individual investors enjoyed a higher level of protection; by contrast, "the rules for professional investors [were] designed to reflect the greater degree of rationality, sophistication and expertise of these actors (such as banks, investment firms, particularly large undertakings etc.)."[110] However, at the same time, pursuant to Annex II of the Directive the member states were given the right, when transposing the Directive into the national legal order, to give private individual investors the possibility to choose the lesser protection granted to professional clients—*opting up*—thus waiving the

107 So rightly Eidenmüller, Widerrufsrechte, pp. 136–137.

108 See also Bachmann, *JZ* (2008), 19; for more detail, see Bechtold, *Die Grenzen zwingenden Vertragsrechts…*, pp. 280 ff., esp. 287 ff.; cf. further Cherednychenko, 10 *ERCL* (2014), 395 ff.

109 See also Bechtold, *Die Grenzen zwingenden Vertragsrechts…*, p. 282 (: "Durch die Kundenklassifikation soll vermieden werden, dass Anleger mit hohem Kenntnisstand und breiter Erfahrung mehr—oftmals belastenden—Schutz erfahren, als sie benötigen. Auch soll vermieden werden, dass unerfahrene Anleger weniger Schutz erhalten, als erforderlich ist.").

110 Hacker, 3 *ERPL* (2017), 675.

enhanced protection scheme initially offered to them.[111] This waiver of the protection could take place only if some procedural and substantive pre-conditions were met, in order to highlight to private individual investors the significance and possible repercussions of downgrading their protection. In particular, the waiver should be considered valid to the extent that the investment firm—after undertaking an adequate assessment of the expertise, experience, and knowledge of the particular client—gave reasonable assurance, in light of the nature of the transactions or services envisaged, that the client was capable of making her own investment decisions and of understanding the risks involved. In addition, clients who wished to waive the benefit of the detailed rules of conduct should state in writing to the investment firm that they wished to be treated as a professional client, either generally or with respect to a particular investment service or transaction, or type of transaction or product; they should also state in writing, in a separate document from the contract, that they were aware of the consequences of losing such protection. In its turn, the investment firm should give them a clear written warning of the protections and investor compensation rights they could lose. This entire *informational nudging* played a very important role in the *opting-up* scheme.

Likewise, according to MiFID I (Annex II), professional clients were also offered the reverse *option*, the right to request non-professional treatment—*opting down*. It was up to the client, considered to be a professional client, to ask for a higher level of protection when she deemed that she was unable to properly assess or manage the risks involved.[112]

The EU legal framework on markets in financial instruments has recently been reformed by Directive 2014/65/EU on markets in financial instruments ('MiFID II') and Regulation (EU) no. 600/2014 on markets in financial instruments ('MiFIR'). Nevertheless, *the new legal framework follows, by and large, the same categorization of the clients of investment firms that MiFID I had already established*. The possibilities of *opting up* and *opting down* have also been preserved: pursuant to Section II of Annex II of MiFID II, a private individual investor may be allowed to waive some of the protections afforded by the conduct of business rules set in MiFID II by requesting to be treated as a professional client. This client must make the request in writing and on her own initiative. This written statement should be in a separate form from contracts or other terms of business. And once again, in accordance with the third paragraph of Section II.1 of Annex II, private individual investors may be treated as professional clients only if an adequate assessment (conducted by the investment firm) of their expertise, experience, and knowledge gives reasonable assurance, in light of the nature of the transactions or services

111 For example, the Greek legislator made use of this discretion and embarked on a relevant provision in Law no. 3606/2007.

112 For both above-mentioned options see, indicatively, Bechtold, *Die Grenzen zwingenden Vertragsrechts...*, pp. 287–288; Fleischer, 76 *RabelsZ* (2012), 239; the same, 10 *BKR* (2006), 394; Hacker, 3 *ERPL* (2017), 675–676.

envisaged, that the client is capable of making investment decisions and of understanding the risks involved.[113]

In all circumstances, though, under the current EU legal framework, investment firms should strictly refrain from implementing any practice that aims at incentivizing, inducing, or pressuring a private individual investor to request to be treated as a professional client.[114]

113 See also the Report of the European Securities and Markets Authorities, *Questions and Answers on MiFID and MiFIR Investor Protection and Intermediaries Topics*, p. 84.

114 See the Report of the European Securities and Markets Authorities, *op.cit.*, pp. 82–83.

5 The clause *'as is where is'* in a sales contract and the application of the mandated-choice model

I. Introductory remarks

In sales contracts (especially in the sale of used cars or vessels, or even real estate properties), legal practitioners often encounter the clause *'as is where is'* (*tel quel*; in German: *'gekauft wie besichtigt'*). By this clause, the purchaser seeks to achieve a low purchase price. She effectively accepts to buy the good with all its evident and latent defects while making clear that she has not received from the seller any kind of warranty, representation, or assurance that the good is fit for a particular use or purpose.[1] Practically, the seller is thus *insured* against the risk of future claims on the purchaser's part deriving from an eventual defectiveness of the good sold; the *insurance premium* the seller pays takes the form of a reduced purchase price, while the purchaser assumes the aforementioned risk against a financial consideration—that is, once again, the reduced purchase price.

If this risk allocation scheme reflects the freely formed contractual will of the parties, the law must respect it. And this is indeed what seems to be the case in most legal systems. In the German and Greek systems, for instance,[2] the clause *'as is where is'* is, in principle, considered valid, for it rests upon the purchaser's exercise of her contractual freedom and freely accepted assumption of risk. The deeper legal underpinning for the acceptance of this type of contractual clause lies in the following thought: a purchaser who chooses to conclude the sales contract and especially to waive her right to the statutory remedies granted to her in the event that the good is defective, thus accepting the possibility of the

1 See, indicatively, Locke, *Representations, Warranties and "As Is" Disclaimers*, pp. 6 ff., wherein *inter alia*: "As a material part of the consideration for this Agreement, Seller and Purchaser agree that Purchaser is taking the Property 'AS IS' with any and all latent defects and that there is no warranty by Seller that the Property is fit for a particular purpose. Purchaser acknowledges that it is not relying upon any representation, statement or other assertion with respect to the Property condition, but is relying upon its examination of the Property. Purchaser takes the Property under the express understanding there are no express or implied warranties..." For the equivalent German clause, *'gekauft wie besichtigt unter Ausschluss jeglicher Gewährleistung,'* see Canaris, 200 *AcP* (2000), 362; Adomeit, *JZ* (2003), 1053–1054; Karampatzos, Haftungsfreizeichnungs-klauseln..., pp. 184 ff.

2 See the previous fn. 1.

subsequent appearance of (latent) defects, cannot later request the activation of those remedies in case of defectiveness, for such conduct would amount to a forbidden *venire contra factum proprium*—that is, in Anglo-American legal terminology, it would violate the *principle of estoppel.* Besides, the same rationale is also encountered in the civil law provisions that exclude the seller's liability when the purchaser *knew* of the existence of a defect at the time the sales contract was concluded [see, for instance, § 442 of the German Civil Code (BGB) and Article 537 of the Greek Civil Code].

In light of the above, it comes as no surprise that also in common law the clause '*as is where is*' is, in principle, held valid.[3]

II. The barrier of EU law on consumer protection

Yet, in EU law, the above holds only for 'B2B' (business-to-business) or 'C2C' (consumer-to-consumer) sales contracts *but not for 'B2C' (business-to-consumer) sales contracts*, which will often be the case in practice. In the latter case the clause '*as is where is*' normally runs contrary to Article 7 para. 1 sent. a' of Directive 1999/44/EC "*on certain aspects of the sale of consumer goods and associated guarantees*," which provides that "[a]ny contractual terms or agreements concluded with the seller before the lack of conformity is brought to the consumer's attention which directly or indirectly waive or restrict the rights resulting from this Directive shall, as provided for by national law, not be binding on the consumer." More specifically:

In German theory the issue has been discussed in detail, mainly on the basis of the following less than inflammatory example, which makes the present analysis a little clearer[4]: a private person interested in acquiring a used car proposes to the salesman to buy the car '*as is where is*,' waiving all her rights deriving from any eventual defectiveness of the car in order to get a lower price[5]; in the past, in many EU countries, including Germany and Greece, it would have sufficed to say that the car was sold under the valid clause '*as is where is*' (in German:

3 See, indicatively, Locke, *Representations, Warranties and "As Is" Disclaimers*, pp. 8 ff. See also the characteristic formulation in *Prudential Ins. Co. of America v. Jefferson Assoc., Ltd.*, 896 S.W.2d 156, 160 (Tex. 1995), which echoes the *principle of self-responsibility* that is prevalent in the Anglo-American world: "The sole cause of a buyer's injury [*scil.* when he agrees to purchase something 'as is'], by his own admission, is the buyer himself. He has agreed to take the full risk of determining the value of the purchase. He is not obliged to do so; he could insist instead that the seller assume part or all of that risk by obtaining warranties to the desired effect. If the seller is willing to give such assurances, however, he will ordinarily insist upon additional compensation. Rather than pay more, a buyer may choose to rely entirely upon his own determination of the condition and value of his purchase."

4 See Canaris, 200 *AcP* (2000), 362–363; Adomeit, *JZ* (2003), 1054; Schürnbrand, *JZ* (2009), 135.

5 See also Wagner, Mandatory Contract Law..., p. 33: "... Particularly among young people with little money, plenty of time and some mechanical skills, it was common to buy a car for a low price without a warranty"; the same, Zwingendes Vertragsrecht, pp. 38–39.

'*gekauft wie besichtigt unter Ausschluss jeglicher Gewährleistung*'). In addition to the thoughts already articulated above (speaking in favor of the general legal validity of the clause), the German Supreme Civil Court (Bundesgerichtshof, BGH) would also underscore that[6] the liability exclusion for latent defects is *commercially reasonable*, since when a used car appears to be defective after the conclusion of the sales contract it is difficult to ascertain whether the defect already existed at the (critical) time the car was handed over to the purchaser, or emerged after that point in time (e.g., due to regular wear and tear).[7]

However, after the enactment of Directive 1999/44/EC this approach can no longer be tenable, since the clause '*as is where is*' entails an exclusion of the purchaser's rights in case of defectiveness of the good, which is prohibited pursuant to Article 7 para. 1 sent. a' of the Directive. The paternalistic motive is here rather evident: it lies, namely, with the abstract need to protect the—seemingly—weaker and inexperienced transacting party, that is, the consumer-purchaser; in other words, the legislator considers it justified in the abstract to restrict freedom of contract to prevent eventual exploitation.[8] The same restrictive spirit survives in the provisions of the newly published *Directive (EU) 2019/771 of 20 May 2019 on certain aspects concerning contracts for the sale of goods, amending Regulation (EU) 2017/2394 and Directive 2009/22/EC, and repealing Directive 1999/44/EC* (OJ 2019 L 136/28—'*the New Sale of Goods Directive*,' which will apply from 1 January 2022 and will then repeal Directive 1999/44/EC).[9]

Thus, mandatory law creates a protective backstop for a person who has freely entered into a specific contractual arrangement, which she deems serves best her interests; this backstop limits, rather than protects, the contractual freedom of the consumer-purchaser, since it does not allow her to pay a low price against the conscious assumption of a higher transactional risk.[10] As is well pointed out in theory, there is definitely "a loss of freedom when consumers are prevented from [...] buying consumer goods from commercial vendors without a 2 year period to claim defects. A well informed consumer may rationally prefer a cheaper good without warranty to the more expensive good with a warranty."[11] (Pursuant to

6 See BGHZ 74, 383 [386]; BGH *NJW* (1966), 1070 [1071]; BGH *NJW* (1970), 29 [31].

7 See Wagner, Mandatory Contract Law..., p. 33.

8 *Cf.* Schweizer, Nudging and the Principle of Proportionality..., pp. 105–106.

9 See, indicatively, Letten, *New Directive on contracts for the sale of goods...*; www.consilium.europa.eu/en/press/press-releases/2019/04/15/eu-adopts-new-rules-on-sales-contracts-for-goods-and-digital-content/; in detail, Stabentheiner/Wendehorst/Zöchling-Jud, *Das neue europäische Gewährleistungsrecht – Zu den Richtlinien (EU) 2019/771 über den Warenkauf sowie (EU) 2019/770 über digitale Inhalte und digitale Dienstleistungen* (2019).

10 See the relevant criticism in the German literature: Wolf/Neuner, *AT des BürgR*[10], § 10 no. 73 (: "... keine hinreichenden sozialen Gründe ersichtlich sind, den Verbraucher gleichsam vor sich selbst beim Aushandeln von Individualvereinbarungen zu schützen"); Canaris, 200 *AcP* (2000), 362 ff.; Adomeit, *JZ* (2003), 1054; Tiedtke/Burgmann, *NJW* (2005), 1154. *Cf.* also Kähler, *Begriff und Rechtfertigung...*, pp. 213 ff.; in a similar vein, see Wein, *Eine Ökonomische Analyse der neuen Verbrauchsgüterkaufrichtlinie...*, p. 19.

11 Schweizer, Nudging and the Principle of Proportionality..., p. 105; see also Bar-Gill/Ben-Shahar, 50 *CML Rev.* (2013), 109–110.

Article 7 para. 1 sent. b' of Directive 1999/44/EC it is, though, possible that the EU member states "provide that, in the case of second-hand goods, the seller and consumer may agree contractual terms or agreements which have a shorter time period for the liability of the seller than that set down in Article 5(1). Such period may not be less than one year." Such a provision was recently introduced into Article 5 para. 1 of the Greek Law on consumer protection, that is, Law no. 2251/1994, and is also included in Article 10 para. 6 of the New Sale of Goods Directive.[12])

What we actually encounter here is a general defect of the mandatory imposition of greater legal protection on the consumer-purchaser: the *nominal* increase in the consumer protection may often not benefit the consumer herself, given that, in general, for any 'legal privilege' granted to her by means of mandatory rules she herself pays the price—that is, an insurance premium that takes the form of a higher price for the goods she acquires. In other words, the excessive consumer protection framework, primarily consisting of abundant mandatory law provisions, not only entails an unacceptable limitation of individuals' private autonomy but also goes against the financial interests of consumers themselves—since it comes at a considerable price. The cost of this enhanced legal protection is always rolled, in part or in full, into the final purchase price of the goods. Legal protection costs are thus shifted to consumers, and this shift may easily be ascertained by comparing the price of a good (e.g., an electronic device) *before* the introduction of a mandatory rule with the price *after*.[13]

12 For more detail, see, further, the Preamble to the New Sale of Goods Directive, recital 43: "As regards certain aspects, different treatment of second-hand goods could be justifiable. Although a liability or limitation period of two years or more usually reconciles the interests of both the seller and the consumer, this might not be the case with regard to second-hand goods. Member States should, therefore, be allowed to enable the parties to agree on a shortened liability or limitation period for such goods. Leaving this question to a contractual agreement between the parties increases contractual freedom and ensures that the consumer has to be informed both about the nature of the good as a second-hand good, and the shortened liability or limitation period. However, such a contractually agreed period should not be shorter than one year."

13 *Cf.* Huber, 4 *ZEuP* (2008), 712, wherein *inter alia*: "Der Verbraucher wird durch den Verbraucherschutz sozusagen gegen Enttäuschung versichert, z.B. dagegen, dass die verkaufte Sache mangelhaft und der dafür bezahlte Kaufpreis verloren ist. Die „Versicherungsprämie" steckt notwendigerweise im Kaufpreis, der natürlich höher sein muss, wenn man mit als wenn man ohne Garantie kauft. Da Verbraucherschutzrecht [...] zwingend sein muss, wird die Versicherung dem Verbraucher zwangsweise auferlegt, ob er will oder nicht. *Dieser Mechanismus gilt für alle Wohltaten, die der Gesetzgeber dem Verbraucher erweist...*" (emphasis added); Wagner, Mandatory Contract Law..., pp. 31–32, wherein *inter alia*: "... the consumers-buyers themselves have to pay for any rights they have under a contract of sale, because the total costs associated with the relevant scheme of remedies will be reflected in the contract price. The more expansive the remedies conferred on the consumer, the higher the price the seller will charge for the product in question"; the same, *ZEuP* (2007), 210; Gill/Ben-Shahar, 50 *CML Rev.* (2013), 110, 113 ff.; Karampatzos, Haftungsfreizeichnungsklauseln..., pp. 188 ff.; Rühl, 207 *AcP* (2007), 624 ff.; Schäfer/Ott, *Lehrbuch der ökonomischen Analyse des Rechts*[4], pp. 8, 138, 345; Schwab, Widerrufsrechte..., pp. 173–174; Haupt, 4 *Ger. Law J.* (2003), 1156, 1159–1160; van Boom/Ogus, Introducing, Defining and Balancing..., p. 5; Eidenmüller/Jansen/Kieninger/Wagner/

Further, these costs turn some goods into financially difficult-to-access goods or even forbidden fruits to low-income consumers. Evidently, such consequences are not welfare-promoting and thus not welcome.[14]

III. Applying the mandated-choice model

The problematic situation discussed above could be easily avoided if we were willing to accept the application of the mandated-choice model in B2C sales contracts. Under this model the consumer-purchaser *would be required to choose* between two products. One would come with greater legal protection—that is, the purchaser's statutory rights in case of defectiveness; the other would have no such protection and therefore cost less. The consumer-purchaser could then sovereignly decide whether to purchase the insurance premium or risk proceeding without it. Thus her private autonomy would be well preserved and more efficient transactions would be advanced. In a nutshell, this mandated option would enhance buyer's freedom of choice, advance the interests of low income consumers, and eliminate *cross-subsidization*—since the enhanced legal protection would be paid only by those risk-averse consumers who would really wish to enjoy such additional protection (and not by the entirety of consumers).[15] At the end of the day, this approach corresponds to the Latin proverb "*invito beneficium non datur*," which means that *no one enjoys a benefit if they do not wish to.*[16]

It is rather self-explanatory, though, that the aforementioned waiver is without importance in the event of fraudulent behavior on the seller's part and especially if there is fraudulent concealment of a defect. Such behavior is prohibited in most modern legal systems; the relevant statutory provisions on fraudulent or deceitful behavior are rightly *ius cogens*[17] and thus set aside the *caveat emptor* rule[18]—or, in principle, any other specific contractual arrangement that runs against them.

Zimmermann, *JZ* (2012), 276 ff., 288–289; Eidenmüller, *Effizienz als Rechtsprinzip*³, p. 308; Riesenhuber, Wandlungen oder Erosion der Privatautonomie?, pp. 9–10. *Cf.* further Wittman, *Economic Foundations of Law...*, pp. 234 ff., esp. 236, 242 ff., 249.

14 See van Boom/Ogus, Introducing, Defining and Balancing..., p. 5: "Such transfer of cost may cause the price of the product to rise and ultimately render it unaffordable for individuals of lower incomes, in which case the object of the legal intervention is defeated"; also Haupt, 4 *Ger. Law J.* (2003), 1159–1160.

15 *Cf.* further, in more general terms, Gill/Ben-Shahar, 50 *CML Rev.* (2013), 113: "... consumers might also prefer to pay a lower price and get lower quality products with a lower level of consumer protection. People often waive warranty programmes, buy non-refundable items, choose slower delivery options, or decline to insure, because it makes the product cheaper."

16 This proverb goes back to the Roman jurist Julius Paulus Prudentissimus; see Rudden, 11 *Cambrian L.Rev.* (1980), 87, 89–90, and Liebs, *Lateinische Rechtsregeln und Rechtssprichwörter*⁷, J 134 (p. 112).

17 *Cf.* also Rudden, 11 *Cambrian L.Rev.* (1980), 95.

18 For the origins and the content of this rule, see, indicatively, Zimmermann, *The Law of Obligations...*, pp. 307 ff.; also Wagner, Zwingendes Vertragsrecht, pp. 37–38; Kleinig, *Paternalism*, pp. 176–177.

6 Strict product liability and mandated-choice model

Why are they incompatible?

Another field in which the European legislator has manifested her willingness to protect consumers is product liability. Directive 85/374/EEC "*on the approximation of the laws, regulations and administrative provisions of the Member States concerning liability for defective products*" was introduced to do this. The arresting question now raised is whether the mandated-choice model could also be applied to product liability; my answer, this time, is no. In what follows I explain why.

I. Framing the question

It appears that the question whether a model similar to the mandated-choice model advanced above may be applied in the field of product liability has already been effectively contemplated in the American literature.[1] The relevant discussion has, though, as starting point the two seminal U.S. decisions on product liability, that is, *Escola v. Coca-Cola Bottling Co. (1944)*[2] and *Grimshaw v. Ford Motor Company (1981)*.[3]

In the first decision, the concurring opinion of Judge Roger Traynor admittedly set the foundations for strict product liability: "Even if there is no negligence [...] public policy demands that responsibility be fixed *wherever it will most effectively reduce the hazards* to life and health inherent in defective products that reach the market. It is evident that *the manufacturer can anticipate some hazards and guard against the recurrence of others, as the public cannot.* [...] The cost of an injury and the loss of time or health may be an overwhelming misfortune to the person injured, and a needless one, *for the risk of injury can be insured by the manufacturer and distributed among the public as a cost of doing business.* It is to the public interest to discourage the marketing of products having defects that are a menace to the public. If such products nevertheless find their way into the market it is to the public interest to place the responsibility

1 See, mainly, Wittman, *Economic Foundations of Law...*, Chapters 24–26 (pp. 231 ff., esp. 233 ff.)—further, the authors referenced in fn. 6 below.

2 24 Cal.2d 453, 150 P.2d 436.

3 119 Cal. App. 3d 757.

for whatever injury they may cause upon the manufacturer, *who, even if he is not negligent in the manufacture of the product, is responsible for its reaching the market.* However intermittently such injuries may occur and however haphazardly they may strike, the risk of their occurrence is a constant risk and a general one. Against such a risk there should be general and constant protection and *the manufacturer is best situated to afford such protection*" (emphasis added). It is clear that, with these remarkable thoughts, Judge Traynor referred both to the manufacturer's ability to deter—that is, control and prevent the relevant risk (in German: *Risikobeherrschbarkeit*)[4]—and to the classical economic analysis of law argument that the manufacturer is here the cheaper insurer—that is, the *cheaper-insurer* argument.[5]

In light of such product liability cases, the question that now arises is whether consumers could be given *the option to choose between two different products* along the lines of the aforementioned mandated-choice model.[6] Specifically, take two kinds of Coke bottles, for example, a safe bottle that (hypothetically) never explodes at a price of $2.20 and an unsafe or risky one that explodes one out of a million times at a price of $2. In such a hypothetical transactional situation, the consumer could protect herself against the explosion risk by paying an insurance premium of 20 cents; thus, the risk-preferring consumer will opt for the less safe and cheaper product, whereas the risk-averse consumer will prefer the safe and more expensive one, paying an additional price for this greater protection. The same holds, *mutatis mutandis*, in a similar scenario where the consumer is offered the option between a product *with a liability assumption* on the part of the manufacturer for injury or damage caused to consumer's health or property due to defectiveness, and a different product *without such a liability assumption* that is cheaper.[7] Let us, further, assume that pursuant to the mandated-choice model, as analyzed above, the manufacturer is *obliged by law* to provide the consumer with such an option between the two products.

4 In general, for this ability to control a risk as a crucial criterion for its allocation, see Koller, *Die Risikozurechnung bei Vertragsstörungen...*, pp. 76, 100 ff.

5 For a critical approach, though, to Judge Traynor's opinion, see Epstein, 14 *J.Leg.Stud.* (1985), 646 ff., who analyzes the significant argument from the *insurability* of the risk; also Wittman, *Economic Foundations of Law...*, p. 237. *Cf.* further Hylton, 88 *Notre Dame L.Rev.* (2013), 2463 ff, according to whom the most influential theories set out by Judge Traynor are "the deterrence rationale, the reliance rationale, the insurance rationale, and the administrative costs rationale."

6 For the examination of this crucial question, see, once more, Wittman, *Economic Foundations of Law...*, Chapters 24–26 (pp. 231 ff., esp. 233 ff.); also Schäfer/Ott, *Lehrbuch der ökonomischen Analyse des Zivilrechts*[4], pp. 335–336, esp. 337–338; Adams, Produkthaftung..., pp. 5 ff.; *cf.*, more recently, Hylton, 88 *Notre Dame L.Rev.* (2013), 2477 ff., 2487–2488.

7 *Cf.* Wittman, *Economic Foundations of Law...*, p. 233: "... Just as there is sugar-free Coke, there may be liability-free (for the consumer) Coke and liability (for the consumer) Coke ... [...] By assuming liability, Coke is providing an insurance policy to the consumer. It is a tied product. The consumer buys both Coke and a specialized insurance policy"; *cf.* also Cooter/Ulen, *Law & Economics*[6], p. 252.

II. Arguments against the application of the mandated-choice model

In my opinion, both variations of mandated choice sketched out above, even if imposed on the manufacturer by law, should be rejected; the current forced strict liability regime must be upheld.[8] Well, here's my take:

First, the manufacturer is admittedly, and pursuant to the traditional assumption of economic analysis of law, the *cheapest cost avoider*. It is regularly the entity that can prevent damage from occurring at the lowest possible cost.[9] The manufacturer has, namely, the necessary organizational and entrepreneurial capacity to test and control the products—a capacity which the consumer normally lacks.[10] At the same time, as discussed above, the manufacturer is regularly, indeed, the *cheaper insurer* against the pertinent risk.[11]

In the same vein, the current forced strict liability regime is further, and foremost, justified by the intense *information asymmetry* between the consumer and the manufacturer:[12] the consumer does not know the probability of damage and has no access to the technical means necessary to identify an eventual defect in

8 Nevertheless, I do not disregard here the fact that there is significant, or even prevalent, law and economics literature suggesting that product liability law is a mistake, and perhaps it should be abolished altogether: see, indicatively, Polinsky/Shavell, 123 *Harv.L.Rev.* (2010), 1437 ff., and Oi, 4 *Bell J.Econ.* (1973), 3 ff. *passim*, esp. 25 ff., who already then opposed the strict product liability regime, being imbued with an antipaternalistic spirit. For a response to the position of Polinsky and Shavell, see Goldberg/Zipurski, 123 *Harv.L.Rev.* (2010), 1919 ff. More recently, in an extensive economic analysis of strict product liability, Hylton [88 *Notre Dame L.Rev.* (2013), 2457 ff., esp. 2470 ff.] proceeds to "a cautious defense of products liability law" (*ibidem*, p. 2513), arguing that "the law probably improves social welfare, though it is in need of reform in several areas" (*ibidem*, p. 2458); such reforms "would be more useful than the broad-brush critiques that have dominated the law and economics literature on law and economics" (*ibidem*, p. 2458). For an initial economic analysis of product liability law, see Landes/R.Posner, 14 *J.Leg. Stud.* (1985), 535 ff. In any case, it is evident that it is beyond the scope of this chapter to critically examine, once again, the entire law and economics debate over product liability.

9 See Quillen, 61 *S.Cal.L.R.* (1988), 1126 ff.; Calabresi, *The Costs of Accidents*..., pp. 136 ff.; also Cooter/Eisenberg, 73 *Cal.L.R.* (1985), 1464; Hacker, 11 *ERCL* (2015), 341; Schäfer/Ott, *Lehrbuch der ökonomischen Analyse des Zivilrechts*[4], pp. 411–412; Eidenmüller, *Effizienz als Rechtsprinzip*[3], pp. 402–403; Mathis, *Effizienz statt Gerechtigkeit?*[3], p. 90.

10 See, indicatively, Adams, Produkthaftung..., pp. 14 ff.

11 For detail on this interesting aspect, see R.Posner, *Economic Analysis of Law*[6], pp. 106 ff., 182–183; Wittman, *Economic Foundations of Law*..., pp. 235 ff., 257 ff. (who notes, however, that it is not at all clear that the manufacturer is in fact the cheaper insurer—*ibidem*, p. 237: "The consumer can buy a medical and/or disability policy that insures the consumer against injury from a variety of risks — manufactured, genetic, and just plain clumsiness. Making the manufacturer liable may be a more costly method of insuring the consumer, especially because manufacturer liability often involves lawyers..."); Adams, Produkthaftung..., pp. 18 ff.; Schäfer/Ott, *Lehrbuch der ökonomischen Analyse des Zivilrechts*[4], pp. 406 ff.

12 See Wittman, *Economic Foundations of Law*..., Chapter 25 (pp. 239 ff.); Landes/R.Posner, 14 *J.Leg.Stud.* (1985), 535 ff. *passim*; Schäfer/Ott, *Lehrbuch der ökonomischen Analyse des Zivilrechts*[4], pp. 339 ff.; Sinn, Kommentar..., pp. 81 ff. *passim*; Drexl, *Die wirtschaftliche Selbstbestimmung*..., pp. 373 ff.

a product each time she makes a purchase. The imposition of mandatory law protects the party suffering from such an information deficit: namely, the consumer (but also the market in general, as we will see in the following lines).[13] For instance, the probability of a bottle exploding is a piece of information that the consumer may only acquire at a high, exorbitant, or prohibitive price (e.g., by testing each bottle herself), whereas this is not the case for the manufacturer, who possesses the relevant organizational, technical, and financial capacity to do such testing—in this respect the manufacturer is indeed the *cheapest cost avoider.*[14]

It is noteworthy that, in the absence of mandatory product liability, such information asymmetry could lead to a race to the bottom (*a downward spiral*), as predicted by *Akerlof's theory on the market for lemons.*[15] Manufacturers, taking advantage of their informational superiority in conjunction with the absence of a liability rule, would have a strong incentive to not do all they could to make products safe in order to increase their profits; thus they would fuel the flow of defective (or less safe) products into the market. Eventually the market would be flooded with bad products (*lemons*) and it would eventually collapse (*market failure*).[16] Nonetheless, such a development might be avoided if there were an exchange of information among the consumers (e.g., via the internet) about the quality of the products sold. Such an exchange of information might, possibly, prevent a downward spiral.

Apart from the above, there is a further consideration: *public interest* also speaks in favor of a forced strict product liability regime. When considering which scheme will efficiently protect consumers, regulators should not restrict their considerations to the mere protection of consumers' *financial interests.*

13 It is submitted that this line of reasoning also justifies the establishment of *liability for the provision of services* (e.g., medical services); see Wittman, *Economic Foundations of Law...*, Chapter 25 (pp. 242 ff.).

14 See also R.Posner, *Economic Analysis of Law*[6], pp. 182–183, who sums up the central argument in an exemplary manner: "There is nothing the consumer can do at reasonable cost to prevent the one in a million product failure. *It would not pay for him to inspect every soft drink bottle that he buys for such a minute hazard*, or to investigate the possibility that there are safer substitutes; the expected accident cost is just too low to incite him to any self-protective measures. [...] All this assumes *an asymmetry of information* between the manufacturer and the consumer. [...] ... product failures that cause serious personal injuries are extremely rare, and *the cost to the consumer of becoming informed about them is apt to exceed the expected benefit*" (emphasis added); Landes/R.Posner, 14 *J.Leg.Stud.* (1985), 544–545, 549–550, 555; see also Wittman, *Economic Foundations of Law...*, Chapter 25 (pp. 239 ff.), who, in general, concludes (p. 242): "... when there is asymmetry in knowledge in favor of the producer, there greater reason for the producer to be liable. But the argument in favor of liability is probably as not as strong as one might think at first because even in the absence of forced liability, the safer producer will want to offer the consumer insurance if it is cost effective to do so"; Schäfer/Ott, *Lehrbuch der ökonomischen Analyse des Zivilrechts*[4], p. 339; Adams, Produkthaftung..., pp. 14 ff. *passim.*

15 See already Chapter 4, pp. 93 ff. above.

16 See also Quillen, 61 *S.Cal.L.R.* (1988), 1134; Schäfer/Ott, *Lehrbuch der ökonomischen Analyse des Zivilrechts*[4], pp. 345–346; Drexl, *Die wirtschaftliche Selbstbestimmung...*, p. 374.

The need to protect life, bodily integrity, and consumers' health in general must also be considered; when they are taken into account, the argument in favor of a forced strict product liability regime is immediately strengthened. In other words, the social usefulness of the mandatory rule outweighs any possible cost-benefit analysis (as cynically performed, for instance, by Ford in *Grimshaw v. Ford Motor Company, 1981*[17])—even more so if we take into account the fact that the mandatory protection also comprises the so-called *innocent bystanders*, not just the consumer-end recipient of the good. The latter consideration clearly amplifies the public interest argument. In a nutshell, the lawmaker cannot be indifferent to the choice that an isolated consumer would make between a 'safe' and an 'unsafe' product, for the circulation and use of an unsafe or defective product may also damage the health or property of *third parties uninvolved in the initial consumer decision to buy said product*—that is, the *innocent bystanders*.

Still, in the context of public interest protection, we should further take into account the healthcare system costs, which are borne by all taxpayers. Those costs would increase if unsafe products were circulated and widely used. This means that granting to the consumer the option to choose would entail severe negative externalities for third parties or for society in general. In contrast, a strict product liability regime contributes to the limitation of such adverse effects.

The last parameter is, in general, very significant for the wide-ranging discussion on paternalism. It is therefore worth pondering it a bit further. In some cases, a regulatory intervention may indeed be justified, not only on grounds of protecting the individual against a particular danger (e.g., of life or health) but also on grounds of safeguarding the general welfare or supra-individual interests. Consider the compulsory use of seat belts, for example. Such a mandatory rule might aim not only at protecting car passengers but also at reducing healthcare costs resulting from car accidents. This may be called *medical paternalism*:[18] according to this type of paternalism, the obligation to wear a seat belt or a motorcycle helmet, or, further, the mandatory labeling on cigarette packaging (which draws our attention to the dangers of smoking) is primarily aimed at the protection of the individuals engaged in the dangerous activity, but at the same time, such rules can also be justified on public interest grounds because such activities produce negative externalities on the healthcare system, on the health of passive smokers, and others.[19] Thus the justifications for paternalistic interference may sometimes have a *mixed character*; and precisely in such cases, where

17 On those very frequent cost-benefit analyses, see in detail Viscusi, 52 *Stan.L.Rev.* (2000), 547 ff., who, examining automobile accident cases, comes, *inter alia*, to the conclusion that "[n]otwithstanding the desirability of using a benefit-cost approach to assess the merits of safety measures, in many court cases juries appear to penalize corporations for having done a risk analysis in instances in which the company decided not to make a safety improvement after the analysis indicated the improvement was unwarranted. Automobile accident cases provide the most prominent examples of such juror sanctions."

18 See R. Dworkin, *Justice for Hedgehogs*, p. 370, and Kalliris, *Autonomy, Well-Being and the Law*, pp. 133, 134.

19 See also van Boom/Ogus, Introducing, Defining and Balancing…, p. 4; van Aaken, Begrenzte Rationalität…, pp. 136–137, esp. fn. 91; Englerth, Vom Wert des Rauchens…, pp. 249–250;

the (positive) consequences of the interference go beyond individual interests (*spillover effects*), a ***mixed paternalism*** is at work.[20]

Nevertheless, such paternalistic interferences have to be carefully justified. Even when possible negative externalities of an individual behavior affecting the society as a whole serve as the basis for justification, the argument might not be as clear as it initially appears to be. The adverse societal effects of an individual behavior will usually depend on a series of specific variables, which might not always offer a basis for safe estimations. And in addition, public policymakers might be tempted to abusively exploit the possible—but not well substantiated—existence of such effects in an attempt to justify paternalistic interferences across a wide range of activities.[21] The multiple variables to be taken into account in the context of a mixed paternalism may indeed create an obscure picture, which may not clearly justify the paternalistic interference. For example, on the issue of whether wearing seat belts should be required, what if we were told that the death of a young person in a traffic accident saves the state a large amount of money, especially the healthcare costs of treating a severely injured person, as well as the social security costs for a person who lives to old age? Should we then oppose the obligatory use of the seat belt, preferring the early death of the passenger?[22] The same cynical cost-benefit analysis could be applied to warnings against smoking and other activities which are deemed potentially harmful to the individual.[23]

In light of the questionable (not merely cynical) character of such estimations, it has been suggested in theory that in such cases the state should shy away from any kind of intervention and at the same time impose the relevant societal costs on the individuals themselves who engage in self-regarding, that is, self-endangering or self-harming activities. From this perspective, for instance, a car driver who refuses to wear a seat belt would be deprived of insurance coverage and would pay her own hospitalization expenses if she were injured. The same rules would apply for the adventurous mountain climber who defies bad weather conditions and is lost in a canyon: if she were saved by a highly qualified, specially trained rescue team, she would be required to cover the relevant expenses herself.[24]

Elster, *Ulysses and the Sirens...*, pp. 84–85; Kalliris, *Autonomy, Well-Being and the Law*, pp. 126 ff.

20 This type of paternalism is juxtaposed to so-called ***unmixed paternalism***, where the interference is justified only on grounds of protecting a particular individual (each time she makes a choice), whereas in the context of ***mixed paternalism*** the interference is justified by the need to protect both the individual and wider social interests (or third-party interests). For this distinction, see Feinberg, *Harm to Self*, p. 8. On mixed paternalism, *cf.* also Saint-Paul, *The Tyranny of Utility...*, pp. 101 ff.; Schweizer, Nudging and the Principle of Proportionality..., pp. 104–105; van Aaken, Judge the Nudge..., pp. 108–109.

21 *Cf.* also van Aaken, Judge the Nudge..., p. 109.

22 See Englerth, Vom Wert des Rauchens..., pp. 249–250. Furthermore, in this respect one would also have to consider the rates of deaths, disabilities, or light injuries related to car accidents in which the passengers do not wear seat belts, and proceed with relevant differentiations, and so forth.

23 See, once again, Englerth, Vom Wert des Rauchens..., p. 250.

24 See van Aaken, Begrenzte Rationalität..., pp. 136–137, esp. fn. 91, and Englerth, Vom Wert des Rauchens..., pp. 235 ff., 250; also G. Dworkin, Paternalism: Some Second Thoughts, p. 109; *cf.* further Schwabe, *JZ* (1998), 72–73.

Further, one can reasonably quibble about the validity of some specific components of the aforementioned line of reasoning. What about the critical *causality issue*, for example? Can we be sure, for example, that the disease of a cancer patient is causally or exclusively related to smoking in order to call her to undertake the costs for her treatment? The answer to this question (as well as similar ones) is no: such a policy would risk holding a person liable for a situation she is not responsible for.

In summary, it is rightly argued that in modern societies Mill's famous dividing line "between actions that harm others and those that do not"—which actually reflects the Millian *harm principle* (see also Chapter 7, pp. 132 ff. below)—is not as clear as it might have been thought in the past: for "in societies where governments may either run the health service or provide the health care of last resort, and where the government may provide social services to those left destitute, *there may no longer be many actions which are purely self-regarding*. For example, if my reckless behaviour leaves me severely injured, the state may end up paying for my medical bills or supporting my children. My action, which on the surface seemed only self-regarding, had effects on those around me, and repercussions to a wider group through increased taxes and insurance premiums."[25] At the same time, though, it is also true that if the *direct* target of a paternalistic intervention is the individual but "the harm to the individual *indirectly* leads to costs for society, the legitimacy of the aim [scil. of the paternalistic interference] is *highly questionable and needs more scrutiny*."[26] Therefore, the—rather frequent—invocation of further social costs in an attempt to justify paternalistic interventions in the behavior of individuals must always be met with cautiousness.

III. The moral hazard issue

Notwithstanding the above, a strict product liability regime, in the context of which the manufacturer is insured against damages claims of the consumers, may entail a severe *moral hazard*. As standard theory suggests, in general insurance can eliminate incentives to minimize risk; policyholders are supposed to have less incentive to invest in safety. Respectively, in our case this moral hazard consists in the assumption that insofar as the manufacturer-policyholder knows beforehand that any product liability will be undertaken by the insurer, she will feel no compunction to act responsibly. In other words, insurance weakens the incentive to show diligent conduct and, as a result, the manufacturer will take less care to prevent product defects or harm to the consumer (just as a car owner who is insured against loss may take less care to prevent car theft).[27] However,

25 Bix, *Jurisprudence: Theory and Context*[7], p. 172 (emphasis added).

26 van Aaken, Judge the Nudge..., p. 109 (emphasis added).

27 In general, on the moral hazard deriving from the acquisition of an insurance policy, see R.Posner, *Economic Analysis of Law*[6], pp. 109, 122; Cooter/Ulen, *Law & Economics*[6], pp. 48, 238 ff.; Wittman, *Economic Foundations of Law...*, pp. 260 ff.; Epstein, 14 *J.Leg.Stud.* (1985), 653; Hylton, 88 *Notre Dame L.Rev.* (2013), 2484–2485; Ben-Shahar/Logue, 111 *Mich. L. Rev.* (2012),

this assumption faces a series of serious counterarguments, which ultimately defeat it:

a The insured manufacturer should not actually have any interest in acting irresponsibly or negligently, for the systematic dissemination of defective products will lead to an *increase in the damages claims* filed by consumers; this, in turn, will *increase the insurer's financial obligations*, which, in the end, will cause the *insurer to raise the insurance premium* to be paid by the manufacturer. This highly plausible chain of events alone gives the manufacturer a powerful incentive to reduce consumer claims by minimizing consumer accidents—that is, by ensuring that it produces and sells high-quality products in the market. From this perspective, strict product liability rules essentially turn the insurance companies into *watchdogs* responsible for the quality of the products sold to the public.[28] Or, in other words, the insurance companies thus become *regulators of safety*.[29]

Nonetheless, it has also been suggested that the aforementioned chain of events, and especially the initial increase of the lawsuits against the manufacturer, *may not always be the case*, since some injured consumers may forgo their right to sue because the litigation costs may exceed the value of their claim for compensation, and "this offsets the litigation cost burden on producers, because some claims will go uncompensated."[30]

b The systematic dissemination of defective or unsafe products will, in all likelihood, ruin the *reputation* and *reliability* of the negligent or reckless manufacturer, driving it, sooner or later, out of the market by making consumers

197 ff. *passim*; Adams, Produkthaftung…, pp. 20 ff.; Rühl, 207 *AcP* (2007), 623–624; Kirchgässner, *Homo Oeconomicus*[4], pp. 75–76; Bechtold, *Die Grenzen zwingenden Vertragsrechts…*, pp. 34–35; Neumann, *Libertärer Paternalismus…*, p. 108; *cf.* further Landsburg, *The Armchair Economist…*, pp. 1 ff.

28 So aptly Cooter/Ulen, *Law & Economics*[6], pp. 238–239 and 243, who also refer to further protective means that the insurance companies employ against instances of opportunistic behavior on the part of their customers, such as the various 'carve-outs' or 'liability exclusions,' which are often provided for in insurance contracts, as well as the various *bonuses* given to their customers for diligent behavior; see also Wittman, *Economic Foundations of Law…*, pp. 260–261, who stresses, though, that such means of protection may only limit the aforesaid moral hazard but not fully eliminate it; R.Posner, *Economic Analysis of Law*[6], p. 109; Adams, Produkthaftung…, pp. 20–21; Kirchgässner, *Homo Oeconomicus*[4], pp. 75–76.

29 Cf. Ben-Shahar/Logue, 111 *Mich.L.Rev.* (2012), 197 ff., who generally contend that through *ex ante* and *ex post* 'private regulation' *insurance creates more incentive to invest in safety* so that it can be a superior regulator of safety.

30 Hylton, 88 *Notre Dame L.Rev.* (2013), 2482–2483, who immediately thereafter, however, clarifies that *this is not the rule* (*ibidem*): "But most cases involving product defects involve designs that can and inevitably will generate large damage claims, considerably greater than the cost to the victim of bringing a claim to the court. The class action device allows attorneys to bundle and bring to court cases involving numerous small claims. Given this, the litigation cost burden is likely to increase the cost burden on producers, even after taking into account the rate at which claims are dropped or not pursued because of the litigation costs on the plaintiff's side."

shift their purchases to other brands in order to avoid damage.[31] This argument, however, may be taken to lend support to the position against a statutory provision of the manufacturer's strict liability because under this approach the market is considered to be able to *self-regulate* and thus such a provision would be redundant. In other words, the rational decision of consumers to choose safer products alone gives manufacturers the necessary incentive to produce and sell safe products and at the same time throws the 'black sheep' out of the market.[32]

Yet, this last argument is rather weak. A fundamental pre-condition for such *market self-regulation* to take place is consumers' access to sufficient information about the black sheep—that is, those manufacturers who produce defective or unsafe products.[33] Otherwise, if there is inadequate information or no information at all, the danger of a 'market for lemons' becomes imminent. And under a regime without mandatory product liability, more and more manufacturers will take advantage of consumers' information deficit and disseminate lower-quality, possibly unsafe, products at the same price, thus increasing their profit margin.[34]

In any event, even if consumers are informed to a degree, for the black sheep to be ostracized we also need to embrace the assumption of completely rational consumer behavior and, especially, of consumers' ability to distance themselves from their overly optimistic predisposition and, more specifically, to defeat their tendency to *underestimate future risks* deriving from a particular activity, which is an integral part of *hyperbolic discounting*. This assumption, though, cannot be endorsed. Findings in behavioral economics and the wide acceptance of the theory of *bounded rationality*, once again, should not be overlooked.[35] Consumers are highly likely to underestimate the risk of harm from a possibly defective product, *even when they are aware of such risk*.[36] For this reason, they might still purchase products known (or suspected) to be occasionally defective or risky, without noticing their 'unobservable' actual purchase price, which would be higher than the 'visible' price, since the risk of suffering damage from the product should be added to the latter. Thus, it seems that market actors and the market itself

31 *Cf.* Wittman, *Economic Foundations of Law*..., p. 261 (: "... Coke, realizing this to be the case, will provide the appropriate level of care in the first place"); also Cooter/Ulen, *Law & Economics*[6], p. 3. More generally, on the so-called *reputation effect* in a certain market, *cf.*, indicatively, Hatzis, An Offer You Cannot Negotiate..., pp. 46 and 49, wherein further references.

32 See Arlen, 52 *Vand.L.Rev.* (1998), 1767 and 1774.

33 See also Quillen, 61 *S.Cal.L.R.* (1988), 1134: "If perfect competition exists and buyers have perfect information about the likelihood that a seller will breach, market forces will cause the seller to take optimal precautions"; further Shavell, 9 *J.Leg.Stud.* (1980), 6; Cooter/Ulen, *Law & Economics*[6], p. 226.

34 See also Cooter/Ulen, *Law & Economics*[6], pp. 226 and 240.

35 See extensively Chapter 1.

36 See also Calabresi, *The Costs of Accidents*..., p. 56.

cannot alone offer the necessary incentive for manufacturers to disseminate safe products.[37]

The aforesaid assumption resting on consumers' over-optimism is also reinforced by the so-called *paradox of safety*. More particularly, as products become safer over time, the market is likely to produce a *paradox of safety*, which means that "as consumers anticipate high levels of safety in general, their expectation of danger diminishes to the point that it is no longer a useful means of distinguishing between products on the market".[38] This *paradox* effectively generates an optimistic predisposition on consumers' part as regards products' quality and safety. Strong empirical evidence backs this claim; therefore the existence of the paradox of safety can hardly be disputed.

c Last but not least, moral hazard may recede if the cost of producing a safe product (e.g., a bottle) is lower than the insurance cost. In this case, and under a mandatory strict liability regime, the manufacturer will rationally opt to produce a safe product. The *precaution*[39] taken by the manufacturer would effectively function as *a substitute for insurance*.[40] However, one might well question whether it is possible to manufacture an *absolutely* safe product in all instances. In all likelihood it is not; therefore, the only realistic option for the manufacturer remains to obtain insurance against the risk of paying damages to the consumers.

In all events, it must be noted at this juncture that insofar as under a mandatory strict liability regime the manufacturer follows the insurance path, *it passes the relevant cost on to all consumers*.[41] However, the only ones who benefit from the manufacturer's liability are those very few consumers who suffer damage from a defective product; the rest of the consumers are forced to pay for the damage suffered by the few who are harmed.[42] Such

37 See Arlen, 52 *Vand.L.Rev.* (1998), 1774 and 1782; Schäfer/Ott, *Lehrbuch der ökonomischen Analyse des Zivilrechts*[4], p. 341; *cf.* also Adams, Produkthaftung..., pp. 10 ff.

38 Hylton, 88 *Notre Dame L.Rev.* (2013), 2499–2500, who goes on and rightly argues that "[a] consumer who must choose between a product that has a dangerous defect in only one out of one million units and another product that has a dangerous defect in only one out of two million units will be inclined to ignore the difference between the two products. Perceptions of risk differences at such a microscopic level effectively fade into the background. Consumer demand will no longer sort dangerous from safe products."

39 In general, on this notion and its importance in tort law, see Cooter/Ulen, *Law & Economics*[6], pp. 199 ff. *passim*.

40 So Wittman, *Economic Foundations of Law...*, p. 235: "Precaution (less-explosive bottles) is a substitute for insurance."

41 See also Wittman, *Economic Foundations of Law...*, p. 236; Adams, Produkthaftung..., p. 6; Weatherill, *EU Consumer Law...*, p. 174; *cf.*, more recently, Hylton, 88 *Notre Dame L.Rev.* (2013), *passim*, esp. 2503.

42 See also Wittman, *Economic Foundations of Law...*, p. 236: "... making Coke liable redistributes income from those who do not have bottles exploding in their faces to those who do but would not have purchased insurance if Coke were not liable. When Coke is liable, everyone pays a higher

a transfer of resources cannot be fair, especially in view of the fact that lower-income consumers, whose exposure to damaging events is low, pay the same additional price—***the insurance premium***—that the wealthy consumers pay (with regard to the same product), ***even though the latter's exposure to damaging events is, in principle, greater.*** And the degree of exposure differs because, in principle, a low-income consumer will want to conserve her money by, for example, using her car less frequently (than a wealthy consumer), thus reducing her chances of getting involved in a car accident and suffering the consequences of a defective airbag. This behavior is in evident contrast to the behavior of a wealthy person who possesses the same car. In other words, because wealthy consumers are regularly associated with a higher potential to suffer damage and thus are more frequently benefited from manufacturer's liability, it is not fair for the low-income consumers to pay the same price the former pay.[43]

Yet, under the mandatory product liability regime, the person who uses a product very rarely and is thus statistically exposed to less risk indeed pays the same risk premium as the person who uses the same product often and is thus exposed to greater risk. This amounts to a *socially unjust cross-subsidization*. Perhaps, a socially just solution would be to call for all consumers to insure themselves against the risk of suffering damage on the basis, for example, of their personal income or the frequency with which they use a product.[44] Or, in the same vein, to call for the manufacturers to differentiate the price of their products on the basis of indices such as personal income or frequency of use of the product on the part of the consumer—thus, they would adjust the insurance premium ***ad hoc***. In this way, though, manufacturers would be called upon to undertake ***a very heavy, often prohibitive administrative cost of price differentiation-personalization*** according to the specific financial-behavioral profile of each consumer; this critical parameter renders the aforementioned suggestion rather unrealistic.[45]

Notwithstanding the above, it is worth noting that the aforementioned socially unjust treatment is typically limited to ***durable consumer goods of a significant economic value*** (cars, household appliances, etc.) for the frequency of

---

price for the Coke because of the added insurance. Only those consumers who have bottles exploding in their faces benefit from this insurance..."

43 See also Schäfer/Ott, *Lehrbuch der ökonomischen Analyse des Zivilrechts*[4], pp. 336, 338; Oi, 4 *Bell J.Econ.* (1973), 27. *Cf.* further Hylton, 88 *Notre Dame L.Rev.* (2013), 2483–2484.

44 See Schäfer/Ott, *Lehrbuch der ökonomischen Analyse des Zivilrechts*[4], pp. 338, 339–340; Adams, Produkthaftung..., pp. 6 (: "... Ein Gewinn an Gerechtigkeit scheint mit einem solchen Vorgang nicht verbunden"), 7–8 (: "... Die Einführung einer Gefährdungshaftung erweist sich somit bei Konsumenten mit unterschiedlichem, ihnen besser als den Herstellern bekannten Schadensaufkommen als Danaergeschenk, mehr als Fluch denn als Segen."); Wittman, *Economic Foundations of Law...*, pp. 236, 242 ff.; Cooter/Ulen, *Law & Economics*[6], p. 252; Oi, 4 *Bell J.Econ.* (1973), 27.

45 *Cf.* also Adams, Produkthaftung..., p. 6.

use of such goods depends on personal or family income. The same, though, does not hold for goods of wide, ordinary use (food, medications, etc.); demand for such goods is *inelastic* (: they are *price insensitive* goods), and they are thus purchased and used by both high- and low-income consumer groups.

IV. Concluding remarks

Despite the downside of socially unjust cross-subsidization—which is limited, though, to durable consumer goods—the mandatory product liability regime is well justified. And this is due, first and foremost, to *information asymmetry* between manufacturers and consumers.[46] The need for such a mandatory law is also reinforced by consumers' *frequent denial of the possibility of severe risk* associated with the use of particular products. This tendency may be mainly attributed to consumers' *overoptimistic predisposition*, which makes the process of restoring a pertinent information deficit difficult, even when the critical information is readily available. In addition, the establishment of a strict liability regime elicits, beyond any doubt, a *desired steering of manufacturers' behavior*.[47] This steering has, primarily, a positive effect on *innocent bystanders*, who may also be harmed by a defective product and who are typically not in a position to avoid the damage.[48] Under a mandated-choice scheme a purchaser's choice to buy an unsafe product—in order to avoid paying an insurance premium—would possibly also cause harm to those innocent bystanders, their fate being, thus, in the hands of the *chooser*-purchaser.

46 *Cf.* also, once again, Wittman, *Economic Foundations of Law...*, chapter 25 (pp. 239 ff.).

47 In general, for the *steering of people's behavior* (in German: *Verhaltenssteuerung*) through legal provisions, *cf.* Schmolke, *JZ* (2015), 121 ff.; and Englerth, Behavioral Law and Economics..., pp. 123–124.

48 See also Schäfer/Ott, *Lehrbuch der ökonomischen Analyse des Zivilrechts*[4], pp. 339 ff.; Landes/R.Posner, 14 *J.Leg.Stud.* (1985), 550–551; *cf.* further Simitis, *Verbraucherschutz: Schlagwort oder Rechtsprinzip?*, p. 53 (who reaches the following conclusion: "Die Verteilung der Risiken auf die Gesamtheit der Konsumenten ist einer Belastung des einzelnen Verbrauchers mit den Konsequenzen eines Schadensfalles vorzuziehen.").

7 Final remarks

The philosophical foundations of freedom of choice and personal autonomy and the specific affiliation of the mandated-choice model to them

I. From Kant's and Mill's perception of personal autonomy to legal paternalism

According to the classic, oft-cited Kantian definition, "Enlightenment is man's emergence from his self-incurred immaturity." The immaturity, Kant argues, is self-inflicted not from a lack of understanding, but from the lack of courage to use one's reason, intellect, and wisdom without the guidance of another; so, the key to throwing off these chains of mental immaturity is reason, free thinking, and acting.[1] This Kantian definition is, in historical terms, the deeper ideological background of the fundamental private law principles of private autonomy and freedom of contract,[2] which, in turn, reflect the more general and comprehensive *freedom of self-determination*.[3] The philosophical background underpinning private autonomy and freedom of self-determination may also be traced to Kant's *second version of the categorical imperative*, according to which the individual must not be treated as an object or a means to an end, but as an *end in itself*—that is, as bearing an autonomous will along with full moral dignity.[4]

1 Kant, Beantwortung der Frage: Was ist Aufklärung?, pp. 53 ff., esp. 53.

2 *Cf.* also Bruns, *JZ* (2007), 386. On this fundamental pair of principles (i.e., private automomy and freedom of contract), see, indicatively, Flume, *AT des BürgR – Das Rechtsgeschäft*[4], pp. 1 ff., 12 ff., 17 ff.; Raiser, Vertragsfunktion und Vertragsfreiheit, pp. 101 ff.; Wolf/Neuner, *AT des BürgR*[10], § 1 αp. 3, § 2 no. 14, § 3 no. 7, § 5 no. 12, § 10 nos. 27 ff., 33 ff.; Schäfer/Ott, *Lehrbuch der ökonomischen Analyse des Zivilrechts*[4], pp. 393–394, 421 ff.; the same, *JZ* (1988), 220–221; Busche, *Privatautonomie und Kontrahierungszwang*, *passim*, esp. pp. 13 ff., 46 ff.; Enderlein, *Rechtspaternalismus...*, *passim*, esp. pp. 71 ff., 83 ff.; Grundmann, Privatautonomie, Vertragsfunktion..., pp. 875 ff.; Cserne, *Freedom of Contract...*, pp. 82 ff.

3 *Cf.*, indicatively, Flume, *AT des BürgR – Das Rechtsgeschäft*[4], p. 1 (: "Privatautonomie nennt man das Prinzip der Selbstgestaltung der Rechtsverhältnisse durch den einzelnen *nach seinem Willen*. Privatautonomie ist ein Teil des allgemeinen Prinzips der Selbstbestimmung des Menschen."); also Stürner, *Der Grundsatz der Verhältnismäßigkeit...*, pp. 5 ff.; Schäfer/Ott, *Lehrbuch der ökonomischen Analyse des Zivilrechts*[4], pp. 421 ff.; Riesenhuber, Privatautonomie und Diskriminierungsverbote..., pp. 20–21, 59. Further, on the so-called "Self-Determination Theory" (SDT), one of the most comprehensive psychological theories of autonomy and well-being, *cf.*, once more, Arvanitis, 47 *New Ideas in Psychology* (2017), 57 ff., Arvanitis/Kalliris, 30 *Philos. Psychol.* (2017), 763 ff., as well as fn. 88, Chapter 2, above.

4 Kant, *Grundlegung zur Metaphysik der Sitten*, esp. paras. 429 (pp. 54–55), 430, 433, 434–435. See also Wolf/Neuner, *AT des BürgR*[10], § 10 no. 3 ff.; Heun, *JZ* (2005), 853; White, 33

Aside from the above, it is probably not widely known but Kant developed a more precise stance on the very idea of *personal autonomy*. He expressed this in an essay that is not as famous as his other writings, published in 1793. In that essay he extols the *a priori* value of personal autonomy (or individual freedom). Personal autonomy, Kant argues, needs to be protected against despotic governance, which would on the basis of its own understanding of individual preferences, tastes, and ways to be happy impose on the individual the actions and choices that 'would best serve her interests and needs.' Kant's words read as follows:

> "No-one can compel me to be happy in accordance with the conception of the welfare of others, for each may seek his happiness in whatever way he sees fit, so long as he does not infringe upon the freedom of others to pursue a similar end which can be reconciled with the freedom of everyone else within a workable general law—i.e., he must accord to others the same right as he enjoys himself. A government might be established on the principle of benevolence towards the people, like that of father towards his children. Under such a paternal government (*imperium paternale*), the subjects, as immature children who cannot distinguish what is truly useful or harmful to themselves, would be obliged to behave purely passively and to rely upon the judgment of the head of state as to how they ought to be happy, and upon his kindness in willing their happiness at all. Such a government is the greatest conceivable despotism, i.e., a constitution which suspends the entire freedom of its subjects, who thenceforth have no rights whatsoever."[5]

J.Socio-Econ. (2004), 93; Wagner, Mandatory Contract Law..., p. 10; Nozick, *Anarchy, State, and Utopia*, pp. 30 ff.

5 Kant, *Political Writings*, p. 74. The quoted passage is from Kant's essay *On the Common Saying: This May be True in Theory, but does not Apply in Practice*—in German: *Über den Gemeinspruch: Das mag in der Theorie richtig sein, taugt aber nicht für die Praxis*, chapter II: Vom Verhältnis der Theorie zur Praxis im Staatsrecht (Gegen Hobbes), pp. 145–146: "Niemand kann mich zwingen, auf seine Art (wie er sich das Wohlsein anderer Menschen denkt) glücklich zu sein, sondern ein jeder darf seine Glückseligkeit auf dem Wege suchen, welcher ihm selbst gut dünkt, wenn er nur der Freiheit anderer, einem ähnlichen Zwecke nachzustreben, die mit der Freiheit von jedermann nach einem möglichen allgemeinen Gesetze zusammen bestehen kann, (d.i. diesem Rechte des andern) nicht Abbruch tut.—Eine Regierung, die auf dem Prinzip des Wohlwollens gegen das Volk als eines *Vaters* gegen seine Kinder errichtet wäre, d.i. eine *väterliche Regierung* (imperium paternale), wo also die Untertanen als unmündige Kinder, die nicht unterscheiden können, was ihnen wahrhaftig nützlich oder schädlich ist, sich bloß passiv zu verhalten genötigt sind, um, wie sie glücklich sein *sollen*, bloß von dem Urteile des Staatsoberhaupts, und, daß dieser es auch wolle, bloß von seiner Gütigkeit zu erwarten: ist der größte denkbare *Despotismus* (Verfassung, die alle Freiheit der Untertanen, die alsdann gar keine Rechte haben, aufhebt)." See also Kant, *ibidem*, pp. 155 (: "... [jedem] unbenommen bleibt, seine Glückseligkeit auf jedem Wege, welcher ihm der beste dünkt, zu suchen, wenn er nicht jener allgemeinen gesetzmäßigen Freiheit, mithin dem Rechte anderer Mituntertanen, Abbruch tut.") and 159 (: "Der Souverän will das Volk nach seinen Begriffen glücklich machen, und wird Despot; das Volk will sich den allgemeinen menschlichen Anspruch auf eigene Glückseligkeit nicht nehmen lassen, und wird Rebell."). See further G.Dworkin, Paternalism, Chapter 3; Schmolke, *Grenzen der Selbstbindung...*, pp. 1–2, 15–16.

Six decades later, in 1859, John Stuart Mill would build on this idea and develop his own position on state interventions in individual freedom: the latter *are only then justified when they seek to prevent harm to third persons.* Mill thus articulated the so-called *harm principle*[6]—which, however, may already be traced back to Democritus.[7] The harm principle survives, of course, in modern theory of law, whereby it is taken to suggest that in an open, liberal society the individual is in principle free to carry out self-regarding, that is, self-harming or self-endangering, acts, and that restrictions are imposed only on acts that have socially harmful or damage-inflicting repercussions—that is, when they harm third parties or, more broadly, society as a whole.[8] Modern liberal societies tend to embrace the fundamental assumption that insofar as an individual does not violate the rights of others she is free to strive for the realization of her own personal beliefs about good or well-being. Individuals themselves are free to decide what gives meaning to their lives, while the legal order must in principle be neutral in its treatment of individual ideals about happiness, without expressing approval or disapproval on the basis of their *intrinsic value.*[9]

6 See Mill, On Liberty, esp. chapter I, pp. 14, wherein *inter alia*: "... the only purpose for which power can be rightfully exercised over any member of a civilized community, against his will, is *to prevent harm to others.* [...] He cannot rightfully be compelled to do or forbear because it will be better for him to do so, because it will make him happier, because, in the opinion of others, to do so would be wise, or even right" (emphasis added); also chapter I, p. 17, chapter III, p. 62, chapter IV, pp. 83 ff. On Mill's approach, see, indicatively, Bix, *Jurisprudence: Theory and Context*[7], pp. 171 ff.; Archard, 40 *Philos.Q.* (1990), 453 ff.; Eidenmüller, *Effizienz als Rechtsprinzip*, pp. 329 ff., esp. 352 ff. However, a significant caveat is in order here, since according to Mill himself (On Liberty, chapter I, p. 14), "... this doctrine is meant to apply *only to human beings in the maturity of their faculties*" (emphasis added); also *ibidem*, chapter IV, pp. 83–84: "As soon as any part of a person's conduct affects prejudicially the interests of others, society has jurisdiction over it, and the question whether the general welfare will or will not be promoted by interfering with it, becomes open to discussion. But there is no room for entertaining any such question when a person's conduct affects the interests of no persons besides himself, or needs not affect them unless they like (*all the persons concerned being of full age, and the ordinary amount of understanding*)" (emphasis added). See also Trebilcock/Elliott, The Scope and Limits..., p. 48.

7 Stobaeus, *Iōannou Stobaiou Anthologion*, On Envy, 38/57.

8 See Di Fabio, Article 2 § 1 nos. 50–51, and the same, *Die Kultur der Freiheit*, *passim*, esp. pp. 79 ff. and 268 ff.; also Wiedemann/Wank, *JZ* (2013), 341. The above holds, for example, even for those who opt out of vaccines (although they can be vaccinated): they, namely, cause harm to others and thus the state is entitled to intervene. In particular, it is rightly suggested that "[t]he ongoing measle outbreaks across the United States and Europe prove definitely that our personal choices affect everybody around us" and that "people who are able to take vaccines but refuse to do so are the moral equivalent of drunk drivers"—see Siegel/Berezow, 3 *Scientific American* (2019), wherein *inter alia*: "There is no moral difference between a drunk driver and a willfully unvaccinated person. Both are selfishly, recklessly and knowingly putting the lives of everyone they encounter at risk. Their behavior endangers the health, safety and livelihood of the innocent bystanders who happen to have the misfortune of being in their path." Therefore in such a case, where we can inflict harm or infringe on the rights and liberties of those around us, state interference is justified on the basis of the aforementioned 'harm principle.' Further, once again on the more general, critical assumption that in modern societies "there can no longer be many actions which are purely self-regarding," see Bix, *Jurisprudence: Theory and Context*[7], pp. 171 ff.—for more detail on this assumption, see also Chapter 6, pp. 124 ff. above.

9 See, indicatively, R.Dworkin, Liberalism, pp. 127 ff., and Kronman, 92 *Yale L.J.* (1983), 794–795. *Cf.* also Locke, *Two Treatises of Government*, p. 306: "... the end of law is not to abolish

Therefore, at least in Western legal systems—which largely share the common tradition of the Enlightenment—private autonomy, self-determination, and self-responsibility are of utmost importance. These principles entail that the sovereign individual may herself determine her life course and future through autonomous, intentional choices (whether they be acts or omissions). In most cases the individuals themselves are in a condition to know, better than any guardian, what their needs are, what makes them happy, what adds to their well-being.[10] Especially in the field of contract law the aforementioned principles are closely connected to the equally important, though more specific, principles of freedom of contract and ***pacta sunt servanda***, as well as to the rule ***casum sentit dominus (the loss lies where it falls)***.[11] Hence, it is a matter of self-responsibility for individuals to act diligently in transactions and to make the necessary effort to ensure each time that they have carefully examined the available options and finally selected the option that best suits their needs and desires.[12]

Given all this, it is clear that, in transactions, self-responsibility of the deciding and acting individual is the rule. This means that ***in principle*** all transactors are ***the architects of their own fortune***; that is, they are responsible for their acts or omissions ***even when their decisions do not appear reasonable to an external (objective) observer***.[13]

Unquestionably, though, ***legal paternalism*** usually points in the opposite direction. It demands that the state interfere with the individual freedom. In many cases it moves the individual to act ***against her own free will***, even when the acts or omissions of an individual do not affect others, even when the will of the individual has been freely formed (at least ***prima facie***). The paternalistic intervention is primarily intended to promote ***personal well-being*** and the general welfare, on the assumption that a careful social planner knows better than we do, as individual citizens, what is in our own best interest, which course of action will serve us best, and is thus entitled to prohibit self-harming or self-endangering acts. In the words of Gerald Dworkin, paternalism is "the interference with a person's liberty of action justified by reasons referring exclusively to the welfare, good,

---

or restrain, but ***to preserve and enlarge freedom*** [...]. ...freedom is [...] a liberty to dispose, and order as he lists, his person, actions, possessions, and his whole property, within the allowance of those laws under which he is, and therein ***not to be subject to the arbitrary will of another, but freely follow his own***" (emphasis added). *Cf.* further Schiller, III ***Thalia*** (1790), p. 46 (: "Der Staat selbst ist niemals Zweck, er ist nur wichtig als eine Bedingung, unter welcher der Zweck der Menschheit erfüllt werden kann, ***und dieser Zweck der Menschheit ist kein andrer, als Ausbildung aller Kräfte des Menschen, Fortschreitung***"—emphasis added).

10 See also Wagner, Mandatory Contract Law..., p. 10; Vandenberghe, The Role of Information Deficiencies..., p. 71.

11 See also van Boom/Ogus, Introducing, Defining and Balancing..., p. 1. For the origins of the principle ***the loss lies where it falls***, see Holmes, *The Common Law*, p. 94; also Cohen/Knetsch, 30 *Osgoode Hall L.J.* (1992), 738.

12 So Vandenberghe, The Role of Information Deficiencies..., p. 71.

13 So Wiedemann/Wank, *JZ* (2013), 344 (wherein ***inter alia***: "... *Jeder ist seines Glückes Schmied*"); see also Bruns, *JZ* (2007), 390, 391; Saint-Paul, *The Tyranny of Utility...*, *passim*, esp. 8 ff., 115 ff.

happiness, needs, interests or values of the person being coerced".[14] Within the framework of legal paternalism, in certain circumstances the legislative authority seeks to trump autonomous choice on the assumption that individuals might not exercise the freedom of choice in a prudent manner, thus harming themselves.[15] Paternalism is by definition autonomy-restricting; it interferes with our decision-making process through coercion, manipulation, or the usurpation of decision-making. Its motive, though, is 'benevolent': it seeks, namely, to benefit the individual whose autonomy is restricted. Therefore, in many contexts a short-term restriction of individual autonomy is deemed necessary if it is meant to advance the long-term autonomy and well-being of a person.[16] In a nutshell, in many instances individual autonomy is supposed to be restricted in favor of individual well-being.

In fact, much of the current discussion with respect to the strained relationship between private autonomy and paternalism centers on the question of *the extent to which* the state is entitled to restrict private autonomy for the benefit of individuals themselves. Which degree of state interference with individual choices and self-harming or self-endangering acts might be justifiable? And under what conditions may it be practically effectuated?[17] It is on this critical point that views mostly differ and intense theoretical debates re-impose themselves and flare up. However, for the purposes of the present discussion there is no reason to pursue this question.[18]

14 G.Dworkin, 56 *The Monist* (1972), 65; also the same, Paternalism, wherein, *inter alia*, in the preamble one can find the following (more) comprehensive definition: "Paternalism is the interference of a state or an individual with another person, *against their will*, and defended or motivated by a claim *that the person interfered with will be better off or protected from harm*. [...] At the theoretical level it raises questions of how persons should be treated when they are *less than fully rational*" (emphasis added); R.Dworkin, *Justice for Hedgehogs*, pp. 361–362: "Paternalism means imposing a decision on someone *supposedly for his own good but contrary to his own sense of what that is*" (emphasis added); Blackburn (ed.), *Oxford Dictionary of Philosophy*², p. 269; see also Kronman, 92 *Yale L.J.* (1983), 763 ff.; Cserne, *Freedom of Contract...*, pp. 11 ff.; Schmolke, *Grenzen der Selbstbindung...*, pp. 9 ff.; Enderlein, *Rechtspaternalismus...*, *passim*; van Aaken, Begrenzte Rationalität..., pp. 109 ff., esp. 122 ff., 133 ff.; the same, Judge the Nudge..., pp. 87 ff.; Schwabe, *JZ* (1998), 66 ff.; Eidenmüller, *Effizienz als Rechtsprinzip*³, pp. 358 ff.; the same, *JZ* (2011), 814 ff.; Wagner, Mandatory Contract Law..., pp. 9, 19–20; van Boom/Ogus, Introducing, Defining and Balancing..., pp. 1 ff.; Kalliris, *Autonomy, Well-Being and the Law*, *passim*, esp. pp. 121 ff., 143 ff.

15 See Ogus, 30 *Legal Studies* (2010), 61, 62, and Deakin, Contracts and Capabilities..., p. 127.

16 See G.Dworkin, Paternalism, Chapter 3.

17 See, once again, G.Dworkin, Paternalism; also Waddams, Autonomy and Paternalism..., p. 145.

18 For a strong defense of personal autonomy against any 'protective' state intervention, especially from the viewpoint of criminal law theory, see Feinberg, *Harm to Others*, pp. 47 ff., esp. 54, 55; also the same, *Harm to Self*, esp. pp. 4 ff. *Cf.* further Nozick, *Anarchy, State, and Utopia*, *passim*, esp. pp. ix, 26–27, 58–59, 272–273; Hillgruber, *Der Schutz des Menschen vor sich selbst*; Möller, *Paternalismus und Persönlichkeitsrecht*; Fischer, *Die Zulässigkeit aufgedrängten staatlichen Schutzes vor Selbstschädigung*. For a rebuttal of Nozick's views, from the viewpoint of *analytical Marxism*, see Cohen, *Self-ownership, Freedom and Equality*, pp. 19 ff., 144 ff.

II. Mild paternalism and the visible hand of the mandated-choice model

Now, in the context of a modern and efficient private law, *mild paternalism*, in the specific form of the *mandated-choice model* (in German: *zwingendes Optionsmodell*) discussed above, seems in many cases to be more compatible with private autonomy than other paternalistic interference alternatives, which we have already examined. In fact, mandated choice appears to reinforce freedom of choice, which is indispensable in a free society[19] and is nowadays recognized not merely for its *instrumental value* but also for its *intrinsic value*, for its character as an *end in itself*, as a basic element of human dignity.[20]

Specifically, the mandated-choice model constitutes an innovative, plain-vanilla regulatory means of intervention in the field of private law. It sets aside the traditional way we approach transactional freedom of choice and the classic forms of regulatory intervention. Namely, from a traditional point of view, the legislative authorities, when confronting an issue that could be regulated—or that they are called upon to regulate—are basically faced with three regulatory options: (a) *allow complete freedom of active choosing*: under this option the legislative authority refrains from any kind of intervention; individuals are free to autonomously decide how they may best act and protect themselves in the transactions. This option allows the market to self-regulate—it is the option of *libertarian non-paternalism*. (b) *Introduce default rules (ius dispositivum)*: with this model the legislative authority seeks to gently steer the conduct of the transacting parties, who retain, though, the right to opt out of the default regulatory scheme—the option of *libertarian-mild paternalism*. (c) *Introduce mandatory rules (ius cogens)*: in this case, the legislative authority intervenes openly and imposes a compulsory regulatory scheme that deprives the parties of any freedom to depart from it and the therein contained evaluation—the option of *coercive-hard paternalism*; this option also embraces *disclosure mandates*, mainly aiming to protect consumers. To these three layers of regulatory intervention *we now add a fourth one*: the mandated-choice model. This model may figuratively be located either between the second and third option (i.e., between default and mandatory rules), or between the first and second option (i.e., between freedom of active

19 See here, indicatively, van Aaken, Begrenzte Rationalität..., pp. 125, 135, 138.

20 See Sunstein, 127 *Harv.L.R. Forum* (2014), 210 ff., esp. 211; the same, *Choosing Not to Choose...*, pp. 130, 192, 194; the same, *Forcing People To Choose Is Paternalistic*, 13. Nonetheless, there is also a different approach, according to which securing freedom of *autonomous choice* alone is not sufficient to preserve personal autonomy in its entirety, since freedom of choice is qualified as *shallow autonomy*, refers to secondary matters, decisions or choices of everyday life (e.g., to eat or drink something, to go for a walk) and is juxtaposed to *deep autonomy*—that is, *self-rule* of the individual over her life or *self-authorship*; in other words, freedom of choice has only an instrumental value, for a real intrinsic value may only be ascribed to deep autonomy, of which freedom of choice is one out of many specific instruments—Sneddon, 33 *CRITICA* (2001), 105 ff., and fn. 89, Chapter 2, above.

choosing and default rules). The precise placement on the spectrum is, at the end of the day, a matter of the observer's viewpoint, not a matter of essence.[21]

Yet this novel regulatory option may be better understood as an option that *transcends* the other three traditional options, and at the same time synthesizes elements of all of them.[22] The main concern is still the protection of individual freedom of choice and private autonomy, which under a regime of mandated choice are better preserved than under a traditional default or mandatory law regime. The mandated-choice system does not have the coercive character of mandatory law, where no opting out is possible. It also performs a crucial informative function each time an individual faces transactional risks or options that are statutorily given to her; it allows her to reach a conscious and rational decision in various transactional or other choice situations. This assistance is deemed to be *behaviorally justified*, mainly on the basis of solid findings of behavioral economics. It goes without saying, though, that the mandated-choice scheme is not a panacea, a one-size-fits-all solution; thus it is not applicable to every decision-making situation.

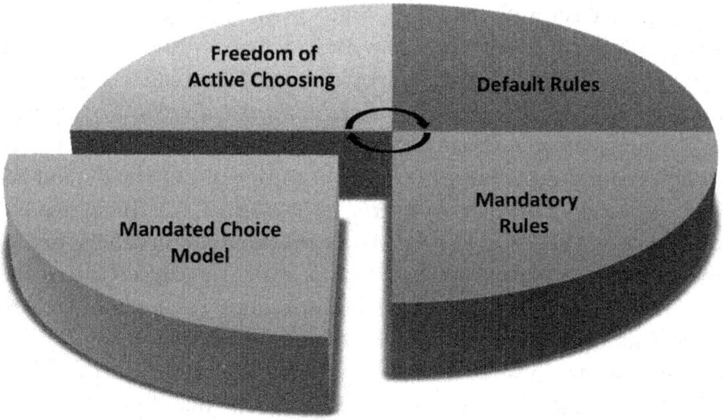

On their part, Sunstein and Thaler, the proponents of libertarian paternalism and of an extensive use of default rules, have initially expressed some reasonable reservations about the mandated-choice model (which they call *required active choosing* or *system of forced choices*).[23] On the one hand, they hold the view

21 We could also add a fifth regulatory tool: namely, the option of *'personalized' default or mandatory rules*, which has recently gained ground in legal scholarship—in detail, see Chapter 2, pp. 71 ff., and Chapter 4, pp. 107 ff. above.

22 *Cf.* further Bechtold, *Die Grenzen zwingenden Vertragsrechts...*, pp. 121 ff., 256 ff., 264–265, 331–332.

23 See Sunstein/Thaler, 70 *U.Chi.L.Rev.* (2003), 1173: "Required active choosing *honors freedom of choice in a certain respect*; but it does not appeal to those who would choose not to choose, and indeed it will seem irritating and perhaps unacceptably coercive by their lights" (emphasis added—see also *ibidem*, pp. 1188–1189); Thaler/Sunstein/Balz, Choice Architecture, p. 431; Thaler/Sunstein, *Nudge...*, pp. 86–87, 109–110, 147, 180, 243; Sunstein, 162 *U.Penn.L.R.* (2013),

that people may often perceive, or feel, that mandated choice is an unnecessary nuisance or burden that demands from them a non-negligible effort cost; on the other hand, they generally support the opt-out system of default rules on the basis of the consequentialist, non-prescriptive standpoint that mandated-choice systems may elicit higher rates of participation in statutory regulation than the *opt-in* systems, *but in any case lower participation than the opt-out (default) systems elicit.*[24]

Nevertheless, Sunstein and Thaler have also conceded that in some contexts the mandated-choice scheme may be the most appropriate and efficient way to deal with a decision-making situation. This may be the case especially when the individual is faced with 'closed questions.' These call for simple yes-or-no decisions, where the effort costs (i.e., mainly time) required for choice-making are innocuous, such as in the case of organ donation.[25] The same further holds in cases where the policymaker has doubts about the efficiency of the opt-out system; in the event of such doubt, the policymaker must prefer the mandated-choice system.[26]

In all cases, Sunstein and Thaler rightly identify and highlight a distinctive, very positive feature of the mandated-choice system[27]: within this system, namely, people feel that their freedom of choice is being respected more than within the opt-out system. *This is actually true and not a mere feeling or impression devoid of substance.* When people are asked to make a choice, they choose the position they expressly agree with. In other words, under the mandated-choice scheme, taking a passive stance does not mean anything, does not allow any inference as regards the individual's will; and what is more important, by being compelled to make an explicit choice the individual cannot become the object of exploitation or manipulation on the part of a clever social planner. *In a nutshell, the mandated-choice system reaches us with a visible hand.* Therefore, it appears to be immune to criticism for manipulating or violating personal autonomy or dignity, unlike some default rules that operate *behind people's back or fly below their radar.*

At the same time, the mandated-choice system is appropriate for eliminating, or at least attenuating, some systematic or persistent behavioral fallacies

39 ff.; the same, *Choosing Not to Choose...*, pp. 87 ff., 114 ff.; the same, *Nudging and Choice Architecture...*, p. 19. Lichtenberg, Paternalism, Manipulation, Freedom, and the Good, p. 496.

24 Sunstein/Thaler, 70 *U.Chi.L.Rev.* (2003), 1194–1195, and *Nudge...*, pp. 86–87, 110, 243; Thaler/Sunstein/Balz, Choice Architecture, p. 431.

25 See Thaler/Sunstein/Balz, Choice Architecture, p. 431, wherein *inter alia*: "A good example where mandated choice has considerable appeal is organ donation. [...] An effective compromise is mandated choice. [...] We believe that required choice, which is favored by many who like freedom, is sometimes the best way to go. [...] ... required choosing is generally more appropriate for simple yes-or-no decisions than for more complex choices"; Lichtenberg, Paternalism, Manipulation, Freedom, and the Good, p. 496 (wherein *inter alia*: "What seems certain is that mandated choice is *more* neutral than opt-in or opt-out default rules. [...] when choices are not binary, yes-no decisions, mandated choice might not even be feasible"); Thaler/Sunstein, *Nudge...*, pp. 86–87, 109–110, 147, 180, 243; Sunstein, *Nudging and Choice Architecture...*, p. 19.

26 Sunstein/Thaler, 70 *U.Chi.L.Rev.* (2003), 1194–1195.

27 See Thaler/Sunstein, *Nudge...*, p. 180, and Thaler/Sunstein/Balz, Choice Architecture..., p. 431—see also fn. 25 above with respect to organ donation.

and mental errors in concrete transactional situations and life decisions. Even in these cases, however, a specific, well-founded justification for the introduction of the mandated-choice scheme is needed.[28]

Indeed, an intervention by means of a mandated choice is intended to defeat, or at least limit, some systematic biases or rationality deficits of individuals, which, in turn, lead to irrational and inefficient choices. Whether such an intervention is acceptable, though, depends mainly on the following criteria (see in detail Chapter 2, pp. 61 ff. above): (a) *the severity of the behavioral bias* that the social planner (mostly the legislator) seeks to address. Practically, this means that the concern of the planner must lie only with severe behavioral biases. The existence and severity of each bias *must be adequately evidenced and substantiated, not just hypothetically assumed* (evidence-based intervention is required). (b) *The intensity of the particular means of paternalistic interference with private autonomy*, which should be *as mild as possible.* Typically, the mandated-choice scheme is milder than mandatory rules that forbid or exclude choices. (c) *The easy, and cheap, process of making the mandated choice*, which implies that the chooser should not get involved in an effort-draining process (see, once again, the issue of organ donation and the attempt to design an efficient mandated-choice scheme, esp. Chapter 3 above). (d) *The transparency of the regulatory intervention*, which therefore must not develop its force in a covert way or deceive the individuals it is intended to protect about their available options, especially by means of a misleading framing of the decision-making situation. And (e) *the possibility of causing severe negative externalities to third parties* who are not the individuals meant to be protected by the paternalistic intervention; if there is such a possibility then the intervention is not acceptable.

If the above criteria are not violated, the regulatory intervention, by means of a mandated choice, is in principle justified. These criteria specify, in essence, the commands of the fundamental *principle of proportionality*, which requires careful balancing on the part of the social planner each time she considers whether to enact a nudging intervention.

III. "*Be Homer's works your study and delight*"[29]: when mild paternalism meets Odysseus

Finally, I would add this postscript, to make the whole scheme crystal clear. The simple, overarching regulatory mechanism I advocate in these pages, as well as the philosophical background that supports it, finds an excellent practical

28 Recently, Sunstein (*Forcing People to Choose Is Paternalistic*, 1 ff.) expressed his general criticism of the idea of forcing people to choose within a system that favors active choosing, arguing that this idea actually reflects a kind of "nonlibertarian paternalism." However, this criticism does not seem to directly affect the mandated-choice model analyzed hereinabove, which may be used in some instances *instead of a default rule or mandatory law*; in my understanding, this specific regulatory option still appears to be legitimate, also in Sunstein's view.

29 Alexander Pope, *An Essay on Criticism* (1709).

illustration in a parable that has been discussed in German theory but actually goes back to Mill and his stance in favor of a type of mild paternalism[30]: A head-over-heels-in-love and brave Odysseus is ready to cross a dangerously dilapidated suspension bridge. The bridge could collapse at any time, but his beloved Penelope is on the other side. He must reach her. Suddenly, mild paternalism comes up behind him, taps him gently on the shoulder and draws his attention to the grave danger he is about to confront. This simple warning does not restrict Odysseus's freedom of choice; to the contrary, he remains in charge of the situation, and it is up to him to decide whether to take the risk. Whether (or not) to engage in a self-endangering or self-harming act remains a matter to be sovereignly decided by the individual actor himself. Odysseus is just the addressee of a benevolent, chiefly *informational, nudging*—a prompting to act in the direction of enhanced self-protection. Nonetheless, he decides to take the risk. Love is to him a higher, overriding value, for which he is ready to risk his life.

Such informational interference sits comfortably in the liberal tradition of Kant and Mill, which we would do well to follow. Specifically, Kant would be supportive and would not force Odysseus to take a different course of action. For, as already illustrated above, according to the great philosopher, *no one can be compelled to follow an 'ideal,' 'objective' notion of happiness against her own free will; instead, every person is free to seek happiness in the way that seems best to her, as long as she does not violate the freedom of others to strive toward a similar end*—or, in modern terms, as long as her actions do not produce *negative externalities* that affect third persons or society as a whole.[31] If, instead, we allowed *hard-coercive paternalism* to take action here and order the arrest or enchaining of Odysseus, then his personal autonomy and the Kantian axiom would suffer a severe, irreparable blow.[32] The only acceptable exception in this context would be the case where there is no time to restore Odysseus's information deficit and warn him that the bridge is not safe and that he is putting his life in grave danger. If the potential harm to Odysseus is imminent and there is no time to warn him, we may legitimately use force, seize him, and turn him back. Even Mill would not object to this, given the special circumstances of the impatient lover's situation.[33] Besides, in the same way we would all instinctively react if we were

30 See Mill, On Liberty, chapter V, pp. 106–107; Kirste, *JZ* (2011), 807 ff. *passim*; van Aaken, Begrenzte Rationalität..., pp. 113 ff. *passim*; G.Dworkin, Paternalism, Chapter 2.

31 *Cf.* also BVerfGE 58, 208, 225: "... unter der Herrschaft des Grundgesetzes [ist] in der Regel jedermann frei, Hilfe zurückzuweisen, sofern dadurch nicht Rechtsgüter anderer oder der Allgemeinheit in Mitleidenschaft gezogen werden."

32 See also G.Dworkin, Paternalism, Chapter 2.

33 Mill, On Liberty, chapter V, pp. 106–107: "... it is a proper office of public authority to guard against accidents. If either a public officer or any one else saw a person attempting to cross a bridge which had been ascertained to be unsafe, *and there were no time to warn him of his danger*, they might seize him and turn him back, without any real infringement of his liberty; *for liberty consists in doing what one desires, and he does not desire to fall into the river.* Nevertheless, when there is not a certainty, but only a danger of mischief, *no one but the person himself can judge of the sufficiency of the motive which may prompt him to incur the risk*: in this case, therefore (unless

standing at a crosswalk and saw the pedestrian next to us start crossing the road directly in the path of an oncoming car: namely, we would not hesitate a minute to grab his hand and pull him to safety.[34]

The latter exceptional case excepted, *respect for freedom of choice and for personal autonomy remains the rule.* Following the path of mild paternalism and, especially, of a mandated-choice system, those fundamental values are in principle preserved. In the original tale of Odysseus, the advice offered by Circe to him about how to resist the bewitching song of the Sirens and sail past them is a form of mild paternalism. Odysseus then resorts to a form of *rational precommitment* by having his men tie him to the mast so he cannot alter the course of the ship and steer toward the Sirens; at the same time, he orders his men to cover their own ears to prevent themselves from hearing the song of the Sirens.[35] As is evident, Circe does not tie herself Odysseus up, but simply provides him with the information that will allow him and his crew to sail safely past the Sirens. *The final decision to follow Circe's advice is Odysseus's alone.* In my opinion, the same somehow holds for the consumer under the mandated-choice model: she is, namely, each time informed of the dangers she faces; it is up to her to weigh the pros and cons, and decide whether the enhanced protection is worth the money.

he is a child, or delirious, or in some state of excitement or absorption incompatible with the full use of the reflecting faculty), he ought, I conceive, *to be only warned of the danger*; not forcibly prevented from exposing himself to it" (emphasis added).

34 See also Englerth, Vom Wert des Rauchens..., p. 238.

35 On this significant issue of *self-precommitment* and the very common reference in literature to the myth of Odysseus, see initially Elster, *Ulysses and the Sirens...*, *passim*, esp. pp. 36 ff., and Strotz, 23 *Rev.Econ.Stud.* (1955–1956), 165 ff., esp. 173 ff. See also Thaler/Sunstein, *Nudge...*, pp. 41–42 and 44 ff., who, *inter alia*, offer the following vivid description (p. 42): "Self-control problems can be illuminated by thinking about an individual as containing two semiautonomous selves, a far-sighted 'Planner' and a myopic 'Doer'. [...] The Planner is trying to promote your long-term welfare but must cope with the feelings, mischief, and strong will of the Doer, who is exposed to the temptations that come with arousal"; Thaler, 1 *J.Econ.Behav.Organ.* (1980), 52 and 54 ff.; the same, *Misbehaving...*, pp. 99 ff.; the same, 125 *J.Polit.Econ.* (2017), 1800–1801; the same, 108 *Am.Econ.Rev.* (2018), 1267–1268; Tversky/Kahneman, 211 *Science* (1981), 457–458; G.Dworkin, 56 *The Monist* (1972), 77 ff.; Schelling, 60 *The Public Interest* (1980), 94 ff.; the same, 74 *Am.Econ.Rev.* (1984), 1 ff.; Korobkin/Ulen, 88 *Cal.L.R.* (2000), 1123–1124; White, 33 *J.Socio-Econ.* (2004), 97–98; Heiner, 73 *Am.Econ.Rev.* (1983), 573–574; Bar-Gill, 98 *Nw.U.L.R.* (2004), 1375; Blackburn (ed.), *Oxford Dictionary of Philosophy*², p. 372; Englerth, Vom Wert des Rauchens..., pp. 252–253. A modern form of self-precommitment offers nowadays the website called "stickK" (www.stickk.com/), which precisely helps people eliminate the gap between having a goal and achieving a goal, by proposing them to sign a "Commitment Contract": this contract is, namely, "a binding agreement you sign with yourself to ensure that you follow through with your intentions—and it does this by utilizing the psychological power of loss aversion and accountability to drive behavior change"; by asking their users to sign such Commitment Contracts, "stickK helps users define their goal (whatever it may be), acknowledge what it'll take to accomplish it, and leverage the power of putting money on the line to turn that goal into a reality" (www.stickk.com/tour).

Bibliography

van Aaken, Anne: Begrenzte Rationalität und Paternalismusgefahr: Das Prinzip des schonendsten Paternalismus, in: Anderheiden/Bürkli/Heinig/Kirste/Seelmann (eds.), *Paternalismus und Recht: In memoriam Angela Augustin (1968–2004)*, 2006, p. 109 [referenced as: van Aaken, Begrenzte Rationalität…].

van Aaken, Anne: Das deliberative Element juristischer Verfahren als Instrument zur Überwindung nachteiliger Verhaltensanomalien—Ein Plädoyer für die Einbeziehung diskursiver Elemente in die Verhaltensökonomik des Rechts, in: Engel/Englerth/Lüdemann/Spiecker-Döhmann (eds.), *Recht und Verhalten—Beiträge zu Behavioral Law and Economics*, 2007, p. 189 [referenced as: van Aaken, Das deliberative Element juristischer Verfahren…].

van Aaken, Anne: Judge the Nudge: In Search of the Legal Limits of Paternalistic Nudging in the EU, in: Alemanno/Sibony (eds.), *Nudge and the Law—A European Perspective*, 2017, p. 83 [referenced as: van Aaken, Judge the Nudge…].

Adams, Michael: Produkthaftung—Wohltat oder Plage—Eine ökonomische Analyse, 31 *BB* (1987), 1. [referenced as: Adams, Produkthaftung…].

Adams, Michael: Ökonomische Begründung des AGB-Gesetzes, *BB* (1989), 781.

Adomeit, Klaus: Die gestörte Vertragsparität—ein Trugbild, *NJW* (1994), 2467.

Adomeit, Klaus: Das Günstigkeitsprinzip—jetzt auch beim Kaufvertrag, oder: der Kfz-Mechaniker von Canaris, *JZ* (2003), 1053.

Akerlof, George: The Market for 'Lemons': Quality Uncertainty and the Market Mechanism, 84 *Quart.J.Econ.* (1970), 488. DOI: 10.2307/1879431

Akerlof, George/Dickens, William: The Economic Consequences of Cognitive Dissonance, 72 *Am.Econ.Rev.* (1982), 307.

Akerlof, George: Procrastination and Obedience, 81 *Am.Econ.Rev.* (1991), 1.

Akerlof, George/Shiller, Robert: *Phishing for Phools: The Economics of Manipulation and Deception*, 2015 [referenced as: Akerlof/Shiller, *Phishing for Phools…*]. DOI: 10.1515/9781400873265

Alchian, Armen: Uncertainty, Evolution, and Economic Theory, 58 *J.Polit.Econ.* (1950), 211. DOI: 10.1086/256940

Alemanno, Alberto/Sibony, Anne-Lise (eds.): *Nudge and the Law—A European Perspective*, 2017.

Alemanno, Alberto/Sibony, Anne-Lise: Epilogue: The Legitimacy and Practicability of EU Behavioural Policy-Making, in: Alemanno/Sibony (eds.), *Nudge and the Law—A European Perspective*, 2017, p. 325 [referenced as: Alemanno/Sibony, Epilogue…]. DOI: 10.5040/9781474203463.ch-014

Alexy, Robert: Constitutional Rights, Balancing, and Rationality, 16 *Ratio Juris* (2003), 131. DOI: 10.1111/1467-9337.00228

Altmann, Steffen/Falk, Armin/Marklein, Felix: Eingeschränkt rationales Verhalten: Evidenz und Implikationen, in: Fleischer/Zimmer (eds.), *Beitrag der Verhaltensökonomie (Behavioral Economics) zum Handels- und Wirtschaftsrecht*, 2011, p. 63 [referenced as: Altmann/Falk/Marklein, Eingeschränkt rationales Verhalten...].

Angner, Erik: *A Course in Behavioral Economics*, 2nd ed. 2016. DOI: 10.1111/1475-4932.12162

Archard, David: Freedom Not to Be Free: The Case of the Slavery Contract in J. S. Mill's on Liberty, 40(160) *Philos.Q.* (1990), 453. DOI: 10.2307/2220110

Ariely, Dan: *Predictably Irrational: The Hidden Forces That Shape Our Decisions*, 2010 [referenced as: Ariely, *Predictably Irrational*...].

Arlen, Jennifer: Comment: The Future of Behavioral Economic Analysis of Law, 52 *Vand.L.Rev.* (1998), 1765.

Arrow, Kenneth: Risk Perception in Psychology and Economics, 20 *Econ.Inq.* (1982). DOI: 10.1111/j.1465-7295.1982.tb01138.x

Arvanitis, Alexios: Autonomy and morality: A Self-Determination Theory Discussion of Ethics, 47 *New Ideas in Psychology* (2017), 57. DOI: 10.1016/j.newideapsych.2017.06.001

Arvanitis, Alexios/Kalliris, Konstantinos: A Self-Determination Theory Account of Selfauthorship: Implications for Law and Public Policy, 30 *Philos.Psychol.* (2017), 763. DOI: 10.1080/09515089.2017.1307333

Arvanitis, Alexios/Kalliris, Konstantinos/Kaminiotis, Konstantinos: Are defaults supportive of autonomy? An examination of nudges under the lens of Self-Determination Theory, *Soc.Sci.J.* (2019). DOI: doi.org/10.1016/j.soscij.2019.08.003

Arvanitis, Alexios/Karampatzos, Antonios: Negotiation and Aristotle's Rhetoric: Truth over Interests?, 24 *Philos.Psychol.* (2011), 845. DOI: 10.1080/09515089.2011.569910

Arvanitis, Alexios/Karampatzos, Antonios: Negotiation as an Intersubjective Process: Creating and Validating Claim-Rights, 26 *Philos.Psychol.* (2013), 89. DOI: 10.1080/09515089.2011.633692

Ayres, Ian: Menus Matter, 73 *U.Chi.L.Rev.* (2006), 3.

Ayres, Ian/Gertner, Robert: Filling Gaps in Incomplete Contracts: An Economic Theory of Default Rules, 99 *Yale L.J.* (1989), 87. DOI: 10.2307/796722

Ayres, Ian/Gertner, Robert: Strategic Contractual Inefficiency and the Optimal Choice of Legal Rules, 101 *Yale L.J.* (1992), 729. DOI: 10.2307/796873

Bachmann, Gregor: *Private Ordnung—Grundlagen ziviler Regelsetzung*, 2006 [referenced as: Bachmann, *Private Ordnung*...].

Bachmann, Gregor: Optionsmodelle im Privatrecht, *JZ* (2008), 11. DOI: 10.1628/002268808783355591

von Bar, Christian/Clive, Eric/Schulte-Nölke, Hans, et al. (eds.): *Principles, Definitions and Model Rules of European Private Law—Draft Common Frame of Reference (DCFR)*, vol. I, 2009 [referenced as: von Bar/Clive/Schulte-Nölke et al., *Principles, Definitions and Model Rules*...].

Barberis, Nicholas: Richard Thaler and the Rise of Behavioral Economics, 120 *Scand.J.Econ.* (2018), 661. DOI: 10.1111/sjoe.12313

Bar-Gill, Oren: Seduction by Plastic, 98 *Nw.U.L.R.* (2004), 1373.

Bar-Gill, Oren: The Behavioral Economics of Consumer Contracts, 92 *Minn.L.Rev.* (2008), 749.

Bar-Gill, Oren: *Seduction by Contract: Law, Economics, and Psychology in Consumer Markets*, 2012 [referenced as: Bar-Gill, *Seduction by Contract*...]. DOI: 10.1093/acprof:oso/9780199663361.003.0002

Bar-Gill, Oren: Consumer Transactions, in: Zamir/Teichman (eds.), *The Oxford Handbook of Behavioral Economics and the Law*, 2014, p. 465. DOI: 10.1093/oxfordhb/9780199945474.013.0018

Bar-Gill, Oren/Ben-Shahar, Omri: Regulatory Techniques in Consumer Protection: A Critique of European Consumer Contract Law, 50 *CML Rev.* (2013), 109. DOI: 10.2139/ssrn.2061148

Barr, Michael/Mullainathan, Sendhil/Shafir, Eldar: Behaviorally Informed Regulation, in: Shafir (ed.), *Behavioral Foundations of Public Policy*, 2012, p. 440. DOI: 10.2307/j.ctv550cbm.32

van Bavel, René/Herrmann, Benedikt/Esposito, Gabriele/Proestakis, Antonios (European Commission, Joint Research Centre, Institute for Prospective Technological Studies): *Applying Behavioural Sciences to EU Policy-making, JRC Scientific and Policy Reports (EUR 26033 EN)*, 2013, www.capire.org/capireinforma/scaffale/30092013_jrc_scientific_policy_report_en.pdf [referenced as: *Applying Behavioral Sciences to EU Policy-making (EU 26033 EN)*].

Becher, Shmuel: Behavioral Science and Consumer Standard Form Contracts, 68 *La.L.Rev.* (2007), 117.

Bechtold, Stefan: *Die Grenzen zwingenden Vertragsrechts—Ein rechtsökonomischer Beitrag zu einer Rechtsetzungslehre des Privatrechts*, 2010 [referenced as: Bechtold, *Die Grenzen zwingenden Vertragsrechts*...]. DOI: 10.1628/978-3-16-151226-1

Becker, Gary: *The Economic Approach to Human Behavior*, 1976 (reprinted in 1990). DOI: 10.7208/chicago/9780226217062.001.0001

Becker, Gary: A Theory of Competition among Pressure Groups for Political Influence, 98 *Quart.J.Econ.* (1983), 371. DOI: 10.2307/1886017

Becker, Gary: The Economic Way of Looking at Behavior, 110 *J.Polit.Econ.* (1993), 385. DOI: 10.1086/261880

Becker, Gary/Elias, Julio: Cash for Kidneys: The Case for a Market for Organs, in: *The Wall Street Journal*, 18.01.2014, www.wsj.com/articles/cash-for-kidneys-the-case-for-a-market-for-organs-1389992925 [referenced as: Becker/Elias, Cash for Kidneys...].

Benartzi, Shlomo/Beshears, John/Milkman, Katherine/Sunstein, Cass/Thaler, Richard/Shankar, Maya/Tucker-Ray, Will/Congdon, William/Galing, Steven: Should Governments Invest More in Nudging?, 28 *Psychol.Sci.* (2017), 1041. DOI: 10.2139/ssrn.2982109

Benartzi, Shlomo/Peleg, Ehud/Thaler, Richard: *Choice Architecture and Retirement Saving Plans* (11.07.2007). DOI: 10.2139/ssrn.999420

Benhabib, Jess/Bisin, Alberto/Schotter, Andrew: Present-Bias, Quasi-Hyperbolic Discounting, and Fixed Costs, 69 *GEB* (2010), 205. DOI: 10.1016/j.geb.2009.11.003

Ben-Shahar, Omri: Regulation Through Boilerplate: An Apologia, 112 *Mich.L Rev.* (2014), 883. DOI: 10.2139/ssrn.2255161

Ben-Shahar, Omri/Logue, Kyle: Outsourcing Regulation: How Insurance Reduces Moral Hazard, 111 *Mich. L. Rev.* (2012), 197. DOI: 10.2139/ssrn.2038105

Ben-Shahar, Omri/Porat, Ariel: Personalizing Negligence Law, 91 *N.Y.U.L.Rev.* (2016), 627.

Ben-Shahar, Omri/Porat, Ariel: Personalizing Mandatory Rules in Contract Law, 86 *U.Chi.L.Rev.* (2019), 255.

Ben-Shahar, Omri/Posner, Eric: The Right to Withdraw in Contract Law, 40 *J.Leg.Stud.* (2011), 115. DOI: 10.2139/ssrn.1569753

Ben-Shahar, Omri/Pottow, John: On the Stickiness of Default Rules, 33 *Fla.St.U.L.Rev.* (2006), 651.

Ben-Shahar, Omri/Schneider, Carl: The Failure of Mandated Discourse, 159 *U.Pa.L.Rev.* (2011), 647.

Ben-Shahar, Omri/Schneider, Carl: *More Than You Wanted to Know: The Failure of Mandated Disclosure*, 2014.

Bentham, Jeremy: *An Introduction to the Principles of Morals and Legislation*, 1789 (reprinted in 2007).

Berger, Sebastien: Singapore's Compulsory Organ Transplants, in: *The Telegraph*, 02.03.2007, www.telegraph.co.uk/news/1544379/Singapores-compulsory-organ-transplants.html

van den Bergh, Roger: Wer schützt die europäischen Verbraucher vor dem Brüsseler Verbraucherschutz?—Zu den möglichen adversen Effekten der europäischen Richtlinien zum Schutze des Verbrauchers, in: Ott/Schäfer (eds.), *Effiziente Verhaltenssteuerung und Kooperation im Zivilrecht*, 1996, p. 77 [referenced as: Van den Bergh, Wer schützt die europäischen Verbraucher…].

Bix, Brian: *Jurisprudence: Theory and Context*, 7th ed. 2015.

Blackburn, Simon (ed.): *Oxford Dictionary of Philosophy*, 2nd ed. 2008. DOI: 10.1093/acref/9780199541430.001.0001

Blumenthal-Barby, Jennifer: Choice Architecture: A Mechanism for Improving Decisions While Preserving Liberty?, in: Coons/Weber (eds.), *Paternalism—Theory and practice*, 2013, p. 178 [referenced as: Blumenthal-Barby, Choice Architecture…]. DOI: 10.1017/cbo9781139179003.010

van Boom, Willem H./Ogus, Anthony: Introducing, Defining and Balancing 'Autonomy versus Paternalism', in: Ogus/van Boom, *Juxtaposing Autonomy and Paternalism in Private Law*, 2011, p. 1 [referenced as: van Boom/Ogus, Introducing, Defining and Balancing…]. DOI: 10.553/ELR221026712010003001001

Borges, Georg/Irlenbusch, Bernd: Fairness Crowded Out by Law: An Experimental Study on Withdrawal Rights, 163 *J.Inst.Theor.Econ.* (2007), 84. DOI: 10.1628/093245607780181937

Brest, Paul: Quis custodiet ipsos custodes? Debiasing the Policy Makers Themselves, in: Shafir (ed.), *The Behavioral Foundations of Public Policy*, 2013, p. 481 [referenced as: Quis custodiet ipsos custodies?…]. DOI: 10.2307/j.ctv550cbm.35

Bruns, Alexander: Die Vertragsfreiheit und ihre Grenzen in Europa und den USA—Movement from Contract to Status?, *JZ* (2007), 385. DOI: 10.1628/00226880 7782017778

Bubb, Ryan/Pildes, Richard: How Behavioral Economics Trims its Sails and Why, 127 *Harv.L.R.* (2014), 1594.

Buchanan, James: The Domain of Constitutional Economics, 1 *Const.Polit.Econ.* (1990), 1. DOI: 10.1007/bf02393031

Buchanan, James: *Public Choice: The Origins and Development of a Research Program*, 2003.

Buchanan, James: Afraid to Be Free: Dependency as Desideratum, 124 *Public Choice* (2005), 19. DOI: 10.1007/s11127-005-4743-2

Buchanan, James/Tullock, Gordon: *The Calculus of Consent*, 1962. DOI: 10.3998/mpub.7687

Buckley, Francis: *Fair Governance*, 2009. DOI: 10.1093/acprof:oso/9780195341263.001.0001

Busche, Jan: *Privatautonomie und Kontrahierungszwang*, 1999.

Calabresi, Guido: *The Costs of Accidents: A Legal and Economic Analysis*, 1970 [referenced as: Calabresi, *The Costs of Accidents...*].

Calliess, Gralf-Peter: Coherence and Consistency in European Consumer Contract Law: A Progress Report, 4 *Ger. Law J.* (2003), 337. DOI: 10.1017/s2071832200016011

Camerer, Colin: Prospect Theory in the Wild: Evidence from the Field, in: Kahneman/ Tversky (eds.), *Choices, Values, and Frames*, 2009, p. 288 [referenced as: Camerer, Prospect Theory in the Wild...]. DOI: 10.1017/cbo9780511803475.017

Camerer, Colin/Issacharoff, Samuel/Loewenstein, George/O'Donoghue, Ted/Rabin, Matthew: Regulation for Conservatives: Behavioral Economics and the Case for "Asymmetric Paternalism", 151 *U.Penn.L.R.* (2003), 1211. DOI: 10.2307/3312889

Campbell, John: Restoring Rational Choice: The Challenge of Consumer Financial Regulation, 106 *Am.Econ.Rev.* (2016), 1. DOI: 10.1257/aer.p20161127

Canaris, Claus-Wilhelm: Wandlungen des Schuldvertragsrechts—Tendenzen zu seiner „Materialisierung", 200 *AcP* (2000), 273. DOI: 10.1515/9783110274035.2141

Cartwright, Edward: *Behavioral Economics*, 2nd ed. 2014. DOI: 10.4324/9781315817897

Casey, Anthony/Niblett, Anthony: The Death of Rules and Standards, 92 *Ind.L.J.* (2017), 1401. DOI: doi.org/10.2139/ssrn.2693826

Charny, David: Hypothetical Bargains: The Normative Structure of Contract Interpretation, 89 *Mich.L.Rev.* (1991), 1815. DOI: 10.2307/1289391

Cherednychenko, Olha: Freedom of Contract in the Post-Crisis Era: Quo Vadis?, 10 *ERCL* (2014), 390. DOI: 10.1515/ercl-2014-0016

Chouhan, Pradeep/Draper, Heather: Modified Mandated Choice for Organ Procurement, 29 *J.Med. Ethics* (2003), 157. DOI: 10.1136/jme.29.3.157

Christman, John: Autonomy in moral and political philosophy, in: *Stanford Encyclopedia of Philosophy* (21.03.2015), https://plato.stanford.edu/entries/autonomy-moral/.

Coase, Ronald: The Problem of Social Cost, 3 *J.L.&Econ.* (1960), 1. DOI: 10.1086/ 466560

Cohen, David/Knetsch, Jack: Judicial Choice and Disparities between Measures of Economic Value, 30 *Osgoode Hall L.J.* (1992), 737.

Cohen, Gerald Allan: *Self-Ownership, Freedom and Equality*, 1995. DOI: 10.1017/ CBO9780511521270

Commission Staff Working Paper, *Consumer Empowerment in the EU*, SEC(2011) 469, https://ec.europa.eu/info/sites/info/files/consumer_empowerment_eu_2011_en.pdf.

Congdon, William: Psychology and Economic Policy, in: Shafir (ed.), *The Behavioral Foundations of Public Policy*, 2013, p. 465.

Conlisk, John: Why Bounded Rationality?, 34 *JEL* (1996), 669.

Conly, Sarah: *Against Autonomy: Justifying Coercive Paternalism*, 2013 [referenced as: Conly, *Against Autonomy...*].

Cooter, Robert/Eisenberg, Melvin: Damages for Breach of Contract, 73 *Cal.L.R.* (1985), 1432. DOI: 10.15779/Z382B1X

Cooter, Robert/Ulen, Thomas: *Law and Economics*, 6th ed. 2011.

Cserne, Péter: *Freedom of Contract and Paternalism, Prospects and Limits of an Economic Approach*, 2012 [referenced as: Cserne, *Freedom of Contract...*]. DOI: 10.1057/9781137000323

Cserne, Péter: Making Sense of Nudge-Scepticism: Three Challenges to EU Law's Learning from Behavioural Sciences, in: Alemanno/Sibony (eds.), *Nudge and the Law—A European Perspective*, 2017, p. 279 [referenced as: Cserne, Making Sense of Nudge-Scepticism...]. DOI: 10.5040/9781474203463.ch-012

Cziupka, Johannes: *Dispositives Vertragsrecht—Funktionsweise und Qualitätsmerkmale gesetzlicher Regelungsmuster*, 2010 [referenced as: Cziupka, *Dispositives Vertragsrecht...*].

Dahlman, Carl: The Problem of Externality, 22 *J.L.&Econ.* (1979), 141. DOI: 10.1086/466936

Darby, Michael R./Karni, Edi: Free Competition and the Optimal Amount of Fraud, 16 *J.L.&Econ.* (1973), 67. DOI: 10.1086/466756

Dasgupta, Partha/Maskin, Eric: Uncertainty and Hyperbolic Discounting, 95 *Am.Econ. Rev.* (2005), 1290. DOI: 10.1257/0002828054825637

Dawnay, Emma/Shah, Hetan: *Behavioural Economics: Seven Principles for Policy-Makers*, 2005, www.i-r-e.org/fiche-analyse-97_en.html [referenced as: Dawnay/Shah, *Behavioural Economics...*].

De Palma, André/Myers, Gordon/Papageorgiou, Yorgos: Rational Choice under an Imperfect Ability to Choose, 84 *Am.Econ.Rev.* (1994), 419.

Deakin, Simon: Contracts and Capabilities: An Evolutionary Perspective on the Autonomy-Paternalism Debate, in: Ogus/van Boom (eds.), *Juxtaposing Autonomy and Paternalism in Private Law*, 2011, p. 127 [referenced as: Deakin, Contracts and Capabilities...]. DOI: 10.553/ELR221026712010003002003

DellaVigna, Stefano: Psychology and Economics: Evidence from the Field, 47 *JEL* (2009), 315. DOI: 10.1257/jel.47.2.315

Dhami, Sanjit: *The Foundations of Behavioral Economic Analysis*, 2016.

Di Fabio, Udo: Article 2, in: Maunz/Dürig (eds.), *Grundgesetz*, 39th ed. 2001.

Di Fabio, Udo: *Die Kultur der Freiheit*, 2005.

Diamond, Peter/Vartiainen, Hannu (eds.): *Behavioral Economics and Its Applications*, 2007.

Dinner, Isaac/Johnson, Eric J./Goldstein, Daniel G./Liu, Kaiya: Partitioning Default Effects: Why People Choose Not to Choose, 17 *J.Exp.Psychol.-Appl.* (2011), 332. DOI: 10.1037/a0024354

Dolan, Paul: Influencing the Financial Behaviour of Individuals: The Mindspace Way, in: Oliver (ed.), *Behavioural Public Policy*, 2013, p. 191 [referenced as: Dolan, Influencing the financial behaviour of individuals...]. DOI: 10.1017/cbo9781107337190.009

Dorf, Michael: *Irrationality, Baselines, and Government "Intervention"* (12.10.2017), www.dorfonlaw.org/2017/10/irrationality-baselines-and-government.html

Drexl, Josef: *Die wirtschaftliche Selbstbestimmung des Verbrauchers—Eine Studie zum Privat- und Wirtschaftsrecht unter Berücksichtigung gemeinschaftsrechtlicher Bezüge*, 1998 [referenced as: Drexl, *Die wirtschaftliche Selbstbestimmung...*].

Dubner, Steven (prod.): Here's Why All Your Projects Are Always Late—and What to Do about It, in: *Freakonomics*, ep. 323 Rebroadcast, http://freakonomics.com/podcast/project-management-rebroadcast/

Dworkin, Gerald: Paternalism, 56 *The Monist* (1972), 64 [= in: Sartorius (ed.), *Paternalism*, 1983, p. 19]. DOI: 10.5840/monist197256119

Dworkin, Gerald: Is More Choice Better than Less?, 7 *Midwest Stud.Philos.* (1982), 47. DOI: 10.1111/j.1475-4975.1982.tb00083.x

Dworkin, Gerald: Paternalism: Some Second Thoughts, in: Sartorius (ed.), *Paternalism*, 1983, p. 105.

Dworkin, Gerald: Paternalism, in: Zalta (ed.), *The Stanford Encyclopedia of Philosophy*, 2014, http://plato.stanford.edu/archives/sum2014/entries/paternalism/ [referenced as: G.Dworkin, Paternalism].

Dworkin, Gerald: *The Theory and Practice of Autonomy*, 1988. DOI: 10.1017/CBO9780511625206

Dworkin, Ronald: Liberalism, in: *Public and Private Morality*, 1978, p. 113. DOI: 10.1017/cbo9780511625329.007

Dworkin, Ronald: *Justice for Hedgehogs*, 2011. DOI: 10.2307/j.ctvjf9vkt

Edwards, Ward: The Theory of Decision Making, 51 *Psychol.Bull.* (1954), 380. DOI: 10.1037/h0053870

Eidenmüller, Horst: Rechtswissenschaft als Realwissenschaft, *JZ* (1999), 53.

Eidenmüller, Horst: Der homo oeconomicus und das Schuldrecht: Herausforderungen durch Behavioral Law and Economics, *JZ* (2005), 216.

Eidenmüller, Horst: *Effizienz als Rechtsprinzip, Möglichkeiten und Grenzen der ökonomischen Analyse des Rechts*, 3rd ed. 2005 [referenced as: Eidenmüller, *Effizienz als Rechtsprinzip*[3]].

Eidenmüller, Horst: Schlusswort, *JZ* (2005), 670.

Eidenmüller, Horst: Forschungsperspektiven im Unternehmensrecht, *JZ* (2007), 487. DOI: 10.1628/002268807781140952

Eidenmüller, Horst: Die Rechtfertigung von Widerrufsrechten, 210 *AcP* (2010), 94. DOI: 10.1628/000389910790787282

Eidenmüller, Horst: Liberaler Paternalismus, *JZ* (2011), 814. DOI: 10.1628/002268811797238466

Eidenmüller, Horst: Why Withdrawal Rights?, 7 *ERCL* (2011), 1. DOI: 10.1515/ercl.2011.1

Eidenmüller, Horst: Widerrufsrechte, in: Eidenmüller/Faust/Grigoleit/Jansen/Wagner/Zimmermann (eds.), *Revision des Verbraucher-acquis*, 2011, p. 109 [= 210 *AcP* (2010), 67] [referenced as: Eidenmüller, Widerrufsrechte].

Eidenmüller, Horst: Was kann an einer Option falsch sein?—Ein optionales gemeinsames europäisches Kaufrecht als Regulierungsinstrument, in: Bruns/Kern/Münch/Piekenbrock/Stadler/Tsikrikas, Festschrift für Rolf Stürner zum 70. Geburtstag, vol. 2, 2013, p. 1025 [referenced as: Eidenmüller, in: *FS Stürner*].

Eidenmüller, Horst/Engel, Martin: *Against False Settlement: Designing Efficient Consumer Rights Enforcement Systems in Europe* (07.07.2013) [referenced as: Eidenmüller/Engel, *Against False Settlement*...]. DOI: 10.2139/ssrn.2290654

Eidenmüller, Horst/Jansen, Nils/Kieninger Eva-Maria/Wagner, Gerhard/Zimmermann, Reinhard: Der Vorschlag für eine Verordnung über ein Gemeinsames Europäisches Kaufrecht, *JZ* (2012), 269.

Elster, Jon: *Ulysses and the Sirens—Studies in Rationality and Irrationality*, 1988 [referenced as: Elster, *Ulysses and the Sirens*...].

Emens, Elizabeth: Changing Name Changing: Framing Rules and the Future of Marital Names, 74 *U.Chi.L.Rev.* (2007), 761.

Emons, Winand: Warranties, Moral Hazard, and the Lemons Problem, 46 *J.Econ.Theory* (1988), 16. DOI: 10.1016/0022-0531(88)90147-0

Enderlein, Wolfgang: *Rechtspaternalismus und Vertragsrecht*, 1996 [referenced as: Enderlein, *Rechtspaternalismus*...].

Engel, Christoph: Zivilrecht als Fortsetzung des Wirtschaftsrechts mit anderen Mitteln, *JZ* (1995), 213.

Engel, Christoph: Rationale Rechtspolitik und ihre Grenzen, *JZ* (2005), 581.

Engel, Christoph/Englerth, Markus/Lüdemann, Jörn/Spiecker-Döhmann, Indra (eds.): *Recht und Verhalten—Beiträge zu Behavioral Law and Economics*, 2007.

Engel, Martin/Stark, Johanna: Buttons, Boxes, Ticks, and Trust: On the Narrow Limits of Consumer Choice, in: Mathis (ed.), *European Perspectives on Behavioural Law and Economics*, 2015, p. 107 [referenced as: Engel/Stark: Buttons, Boxes, Ticks, and Trust...]. DOI: 10.1007/978-3-319-11635-8_6

Englerth, Markus: Behavioral Law and Economics—eine kritische Einführung, in: Engel/Englerth/Lüdemann /Spiecker-Döhmann (eds.), *Recht und Verhalten—Beiträge zu Behavioral Law and Economics*, 2007, p. 60 [referenced as: Englerth, Behavioral Law and Economics…].

Englerth, Markus: Vom Wert des Rauchens und der Rückkehr der Idioten—Paternalismus als Antwort auf beschränkte Rationalität, in: Engel/Englerth/Lüdemann/Spiecker-Döhmann (eds.), *Recht und Verhalten—Beiträge zu Behavioral Law and Economics*, 2007, p. 231 [referenced as: Englerth, Vom Wert des Rauchens…].

Englerth, Markus: Verhaltensökonomie—eine Einführung mit strafrechtlichen Beispielen, in: Towfigh/Petersen (eds.), *Ökonomische Methoden im Recht– Eine Einführung für Juristen*, 2010, p. 165 [referenced as: Englerth, Verhaltensökonomie…].

Epstein, Richard: Products Liability as an Insurance Market, 14 *J.Leg.Stud.* (1985), 645. DOI: 10.1086/467791

Epstein, Richard: The Neoclassical Economics of Consumer Contracts, 92 *Minn.L.Rev.* (2008), 803.

Ernst, Stefan: Widerruf von Anwaltsverträgen im Fernabsatz?, *NJW* (2014), 817.

Etzioni, Amitai: Social Norms: Internalization, Persuasion, and History, 34 *Law Soc.Rev.* (2000), 157. DOI: 10.2307/3115119

European Commission: *Proposal for a Regulation of the European Parliament and of the Council on a Consumer Programme 2014–2020*, COM(2011) 707.

European Commission: *Proposal for a Directive of the European Parliament and of the Council Amending Council Directive 93/13/EEC of 5 April 1993, Directive 98/6/EC of the European Parliament and of the Council, Directive 2005/29/EC of the European Parliament and of the Council and Directive 2011/83/EU of the European Parliament and of the Council as Regards Better Enforcement and Modernisation of EU Consumer Protection Rules*, COM/2018/0185 final-2018/090 (COD).

European Securities and Markets Authorities: *Questions and Answers on MiFID and MiFIR Investor Protection and Intermediaries Topics*, Report ESMA35-43-349, 2019, www.esma.europa.eu/sites/default/files/library/esma35-43-349_mifid_ii_qas_on_investor_protection_topics.pdf.

Falk, Armin/Kosfeld, Michael: The Hidden Costs of Control, 96 *Am.Econ.Rev.* (2006), 1611. DOI: 10.1257/aer.96.5.1611

Fallon, Richard: Should We All Be Welfare Economists?, 101 *Mich.L.Rev.* (2003), 979. DOI: 10.2307/1290513

Farber, Daniel: Toward a New Legal Realism, 68 *U.Chi.L.Rev.* (2001), 279. DOI: 10.2307/1600448

Faure, Michael/ Luth, Hanneke: Behavioural Economics in Unfair Contract Terms-Cautions and Considerations, 34 *J.Consum.Policy* (2011), 337. DOI: 10.1007/s10603-011-9162-9

Feinberg, Joel: *The Moral Limits of the Criminal Law: Harm to Others*, 1986 [referenced as: Feinberg, *Harm to Others*]. DOI: 10.1093/0195046641.001.0001

Feinberg, Joel: *The Moral Limits of the Criminal Law: Harm to Self*, 1986 [referenced as: Feinberg, *Harm to Self*]. DOI: 10.1093/0195059239.001.0001

Feldman, Yuval/Lobel, Orly: Behavioural Trade-Offs: Beyond the Land of Nudges Spans the World of Law and Psychology, in: Alemanno/Sibony (eds.), *Nudge and the Law—A European Perspective*, 2017, p. 301 [referenced as: Feldman/Lobel, Behavioural Trade-Offs…]. DOI: 10.5040/9781474203463.ch-013

Feldman, Yuval/Schurr, Amos/Teichman, Doron: Anchoring Legal Standards, 13 *J.Emp.Leg.Stud.* (2016), 298. DOI: 10.1111/jels.12116

Ferrari, Franco: Zum vertraglichen Ausschluss des UN-Kaufrechts, 4 *ZEuP* (2002), 737.

Festinger, Leon: *A Theory of Cognitive Dissonance*, 1957.

Finnis, John: *Natural Law and Natural Rights*, 1980 (also 2nd ed. 2011).

Fischer, Kai: *Die Zulässigkeit aufgedrängten staatlichen Schutzes vor Selbstschädigung*, 1997.

Fischer, Nikolaj: Das verbraucherschützende Widerrufsrecht und die Schuldrechtsreform, *DB* (2002), 253.

Fischhoff, Baruch/Slovic, Paul/Lichtenstein, Sarah: Knowing with Certainty: The Appropriateness of Extreme Confidence, 3 *J.Exp.Psychol.-Hum.Percept.Perform.* (1977), 552. DOI: 10.1037//0096-1523.3.4.552

Fleischer, Holger: *Informationsasymmetrie im Vertragsrecht*, 2001 [referenced as: Fleischer, *Informationsasymmetrie...*].

Fleischer, Holger: Behavioral Law and Economics im Gesellschafts- und Kapitalmarktsrecht—ein Werkstattbericht, in: Fuchs/Schwintowski/Zimmer (eds.), *Wirtschafts- und Privatrecht im Spannungsfeld von Privatautonomie, Wettbewerb und Regulierung. Festschrift für Ulrich Immenga zum 70. Geburtstag*, 2004, p. 575 [referenced as: Fleisher, in: *FS Immenga*].

Fleischer, Holger: Gesetz und Vertrag als alternative Problemlösungsmodelle im Gesellschaftsrecht, 168 *ZHR* (2004), 673.

Fleischer, Holger: Die Richtlinie über Märkte für Finanzinstrumente und das Finanzmarkt-Richtlinie-Umsetzungsgesetz—Entstehung, Grundkonzeption, Regelungsschwerpunkte, 10 *BKR* (2006), 389.

Fleischer, Holger: The Optional Instrument in European Private Law ("28th Regime"), 76 *RabelsZ* (2012), 235.

Fleischer, Holger/Schmolke, Klaus/Zimmer, Daniel: Verhaltensökonomik als Forschungsinstrument für das Wirtschaftsrecht, in: Fleischer/Zimmer (eds.), *Beitrag der Verhaltensökonomie (Behavioral Economics) zum Handels- und Wirtschaftsrecht*, 2011, p. 9 [referenced as: Fleischer/Schmolke/Zimmer, Verhaltensökonomik als Forschungsinstrument...].

Fleischer, Holger/Zimmer, Daniel (eds.): *Beitrag der Verhaltensökonomie (Behavioral Economics) zum Handels- und Wirtschaftsrecht*, 2011.

Flume, Werner: *Allgemeiner Teil des Bürgerlichen Rechts—Das Rechtsgeschäft*, vol. 2, 4th ed. 1992 [referenced as: Flume, *AT des BürgR—Das Rechtsgeschäft*^{4}].

Förster, Christian: Die Umsetzung der Verbraucherrechterichtlinie in §§ 312 ff. BGB—Eine systematische Darstellung für Studium und Examen—Teil I, *JA* (2014), 721.

Förster, Christian: Die Umsetzung der Verbraucherrechterichtlinie in §§ 312 ff. BGB—Eine systematische Darstellung für Studium und Examen—Teil II, *JA* (2014), 801.

Foka-Kavalieraki, Yulie/Hatzis, Aristides: Rational After All: Toward an Improved Theory of Rationality in Economics, 12 *Rev.phil.écon.* (2011), 3. DOI: 10.3917/rpec.121.0003

Formaini, Robert: James M. Buchanan – The Creation of Public Choice Theory, 8 *Econ. Insights* (2003), 1.

Frederick, Shane/Loewenstein, George/O'Donoghue, Ted: Time Discounting and Time Preference: A Critical Review, 40 *JEL* (2002), 351. DOI: 10.1257/002205102320161311

Frey, Bruno/Gallus, Jana: Beneficial and Exploitative Nudges, in: Mathis/Tor (eds.), *Nudging—Possibilities, Limitations and Applications in European Law and Economics*, 2016, p. 11. DOI: 10.1007/978-3-319-29562-6_2

Friedman, Milton/Savage, Leonard: The Utility Analysis of Choices Involving Risk, 56 *J.Polit.Econ.* (1948), 279. DOI: 10.1086/256692

Fuchs, Andreas: Zur Disponibilität gesetzlicher Widerrufsrechte im Privatrecht, 196 *AcP* (1996), 313.

Gächter, Simon: Human Prosocial Motivation and the Maintenance of Social Order, in: Zamir/Teichman (eds.), *The Oxford Handbook of Behavioral Economics and the Law*, 2014, p. 28 [referenced as: Gächter, Human Prosocial Motivation…]. DOI: 10.1093/oxfordhb/9780199945474.013.0002

Gardner, John: Liberals and Unlawful Discrimination, 9 *Oxf.J.Leg.Stud.* (1989), 1. DOI: 10.1093/ojls/9.1.1

Georgakopoulos, Nicholas: *Principles and Methods of Law and Economics, Basic Tools for Normative Reasoning*, 2005 [referenced as: Georgakopoulos, *Principles and Methods of Law and Economics…*]. DOI: 10.1017/CBO9780511511455

Gernhuber, Joachim: Verbraucherschutz durch Rechte zum Widerruf von Willenserklärungen—Eine rechtsdogmatische Studie, *WM* (1998), 1797.

Ghisellini, Fabrizio/Chang, Beryl: *Behavioral Economics—Moving Forward*, 2018 [referenced as: Ghisellini/Chang, *Behavioral Economics…*].

Ginsburg, Tom/Masur, Jonathan/McAdams, Richard: Libertarian Paternalism, Path Dependence, and Temporary Law, 81 *U.Chi.L.Rev.* (2014), 291. www.researchgate.net/publication/265013226_Libertarian_Paternalism_Path_Dependence_and_Temporary_Law

Glaeser, Edward: Paternalism and Psychology, 29 *Regulation* (2006), 32.

Goldberg, John/Zipurski, Benjamin: The Easy Case for Products Liability Law: A Response to Professors Polinsky and Shavell, 123 *Harv.L.Rev.* (2010), 1919. DOI: 10.2307/20788299

Goodwin, Tom: Why We Should Reject 'Nudge', 32 *Politics* (2012), 85. DOI: 10.1111/j.1467-9256.2012.01430.x

Graddy, Kathryn/Loewenstein, Lara/Mei, Jianping/Moses, Mike/Pownall, Rachel: Anchoring or Loss Aversion? Empirical Evidence from Art Auctions, in: *Working Paper Series 2014/73*, 1, www.semanticscholar.org/paper/Anchoring-or-Loss-Aversion-Empirical-Evidence-from-Graddy-Loewenstein/145e171e86f01cc3bbf56cc3acf9391fa7d23c62 [referenced as: Graddy/Loewenstein/Mei/Moses/Pownall, Anchoring or Loss Aversion?…].

Graffi, Leonardo: Overview of Recent Italian Court Decisions on the CISG, 4 *Eur.L.For.* (2000–2001), 240.

Gray, John: *The Soul of the Marionette: A Short Inquiry into Human Freedom*, 2015 [referenced as: Gray, *The Soul of the Marionette…*].

Grigoleit, Hans: Besondere Vertriebsformen im BGB, *NJW* (2002), 1151.

Grigoleit, Hans Christoph: Zwingendes Recht (Regelungsstrukturen), in: Basedow/Hopt/Zimmermann (eds.), *Handwörterbuch der Europäischen Privatrechts*, vol. II, 2009, p. 1822 [referenced as: Grigoleit, Zwingendes Recht…].

Grundmann, Stefan: Die EU-Verbraucherrechte-Richtlinie, Optimierung, Alternative oder Sackgasse?, *JZ* (2013), 53. DOI: 10.1628/002268813x13560134286957

Grundmann, Stefan: Privatautonomie, Vertragsfunktion und „Richtigkeitschance": Thema, Theorien und Kontext, Diskussion, in: Grundmann/Micklitz/Renner (eds.), *Privatrechtstheorie*, vol. I, 2015, p. 875 [referenced as: Grundmann, Privatautonomie, Vertragsfunktion…].

Grundmann, Stefan: Wissen und Information: Thema, Theorien und Kontext, Diskussion, in: Grundmann/Micklitz/Renner (eds.), *Privatrechtstheorie*, vol. I, 2015, p. 968 [referenced as: Grundmann, Wissen und Information…].

Grundmann, Stefan/Möslein, Florian/Riesenhuber, Karl: Contract Governance: Dimensions in Law and Interdisciplinary Research, in: Grundmann/Möslein/Riesenhuber (eds.), *Contract Governance: Dimensions in Law and Interdisciplinary Research*, 2015, p. 3 [referenced as: Grundmann/Möslein/Riesenhuber, Contract Governance...]. DOI: 10.1093/acprof:oso/9780198723202.003.0001

Güth, Werner: On Ultimatum Bargaining Experiments—A Personal Review, 3 *J.Econ. Behav.Organ.* (1995), 329. DOI: 10.1016/0167-2681(94)00071-l

Güth, Werner/Schmittberger, Rolf/Schwarze, Bernd: An Experimental Analysis of Ultimatum Bargaining, 3 *J.Econ.Behav.Organ.* (1982), 367. DOI: 10.1016/0167-2681(82)90011-7

Güth, Werner/von Wangenheim, Georg: Fairness Crowded Out by Law: An Experimental Study on Withdrawal Rights, Comment, 163 *J.Inst.Theor.Econ.* (2007), 102. DOI: 10.1628/093245607780181982

Hacker, Philipp: The Behavioral Divide—A Critique of the Differential Implementation of Behavioral Law and Economics in the US and the EU, 11 *ERCL* (2015), 299. DOI: 10.1515/ercl-2015-0020

Hacker, Philipp: Nudge 2.0: The Future of Behavioural Analysis of Law in Europe and Beyond—A Review of 'Nudge and the Law. A European Perspective', edited by Alberto Alemanno and Anne-Lise Sibony, 2 *ERPL* (2016), 297. DOI: 10.2139/ssrn.2670772

Hacker, Philipp: Personalizing EU Private Law: From Disclosures to Nudges and Mandates, 3 *ERPL* (2017), 651.

Harari, Yuval Noah: *Homo Deus—A Brief History of Tomorrow*, 2016 [referenced as: Harari, *Homo Deus*...].

Hatzis, Aristides: An Offer You Cannot Negotiate: Some Thoughts on the Economics of Standard Form Consumer Contracts, in: Collins (ed.), *Standard Contract Terms in Europe: A Basis for and a Challenge to European Contract Law*, 2008, pp. 43–56 [referenced as: Hatzis, An Offer You Cannot Negotiate...].

Haupt, Stefan: An Economic Analysis of Consumer Protection in Contract Law, 4 *Ger. Law J.* (2003), 1137. DOI: 10.1017/s2071832200012013

Hausman, Daniel/Welch, Brynn: Debate: To Nudge or Not to Nudge, 18 *J.Polit.Philos.* (2010), 123. DOI: 10.1111/j.1467-9760.2009.00351.x

Hayek, Friedrich: The Use of Knowledge in Society, 35 *Am.Econ.Rev.* (1945), 519. DOI: 10.1142/9789812701275_0025

Hayek, Friedrich: *The Constitution of Liberty: The Definitive Edition*, 1960 [referenced as: Hayek, *The Constitution of Liberty*...]. DOI: 10.7208/chicago/9780226320519.001.0001

Heck, Philipp: Wie ist den Missbräuchen, welche sich bei den Abzahlungsgeschäften herausgestellt haben, entgegen zu wirken?, in: *Verhandlungen des 21. Deutschen Juristentages*, vol. II, 1891, p. 131 [referenced as: Heck, Wie ist den Missbräuchen...].

Heiner, Ronald: The Origin of Predictable Behavior, 73 *Am.Econ.Rev.* (1983), 560.

Hellgardt, Alexander: Privatautonome Modifikation der Regeln zu Abschluss, Zustandekommen und Wirksamkeit des Vertrags, Möglichkeit und Grenzen der Abdingbarkeit der §§ 116 ff., 145 ff. BGB innerhalb von Geschäftsbeziehungen und auf privaten Marktplätzen, 213 *AcP* (2013), 760. DOI: 10.1628/000389914x13920224936258

Herresthal, Carsten: Consumer Law in the DCFR, in: Wagner (ed.), *The Common Frame of Reference: A View from Law & Economics*, 2009, p. 163. DOI: 10.1515/9783866538665.163

Hesse, Konrad: *Grundzüge des Verfassungsrechts der Bundesrepublik Deutschland*, 20th ed. 1995 [referenced as: Hesse, *Grundzüge des Verfassungsrechts*[20]].

Heun, Werner: Die grundgesetzliche Autonomie des Einzelnen im Lichte der Neurowissenschaften, *JZ* (2005), 853.

Heyers, Johannes: Unbergrenzter Widerruf von Lebensversicherungsverträgen?—Richtlinienkonforme Derogation der Ausschlussfrist für das Widerspruchsrecht, *NJW* (2014), 2619.

Hill, Peter: Public Choice: A Review, 34 *Faith & Economics* (1999), 1.

Hillgruber, Christian: *Der Schutz des Menschen vor sich selbst*, 1992.

Hinnosaar, Marit/Hinnosaar, Toomas: *Authority Bias* (31.08.2012), www.academia.edu/2108445/Authority_Bias

Hochma, Tomer: *Endowment Effect: A Guide to the Emotional Trigger That Influences Your Customers' Minds* (10.05.2017), http://humanhow.com/en/endowment-effect/ [referenced as: Hochma, *Endowment Effect...*].

Hoffman, David: From Promise to Form: How Contracting Online Changes Consumers, 91 *N.Y.U.L.Rev.* (2016), 1595. DOI: 10.2139/ssrn.2724661

Hoffman, Elizabeth/Spitzer, Matthew: Willingness to Pay vs. Willingness to Accept: Legal and Economic Implications, 71 *Wash.U.L.Q.* (1993), 59.

Holmes, Oliver Wendell: *The Common Law*, 1881.

Howells, Geraint/Wilhelmsson, Thomas: *EC Consumer Law*, 1997. DOI: 10.4324/9781315257105

Huber, Ulrich: Modellregeln für ein Europäisches Kaufrecht, 4 *ZEuP* 2008, 708.

Husak, Douglas: Paternalism and Autonomy, 10 *Phil.&Pub.Aff.* (1981), 27.

Huxley, Aldous: *Brave New World*, 1932.

Hylton, Keith: The Law and Economics of Products Liability, 88 *Notre Dame L.Rev.* (2013), 2457. DOI: 10.2139/ssrn.2117245

Issacharoff, Samuel: Contracting for Employment: The Limited Return of the Common Law, 74 *Tex.L.Rev.* (1996), 1783.

Issacharoff, Samuel: Can There Be a Behavioral Law and Economics?, 51 *Vand.L.Rev.* (1998), 1729.

Jensen, Michael/Meckling, William: Theory of the Firm: Managerial Behavior, Agency Costs and Ownership Structure, 3 *JFE* (1976), 305. DOI: 10.1016/0304-405x(76)90026-x

Johnson, Eric/Goldstein, Daniel: Do Defaults Save Lives?, 302 *Science* (2003), 1338. DOI: 10.1126/science.1091721

Johnson, Eric/Goldstein, Daniel: Defaults and Donation Decisions, 78 *Transplantation* (2004), 1713. DOI: 10.1097/01.tp.0000149788.10382.b2

Johnson, Eric/Goldstein, Daniel: Decisions by Default, in: Shafir (ed.), *The Behavioral Foundations of Public Policy*, 2013, p. 417. DOI: 10.2307/j.ctv550cbm.30

Jolls, Christine: Behavioral Economic Analysis of Redistributive Legal Rules, in: Sunstein (ed.), *Behavioral Law & Economics*, 2007, p. 288 [referenced as: Jolls, Behavioral Economic Analysis...]. DOI: 10.1017/cbo9781139175197.012

Jolls, Christine: Behavioral Law and Economics, in: Diamond/Vartiainen (eds.), *Behavioral Economics and Its Applications*, 2007, p. 115. DOI: 10.2307/j.ctvd58v0s.8

Jolls, Christine/Sunstein, Cass/Thaler, Richard: A Behavioral Approach to Law and Economics, 50 *Stan.L.Rev.* (1998), 1471. DOI: 10.2307/1229304

Jud, Brigitta/Wendehorst, Christiane: Proposal for a Directive on Consumer Rights—An Academic Position Paper, 6 *GPR* (2009), 68. DOI: 10.1515/gpr.2009.6.2.68

Julius, Patrick: *Prospect Theory: Why We Buy Insurance and Lottery Tickets* (08.02.2015), https://patrickjuli.us/2015/02/08/prospect-theory-why-we-buy-insurance-and-lottery-tickets/ [referenced as: Julius, *Prospect Theory...*].

Kähler, Lorenz: *Begriff und Rechtfertigung abdingbaren Rechts*, 2012 [referenced as: Kähler, *Begriff und Rechtfertigung…*]. DOI: 10.1628/978-3-16-152096-9

Kahneman, Daniel: A Perspective on Judgment and Choice—Mapping Bounded Rationality, 58 *Am.Psychol.* (2003), 697. DOI: 10.1037/0003-066x.58.9.697

Kahneman, Daniel: Maps of Bounded Rationality: Psychology for Behavioral Economics, 93 *Am.Econ.Rev.* (2003), 1449. DOI: 10.1257/000282803322655392

Kahneman, Daniel: New Challenges to the Rationality Assumption, in: Kahneman/Tversky (eds.), *Choices, Values, and Frames*, 2009. DOI: 10.1017/cbo9780511803475.043

Kahneman, Daniel: *Thinking, Fast and Slow*, 2013.

Kahneman, Daniel/Knetsch, Jack/Thaler, Richard: Fairness and the Assumptions of Economics, 59 *J.Bus.* (1986), 285. DOI: 10.1086/296367

Kahneman, Daniel/Knetsch, Jack/Thaler, Richard: Experimental Tests of the Endowment Effect and the Coase Theorem, 98 *J.Polit.Econ.* (1990), 1325 [= in: Sunstein (ed.), *Behavioral Law & Economics*, 2007, p. 211] [referenced as: Kahneman/Knetsch/Thaler, Experimental Tests of the Endowment Effect…]. DOI: 10.1086/261737 [= DOI: 10.1017/cbo9781139175197.009]

Kahneman, Daniel/Knetsch, Jack/Thaler, Richard: Anomalies: The Endowment Effect, Loss Aversion, and Status Quo Bias, 5 *J.Econ.Persp.* (1991), 193 [= Kahneman/Tversky (eds.), *Choices, Values, and Frames*, 2009, p. 159]. DOI: 10.1257/jep.5.1.193 [= DOI: 10.1017/cbo9780511803475.009]

Kahneman, Daniel/Tversky, Amos: Prospect Theory: An Analysis of Decision under Risk, 47 *Econometrica* (1979), 263 [= in: Kahneman/Tversky (eds.), *Choices, Values, and Frames*, 2009, p. 17]. DOI: 10.2307/1914185 [= DOI: 10.1017/cbo9780511803475.003]

Kahneman, Daniel/Tversky, Amos: Choices, Values, and Frames, in: Kahneman/Tversky (eds.), *Choices, Values, and Frames*, 2009, p. 1. DOI: 10.1017/cbo9780511803475.002

Kalliris, Konstantinos: *Autonomy, Well-Being and the Law* (University of Oxford Doctoral Thesis) 2011, available at https://ethos.bl.uk/OrderDetails.do?uin=uk.bl.ethos.560465).

Kalliris, Konstantinos: Self-Authorship, Well-Being and Paternalism, 8 *Jurisprudence* (2017), 23. DOI: 10.1080/20403313.2015.1116200

Kant, Immanuel: Beantwortung der Frage: Was ist Aufklärung? (1784), in: Wieschedel (ed.), *Schriften zur Anthropologie, Geschichtsphilosophie, Politik und Pädagogik*, vol. XI, 1977, p. 53.

Kant, Immanuel: Über den Gemeinspruch: Das mag in der Theorie richtig sein, taugt aber nicht für die Praxis (1793), in: Weischedel (ed.), *Schriften zur Anthropologie, Geschichtsphilosophie, Politik und Pädagogik*, vol. XI, 1977, p. 145.

Kant, Immanuel: *Political Writings*, 2nd ed. 1991. DOI: 10.1017/cbo9780511809620

Kant, Immanuel: *Grundlegung zur Metaphysik der Sitten*, 1999.

Karampatzos, Antonios: Haftungsfreizeichnungsklauseln im Griechischen und Deutschen Kaufrecht sowie im DCFR—Die Dichotomie zwischen Individual- und Verbrauchsgüterkauf, in: Riesenhuber/Karakostas (eds.), *Inhaltskontrolle im Nationalen und Europäischen Privatrecht*, 2009, p. 186 [referenced as: Karampatzos, Haftungsfreizeichnungsklauseln…]. DOI: 10.1515/9783899497465.173

Karampatzos, Antonios: Rechtspaternalismus im Europäischen Verbraucherschutzrecht: Lehren aus „Behavioral Law and Economics“—Eine Bestandsaufnahme, in: Hopt/Tzouganatos (eds.), *Das Europäische Wirtschaftsrecht vor neuen Herausforderungen*, 2014, p. 205 [referenced as: Karampatzos, Rechtspaternalismus im Europäischen Verbraucherschutzrecht…].

Karampatzos, Antonios: Private Autonomy and Consumer Protection – A Contribution to Behavioral Economic Analysis of Law, in Greek (P.N. Sakkoulas Publishers), 2016.

Kelman, Mark: Law and Behavioral Science: Conceptual Overviews, 97 *Nw.U.L.R.* (2003), 1347.

Kelman, Mark/Rottenstreich, Yuval/Tversky, Amos: Context-Dependence in Legal Decision Making, in: Sunstein (ed.), *Behavioral Law & Economics* (2007), p. 73 [referenced as: Kelman/Rottenstreich/Tversky, Context-Dependence...]. DOI: 10.1017/cbo9781139175197.003

Kenrick, Douglas/Griskevicius, Vladas: *The Rational Animal—How Evolution Made Us Smarter Than We Think*, 2013 [referenced as: Kenrick/Griskevicius, *The Rational Animal...*].

Kirchgässner, Gebhard: *Homo Oeconomicus: Das ökonomische Modell individuellen Verhaltens und seine Anwendung in den Wirtschafts- und Sozialwissenschaften*, 4th ed. 2013 [referenced as: Kirchgässner, *Homo economicus*[4]].

Kirste, Stephan: Harter und weicher Rechtspaternalismus, *JZ* (2011), 805. DOI: 10.1628/002268811797238457

Kittner, Michael: *Schuldrecht*, 2nd ed. 2002.

Klassen, Ann/Klassen, David: Who Are the Donors in Organ Donation? The Family's Perspective in Mandated Choice, 125 *Ann.Intern.Med.* (1996), 70. DOI: 10.7326/0003-4819-125-1-199607010-00011

Kleinig, John: *Paternalism*, 1983.

Klick, Jonathan/Mitchell, Gregory: Government Regulation of Irrationality: Moral and Cognitive Hazards, 90 *Minn.L.Rev.* (2006), 1620.

Knetsch, Jack: The Endowment Effect and Evidence of Nonreversible Indifference Curves, 79 *Am.Econ.Rev.* (1989), 1277.

Kötz, Hein: Der Schutzzweck der AGB-Kontrolle—Eine rechtsökonomische Skizze, *JuS* (2003), 209.

Koller, Ingo: *Die Risikozurechnung bei Vertragsstörungen in Austauschverträgen*, 1979 [referenced as: Koller, *Die Risikozurechnung bei Vertragsstörungen...*].

Korobkin, Russell: The Status Quo Bias and Contract Default Rules, 83 *Cornell L.Rev.* (1998), 608.

Korobkin, Russell: Inertia and Preference in Contract Negotiation: The Psychological Power of the Default Rules and Form Terms, 51 *Vand.L.Rev.* (1998), 1583.

Korobkin, Russell: Bounded Rationality, Standard Form Contracts, and Unconscionability, 70 *U.Chi.L.Rev.* (2003), 1203. DOI: 10.2307/1600574

Korobkin, Russell: The Endowment Effect and Legal Analysis, 97 *Nw.U.L.R.* (2003), 1227. DOI: 10.2139/ssrn.326360

Korobkin, Russell: Behavioral Economics, Contract Formation, and Contract Law, in: Sunstein (ed.), *Behavioral Law & Economics*, 2007, p. 116 [referenced as: Korobkin, Behavioral Economics...]. DOI: 10.1017/cbo9781139175197.005

Korobkin, Russell: Wrestling with the Endowment Effect, or How to Do Law and Economics without the Coase Theorem, in: Zamir/Teichman (eds.), *The Oxford Handbook of Behavioral Economics and the Law*, 2014, p. 300 [referenced as: Korobkin, Wrestling with the Endowment Effect...]. DOI: 10.1093/oxfordhb/9780199945474.013.0012

Korobkin, Russell/Ulen, Thomas: Law and Behavioral Science: Removing the Rationality Assumption from Law and Economics, 88 *Cal.L.R.* (2000), 1051. DOI: 10.2307/3481255

Kroll-Ludwigs, Kathrin: Die Zukunft des verbraucherschützenden Widerrufsrechts in Europa, 18 *ZEuP* (2010), 509.

Kronman, Anthony: Paternalism and the Law of Contracts, 92 *Yale L.J.* (1983), 763. DOI: 10.2307/796144

Kuran, Timur/Sunstein, Cass: Availability Cascades and Risk Regulation, 51 *Stan.L.Rev.* (1999), 683. DOI: 10.2307/1229439

Laibson, David: Golden Eggs and Hyperbolic Discounting, 112 *Quart.J.Econ.* (1997), 443. DOI: 10.1162/003355397555253

Landes, William/Posner, Richard: A Positive Economic Analysis of Products Liability, 14 *J.Leg.Stud.* (1985), 535. DOI: 10.1086/467785

Landsburg, Steven: *The Armchair Economist: Economics and Everyday Life*, 1993 [referenced as Landsburg, *The Armchair Economist*...].

Larionova, Olga/Monroe, Karen: *CISG: To Include or Exclude?—That Is the Question* (05.04.2017), www.lexology.com/library/detail.aspx?g=7ae22d0a-2873-425a-962e-3b32a0701529

Leggett, Will: The Politics of Behavior Change: Nudge, Neoliberalism and the State, 42 *Policy Polit.* (2014), 3. DOI: 10.1332/030557312x655576

Letsas, George: Accommodating What Needn't Be Special, 10 *L. Ethics Hum. Rights* (2016), 319. DOI: 10.1515/lehr-2016-0015

Letten, Ine: *New Directive on Contracts for the Sale of Goods*, www.lexgo.be/en/papers/tax-law/european-law/new-directive-on-contracts-for-the-sale-of-goods, 128911.html

Lettl, Tobias: Die wirksame Ausübung eines Widerrufsrechts nach §§ 312 ff. BGB und dessen Rechtsfolgen (§§ 355, 357 BGB), *JA* (2011), 9.

Levitt, Steven/Dubner, Stephen: *Freakonomics—A Rogue Economist Explores the Hidden Side of Everything*, 2009 [referenced as: Levitt/Dubner, *Freakonomics*...].

Lichtenberg, Judith: Paternalism, Manipulation, Freedom, and the Good, in: Shafir (ed.), *The Behavioural Foundations of Public Policy*, 2013, p. 494. DOI: 10.2307/j.ctv550cbm.36

Liebs, Detlef: *Lateinische Rechtsregeln und Rechtssprichwörter*, 7th ed. 2007.

Locke, John: *Two Treatises of Government*, 1690 (reprinted in 1988). DOI: 10.1017/CBO9780511810268

Locke, William: *Representations, Warranties and "As Is" Disclaimers*, 2008.

Loos, Marco: Rights of Withdrawal, in: *Centre for the Study of European Contract Law Working Paper Series No. 2009/04*, p. 1. DOI: 10.2139/ssrn.1350224

Lüdemann, Jörn: Die Grenzen des homo oeconomicus und die Rechtswissenschaft, in: Engel/Englerth/Lüdemann/Spiecker-Döhmann (eds.), *Recht und Verhalten—Beiträge zu Behavioral Law and Economics*, 2007, p. 12 [referenced as: Lüdemann, Die Grenzen des homo oeconomicus...].

Magen, Stefan: Fairness, Eigennutz und die Rolle des Rechts—Eine Analyse aufGrundlage der Verhaltensökonomik, in: Engel/Englerth/Lüdemann/Spiecker-Döhmann (eds.), *Recht und Verhalten—Beiträge zu Behavioral Law and Economics*, 2007, p. 261 [referenced as: Magen, Fairness, Eigennutz und die Rolle des Rechts...].

Malhotra, Naresh: Information Load and Consumer Decision Making, 8 *J.Cons.Res.* (1982), 419. DOI: 10.1086/208882

Mankowski, Peter: Schwebende Wirksamkeit unter § 361a BGB–Probleme, Reaktionsmöglichkeiten, Kritik und Korrektur– Teil I, 16 *WM* (2001), 793.

Mankowski, Peter: *Beseitigungsrechte—Anfechtung, Widerruf und verwandte Institute*, 2003 [referenced as: Mankowski, *Beseitigungsrechte*...].

Mankowski, Peter: Widerrufsrecht, in: Basedow/Hopt/Zimmermann (eds.), *Handwörterbuch der Europäischen Privatrechts*, vol. II, 2009, p. 1792.

Martinek, Michael: Verbraucherschutz im Fernabsatz—Lesehilfe mit Merkpunkten zur neuen EU-Richtlinie, *NJW* (1998), 207.

Mathis, Klaus: *Effizienz statt Gerechtigkeit?—Auf der Suche nach den philosophischen Grundlagen der Ökonomischen Analyse des Rechts*, 3rd· ed. 2009 [referenced as: Mathis, *Effizienz statt Gerechtigkeit?*[3]]. DOI: 10.3790/978-3-428-52724-3

Mathis, Klaus (ed.): *European Perspectives on Behavioural Law and Economics*, 2015. DOI: 10.1007/978-3-319-11635-8

Mathis, Klaus/Steffen, Ariel David: From Rational Choice to Behavioural Economics, in: Mathis (ed.), *European Perspectives on Behavioural Law and Economics*, 2015, p. 31 [referenced as: Mathis/Steffen: From Rational Choice...]. DOI: 10.1007/978-3-319-11635-8_3

Medicus, Dieter/Lorenz, Stephan: *Schuldrecht I—Allgemeiner Teil*, 18th ed. 2008 [referenced as: Medicus/Lorenz, *Schuldr I—AT*[18]].

Meier, Patrick: Der Verbraucherbegriff nach der Umsetzung der Verbraucherrechterichtlinie, *JuS* (2014), 777.

Micklitz, Hans-Wolfgang: Zur Notwendigkeit eines neuen Konzepts für die Fortentwicklung des Verbraucherrechts in der EU, *VuR* (2003), 2.

Micklitz, Hans-Wolfgang/Reich, Norbert: Der Kommissionsvorschlag vom 8.10.2008 für eine Richtlinie über „Rechte der Verbraucher“ oder „der Beginn des Endes einer Ära...“, *EuZW* (2009), 279.

Mill, John Stuart: On Liberty, in: Gray (ed.), *On Liberty and Other Essays*, 1998, p. 5.

Mitchell, Gregory: Libertarian Paternalism Is an Oxymoron, 99 *Nw.U.L.R.* (2005), 1245.

Mitchell, Gregory: Alternative Behavioral Law and Economics, in: Zamir/Teichman (eds.), *The Oxford Handbook of Behavioral Economics and the Law*, 2014, p. 167. DOI: 10.1093/oxfordhb/9780199945474.013.0007

Möller, Kai: *Paternalismus und Persönlichkeitsrecht*, 2005. DOI: 10.3790/978-3-428-51679-7

Möllers, Thomas: Europäische Richtlinien zum Bürgerlichen Recht, *JZ* (2002), 121.

Moller, Arlen/Ryan, Richard/Deci, Edward: Self-Determination Theory and Public Policy: Improving the Quality of Consumer Decisions without Using Coercion, 25 *JPP&M* (2006), 104. DOI: 10.1509/jppm.25.1.104

Mols, Frank/Haslam, Alexander/Jetten, Jolanda/Steffens, Niklas: Why a Nudge Is Not Enough: A Social Identity Critique of Governance by Stealth, 54 *EJPR* (2015), 81. DOI: 10.1111/1475-6765.12073

Möslein, Florian: *Dispositives Recht—Zwecke, Strukturen und Methoden*, 2011 [referenced as: Möslein, *Dispositives Recht...*]. DOI: 10.1628/978-3-16-151759-4

Möslein, Florian: Privatrechtliche Regelsetzung, Governance und Verhaltensökonomik, 1 *ALJ* (2014), 135. DOI: 10.25364/1.1:2014.1.12

Morrison, William/Taubinksy, Dmitry: Rules of Thumb and Attention Elasticities: Evidence from Under- and Overreaction to Taxes, *NBER Working Paper No. 26180* (issued in August 2019), www.nber.org/papers/w26180. DOI: 10.3386/w26180

Nelson, Philip: Information and Consumer Behavior, 78 *J.Polit.Econ.* (1970), 311. DOI: 10.1086/259630

Neumann, Robert: *Libertärer Paternalismus, Theorie und Empirie staatlicher Entscheidungsarchitektur*, 2013 [referenced as: Neumann, *Libertärer Paternalismus...*]. DOI: 10.1628/978-3-16-152882-8

Nicklisch, Andreas/Petersen, Niels: Vertragstheorie, in: Towfigh/Petersen (eds.), *Ökonomische Methoden im Recht*, 2010, p. 117.

Noll, Roger/Krier, James: Some Implications of Cognitive Psychology for Risk Regulation, in: Sunstein (ed.), *Behavioral Law & Economics*, 2007, p. 325 [referenced as: Noll/Krier, Some Implications of Cognitive Psychology…]. DOI: 10.1017/cbo9781139175197.014

Note, Round: Round the Bramble Bush: From Legal Realism to Critical Legal Scholarship, 95 *Harv.L.R.* (1982), 1669. DOI: 10.2307/1340723

Nozick, Robert: *Anarchy, State, and Utopia*, 1974.

Oechsler, Jürgen: *Gerechtigkeit im modernen Austauschvertrag, Die theoretischen Grundlagen der Vertragsgerechtigkeit und ihr praktischer Einfluß auf Auslegung, Ergänzung und Inhaltskontrolle des Vertrages*, 1997 [referenced as: Oechsler, *Gerechtigkeit im modernen Austauschvertrag…*].

Ogus, Anthony: The Paradoxes of Legal Paternalism and How to Resolve Them, 30 *Leg. Stud.* (2010), 61. DOI: 10.1111/j.1748-121x.2009.00146.x

Oi, Walter: The Economics of Product Safety, 4 *Bell J.Econ.* (1973), 3.

Oliver, Adam (ed.), *Behavioural Public Policy*, 2013. DOI: 10.1017/cbo9781107337190

Paparseniou, Paraskevi: *Griechisches Verbrauchervertragsrecht—Eine Untersuchung vor dem Hintergrund des Gemeinschaftsprivatrechts*, 2008 [referenced as: Paparseniou, *Griechisches Verbrauchervertragsrecht…*].

Paredes, Troy: Blinded by the Light: Information Overload and Its Consequences for Securities Regulation, 81 *Wash.U.L.Q.* (2003), 417. DOI: 10.2139/ssrn.413180

Parisi, Francesco: The Harmonization of Legal Warranties in European Sales Law: An Economic Analysis, in: *George Mason Law & Economics Working Paper Series 01-20*, 2001[referenced as: Parisi, The Harmonization of Legal Warranties…]. DOI: 10.2139/ssrn.276993

Pavey, Louisa/Sparks, Paul: Reactance, Autonomy, and Paths to Persuasion: Examining Perceptions of Threats to Freedom and Informational Value, 33 *Motiv.Emot.* (2009), 277. DOI: 10.1007/s11031-009-9137-1

Perez, Oren: Can Experts be Trusted and What Can Be Done about It?—Insights from the Biases and Heuristics Literature, in: Alemanno/Sibony (eds.), *Nudge and the Law—A European Perspective*, 2017, p. 115 [referenced as: Perez, Can Experts be Trusted…]. DOI: 10.5040/9781474203463.ch-005

Persson, Petra: Attention Manipulation and Information Overload, 2 *BPP* (2018), 78. DOI: 10.1017/bpp.2017.10

Polinsky, Mitchell/Shavell, Steven: Punitive Damages: An Economic Analysis, 111 *Harv.L.R.* (1998), 869. DOI: 10.2307/1342009

Polinsky, Mitchell/Shavell, Steven: The Uneasy Case for Product Liability, 123 *Harv.L.Rev.* (2010), 1437. DOI: 10.2307/40648374

Pope, Alexander: *An Essay on Criticism*, 1709.

Pope, Thaddeus Mason: Counting the Dragon's Teeth and Claws: The Definition of Hard Paternalism, 20 *Ga.St.U.L.Rev.* (2004), 699.

Popper, Karl: *The Poverty of Historicism*, 2002. DOI: 10.4324/9780203538012

Porat, Ariel/Strahilevitz, Lior: Personalizing Default Rules and Disclosure with Big Data, 112 *Mich.L.Rev.* (2014), 1417. DOI: 10.2139/ssrn.2217064

Posner, Eric: There Are No Penalty Default Rules in Contract Law, 33 *Fla.St.U.L.Rev.* (2006), 563.

Posner, Richard: Retribution and Related Concepts of Punishment, 9 *J.Leg.Stud.* (1980), 71. DOI: 10.2139/ssrn.690403

Posner, Richard: What Has Pragmatism to Offer Law?, 63 *S.Cal.L.R.* (1990), 1653.

Posner, Richard: Rational Choice, Behavioral Economics and the Law, 50 *Stan.L.Rev* (1998), 1551. DOI: 10.2307/1229305

Posner, Richard: *Economic Analysis of Law*, 6th ed. 2003.
Posner, Richard: Treating Financial Consumers as Consenting Adults, in: *The Wall Street Journal*, 23.07.2009, p. A15.
Priest, George: The Current Insurance Crisis and Modern Tort Law, 96 *Yale L.J.* (1987), 1521. DOI: 10.2307/796494
ProMarket (The blog of the Stigler Center at the University of Chicago Booth School of Business): *How to Address the Privacy and Security Challenges Posed by Big Tech*, https://promarket.org/how-to-protect-privacy-in-the-age-of-digital-platforms/.
Purnhagen, Kai: Why Do We Need Responsive Regulation and Behavioural Research in EU Internal Market Law?, in: Mathis (ed.), *European Perspectives on Behavioural Law and Economics*, 2015, p. 51 [referenced as: Purnhagen, Why Do We Need Responsive Regulation…]. DOI: 10.1007/978-3-319-11635-8_4
Quillen, Gwyn: Contract Remedies and Cross-Subsidization, 61 *S.Cal.L.R.* (1988), 1125.
Rabin, Matthew: Cognitive Dissonance and Social Change, 23 *J.Econ.Behav.Organ.* (1994), 178. DOI: 10.1016/0167-2681(94)90066-3
Rachlinski, Jeffrey: The "New" Law and Psychology, 85 *Cornell L.Rev.* (2000), 739.
Rachlinski, Jeffrey: Cognitive Errors, Individual Differences, and Paternalism, 73 *U.Chi.L.Rev.* (2006), 207. DOI: 10.1093/acprof:oso/9780199211395.003.0008
Rachlinski, Jeffrey (ed.): *Behavioral Law & Economics*, 2009. DOI: 10.4337/9781785362774
Raiser, Ludwig: Vertragsfunktion und Vertragsfreiheit, in: Grundmann/Micklitz/Renner (eds.), *Privatrechtstheorie*, vol. I, 2015, p. 903 [= in: Caemmerer/Friesenhahn/Lange, *Deutscher Juristentag —Hundert Jahre deutsches Rechtsleben, Festschrift zum hundertjährigen Bestehen des Deutschen Juristentages 1860–1960*, 1960, p. 101].
Raz, Joseph: *The Morality of Freedom*, 1986 (reprinted in 2009).
Rebonato, Riccardo: A Critical Assessment of Libertarian Paternalism, 37 *J.Consum.Policy* (2014), 357. DOI: 10.1007/s10603-014-9265-1
Reich, Norbert: Abzahlungsrecht und Verbraucherschutz, *JZ* (1975), 550.
Reiner, Günter: Der verbraucherschützende Widerruf im Recht der Willenserklärungen, 203 *AcP* (2003), 1. DOI: 10.1628/000389903780265343
Rekaiti, Pamaria/van den Bergh, Roger: Cooling-Off Periods in the Consumer Laws of the EC Member States—A Comparative Law and Economics Approach, 23 *J.Consum. Policy* (2000), 371. DOI: 10.1023/a:1007203426046
Reuter, Dieter: Die ethischen Grundlagen des Privatrechts—formale Freiheitsethik oder materiale Verantwortungsethik, 189 *AcP* (1989), 199.
Ricciardi, Victor/Simon, Helen: What is Behavioral Finance?, 2 *Bus.Educ.&Tech.J.* (2000), 1.
Riesenhuber, Karl: *System und Prinzipien des Europäischen Vertragsrechts*, 2003.
Riesenhuber, Karl: Privatautonomie und Diskriminierungsverbote—Grundlagen im deutschen Recht und europäische Regulierung, in: Riesenhuber/Nishitani (eds.), *Wandlungen oder Erosion der Privatautonomie?*, 2007, p. 19 [referenced as: Riesenhuber, Privatautonomie und Diskriminierungsverbote…]. DOI: 10.1515/9783110971217.19
Riesenhuber, Karl: Wandlungen oder Erosion der Privatautonomie?, in: Riesenhuber/Nishitani (eds.), *Wandlungen oder Erosion der Privatautonomie?*, 2007, p. 1. DOI: 10.1515/9783110971217.1
Ringe, Wolf-Georg: Menügesetzgebung im Privatrecht, 213 *AcP* (2013), 98. DOI: 10.1628/000389913x13591069863565
Rittner, Fritz: Das Modell des homo oeconomicus und die Jurisprudenz, *JZ* (2005), 668.

Rizzo, Mario/Whitman, Douglas: The Knowledge Problem of New Paternalism, 2009 *B.Y.U.L.Rev.* (2009), 905. DOI: 10.2139/ssrn.1310732

Rockenbach, Bettina: Fairness Crowded Out by Law: An Experimental Study on Withdrawal Rights, 163 *J.Inst.Theor.Econ.* (2007), 106. DOI: 10.1628/093245607780181964

Röhl, Klaus/Röhl, Hans: *Allgemeine Rechtslehre*, 3rd ed. 2008.

Roland Berger Strategy Consultants: *Aktueller Status der Retourensituation im Versandhandel: Ergebnisse 2004, Studie im Auftrag des Bundesverbandes des Deutschen Versandhandels*, 2005 [Roland Berger Strategy Consultants, *Aktueller Status der Retourensituation*...].

Romeo, Nick: *Platonically Irrational* (15.05.2017), https://aeon.co/essays/what-plato-knew-about-behavioural-economics-a-lot

Rudden, Bernard: Ius Cogens, Ius Dispositivum, 11 *Cambrian L.Rev.* (1980), 87.

Rühl, Giesela: Die Verjährung kaufrechtlicher Gewährleistungsansprüche, 207 *AcP* (2007), 614. DOI: 10.1628/000389907783429182

Russell, Thomas/Thaler, Richard: The Relevance of Quasi Rationality in Competitive Markets, 75 *Am.Econ.Rev.* (1985), 1071.

Sah, Sunita/Cain, Daylian/Loewenstein, George: Confessing One's Sins but Still Committing Them: Transparency and the Failure of Disclosure, in: Oliver (ed.), *Behavioural Public Policy*, 2013, p. 148 [referenced as: Sah/Cain/Loewenstein, Confessing One's Sins but Still Committing Them...]. DOI: 10.1017/cbo9781107337190.007

Saint-Paul, Gilles: *The Tyranny of Utility—Behavioral Science and the Rise of Paternalism*, 2011 [referenced as: Saint-Paul, *The Tyranny of Utility*...]. DOI: 10.1515/9781400838899

Samuelson, William/Zeckhauser, Richard: Status Quo Bias in Decision Making, 1 *J.Risk Uncertainty* (1988), 7. DOI: 10.1007/bf00055564

Schäfer, Hans-Bernd/Ott, Claus: Die ökonomische Analyse—Irrweg oder Chance wissenschaftlicher Erkenntnis, *JZ* (1988), 213.

Schäfer, Hans-Bernd/Ott, Claus: *Lehrbuch der ökonomischen Analyse des Zivilrechts*, 4th ed. 2005. DOI: 10.1007/3-540-27878-8

Schäfer, Thomas: Widerrufsrechte—Herstellung oder Aushöhlung der Privatautonomie?—Kritische Betrachtung der verbraucherschützenden Widerrufsrechte im deutschen und japanischen Vertragsrecht, in: Riesenhuber/Nishitani (eds.), *Wandlungen oder Erosion der Privatautonomie?*, 2007, p. 187 [referenced as: Schäfer, Widerrufsrechte...]. DOI: 10.1515/9783110971217.187

Schärtl, Christoph: Der verbraucherschützende Widerruf bei außerhalb von Geschäftsräumen geschlossenen Verträgen und Fernabsatzverträgen, *JuS* (2014), 577.

Schelling, Thomas: *Micromotives and Macrobehavior*, 1978.

Schelling, Thomas: The Intimate Contest for Self-Command, 60 *Publ.Int.* (1980), 94.

Schiller, Friedrich: Die Gesetzgebung des Lykurgus und Solon, in: III *Thalia* (1790), 30, https://de.wikisource.org/wiki/Die_Gesetzgebung_des_Lykurgus_und_Solon

Schlag, Pierre: Nudge, Choice Architecture, and Libertarian Paternalism, 108 *Mich.L.Rev.* (2010), 913.

Schmolke, Klaus: *Grenzen der Selbstbindung im Privatrecht*, 2014 [referenced as: Schmolke, *Grenzen der Selbstbindung*...]. DOI: 10.1628/978-3-16-152304-5

Schmolke, Klaus: Zuckerbrot und Peitsche—Eine Annäherung an die Funktionsbedingungen rechtlicher Verhaltenssteuerung durch Sanktion und Belohnung mit Beispielen aus dem Wirtschaftsrecht, *JZ* (2015), 121. DOI: 10.1628/002268815x14189163770173

Schön, Wolfgang: Zwingendes Recht oder informierte Entscheidung—zu einer (neuen) Grundlage unserer Zivilrechtsordnung, in: Heldrich/Prölss/Koller (eds.), *Festschrift für Canaris*, vol. I, 2007, p. 1191 [referenced as: Schön, in: *FS Canaris*].

Schürnbrand, Jan: Zwingender Verbraucherschutz und das Verbot unzulässiger Rechtsausübung, *JZ* (2009), 133. DOI: 10.1628/002268809787360284

Schwab, Martin: Widerrufsrechte im deutschen und europäischen Verbraucherschutzrecht, in: Riesenhuber/Nishitani (eds.), *Wandlungen oder Erosion der Privatautonomie?*, 2007, p. 149 [referenced as ως: Schwab, Widerrufsrechte...]. DOI: 10.1515/9783110971217.149

Schwab, Martin/Hromek, Stefanie: Alte Streitstände im neuen Verbraucherprivatrecht, *JZ* (2015), 271. DOI: 10.1628/002268815x14230366453966

Schwabe, Jürgen: Der Schutz des Menschen vor sich selbst, *JZ* (1998), 66.

Schweizer, Mark: Nudging and the Principle of Proportionality—Obliged to Nudge?, in: Mathis/Tor (eds.), *Nudging—Possibilities, Limitations and Applications in European Law and Economics*, 2016, p. 93 [referenced as: Schweizer, Nudging and the Principle of Proportionality...]. DOI: 10.1007/978-3-319-29562-6_7

Sen, Amartya: *The Idea of Justice*, 2009.

Shafir, Eldar (ed.): *The Behavioral Foundations of Public Policy*, 2013.

Shavell, Steven: Strict Liability Versus Negligence, 9 *J.Leg.Stud.* (1980), 1. DOI: 10.1086/467626

Sibony, Anne-Lise/Helleringer, Geneviève: EU Consumer Protection and Behavioural Sciences: Revolution or Reform, in: Alemanno/Sibony (eds.), *Nudge and the Law—A European Perspective*, 2017, p. 209 [referenced as: Sibony/Helleringer, EU Consumer Protection and Behavioural Sciences...]. DOI: 10.5040/9781474203463.ch-009

Siegel, Ethan/Berezow, Alex: Opting out of Vaccines Should Opt You Out of American Society, 3 *Sci.Am.* (2019), https://blogs.scientificamerican.com/observations/opting-out-of-vaccines-should-opt-you-out-of-american-society/.

Siegal, Gil/Bonnie, Richard: Closing the Organ Gap: A Reciprocity-Based Social Contract Approach, 34 *J.L.Med.&Ethics* (2006), 415. DOI: 10.1111/j.1748-720x.2006.00048.x

Siegal, Gil/Bonnie, Richard/Appelbaum, Paul: Personalized Disclosure by Information on Demand: Attending to Patients' Needs in the Informed Consent Process, 40 *J.L.Med.&Ethics* (2012). 359. DOI: 10.1111/j.1748-720x.2012.00669.x

Simitis, Konstantin: *Verbraucherschutz, Schlagwort oder Rechtsprinzip?*, 1976.

Simmonds, Nigel: *Central Issues in Jurisprudence: Justice, Laws and Rights*, 5th ed. 2018 [referenced as: Simmonds, *Central Issues in Jurisprudence*].

Simon, Herbert: A Behavioral Model of Rational Choice, 69 *Quart.J.Econ.* (1955), 99. DOI: 10.2307/1884852

Simon, Herbert: *Models of Man: Social and Rational—Mathematical Essays on Rational Human Behavior in a Social Setting*, 1957 [referenced as: Simon, *Models of Man: Social and Rational...*].

Simon, Herbert: Rational Decision Making in Business Organizations, 69 *Am.Econ.Rev.* (1979), 493.

Simon, Herbert: *Reason in Human Affairs*, 1983.

Simon, Herbert: Rationality in Psychology and Economics, 59 *J.Bus.* (1986), 209.

Simon, Herbert: Bounded Rationality, in: Eatwell/Milgate/Newman (eds.), *The New Palgrave Dictionary of Economics*, 1987, p. 266 [= in: Eatwell/Milgate/Newman (eds.), *Utility and Probability*, 1990, p. 15]. DOI: 10.1057/978-1-349–95121-5_472-1 [= DOI; 10.1007/978-1-349-20568-4_5].

Simon, Herbert: Altruism and Economics, 83 *Am.Econ.Rev.* (1993), 156.

Sinn, Hans-Werner: Kommentar zu Magoulas' „Verbraucherschutz als Problem asymmetrischer Informationskosten", in: Ott/Schäfer (eds.), *Allokationseffizienz in der Rechtsordnung—Beiträge zur ökonomischen Analyse des Zivilrechts*, 1989, p. 81 [referenced as: Sinn, Kommentar...].

Smith, Vernon: Economics in the Laboratory, in: Hausman (ed.), *The Philosophy of Economics, An anthology*, 3rd ed. 2008, p. 334. DOI: 10.1017/cbo9780511819025.023

Sneddon, Andrew: What's Wrong with Selling Yourself into Slavery?—Paternalism and Deep Autonomy, 33 *CRITICA* (2001), 97.

Stabentheiner, Johannes/Wendehorst, Christiane/Zöchling-Jud, Brigitta: *Das neue europäische Gewährleistungsrecht—Zu den Richtlinien (EU) 2019/771 über den Warenkauf sowie (EU) 2019/770 über digitale Inhalte und digitale Dienstleistungen*, 2019.

Steinbeck, Anja/Lachenmaier, Andreas: Verhaltensökonomik im Gerichtssaal, 29 *NJW* (2014), 2086.

Stewart, Sharla: Can Behavioral Economics Save Us from Ourselves?, 97 *U. Chi.Mag.* (2005), https://magazine.uchicago.edu/0502/features/economics.shtml.

Stobaeus, Joannis: *Iōannou Stobaiou Anthologion* (Joannis Stobaei Anthologium), vol. II, 1822, https://archive.org/details/iannoustobaioua02stobgoog [referenced as: Stobaeus, *Iōannou Stobaiou Anthologion*].

Strotz, Robert: Myopia and Inconsistency in Dynamic Utility Maximization, 23 *Rev. Econ.Stud.* (1955–1956), 165. DOI: 10.2307/2295722

Stürner, Michael: Die Qual der (Ab)-Wahl: Der Ausschluss des UN-Kaufrechts aus Sicht des deutschen Importeurs, *BB* (2006), 2029.

Stürner, Michael: *Der Grundsatz der Verhältnismäßigkeit im Schuldvertragsrecht—Zur Dogmatik einer privatrechtsimmanenten Begrenzung von vertraglichen Rechten und Pflichten*, 2010 [referenced as: Stürner, *Der Grundsatz der Verhältnismäßigkeit*...].

Sturn, Richard: Libertärer Paternalismus und Vertragsfreiheit: Potential, Prämissen und Probleme im liberalen Verfassungsstaat, 1 *ALJ* (2014), 48. DOI: 10.25364/1.1:2014.1.4

Sunstein, Cass: Behavioral Analysis of Law, 64 *U.Chi.L.Rev.* (1997), 1175. DOI: 10.2307/1600213

Sunstein, Cass: Behavioral Law and Economics: A Progress Report, 1 *Am.L.&Econ.Rev.* (1999), 115. DOI: 10.1093/aler/1.1.115

Sunstein, Cass: Switching the Default Rule, 77 *N.Y.U.L.Rev.* (2002), 106. DOI: 10.2139/ssrn.255993

Sunstein, Cass: Boundedly Rational Borrowing, 73 *U.Chi.L.Rev.* (2006), 249.

Sunstein, Cass (ed.): *Behavioral Law & Economics*, 2007. DOI: 10.1017/CBO9781139175197

Sunstein, Cass: Introduction, in: Sunstein (ed.), *Behavioral Law & Economics*, 2007, p. 4. DOI: 10.1017/cbo9781139175197.001

Sunstein, Cass: Deciding by Default, 162 *U.Penn.L.R.* (2013), 1.

Sunstein, Cass: The Storrs Lectures: Behavioral Economics and Paternalism, 122 *Yale L.J.* (2013), 1826. DOI: 10.2139/ssrn.2182619

Sunstein, Cass: *Behaviorally Informed Health Policy?—Patient Autonomy, Active Choosing, and Paternalism*, 2014 [referenced as: Sunstein, *Behaviorally Informed Health Policy?*...]. DOI: 10.2139/ssrn.2533700

Sunstein, Cass: Choosing Not to Choose, 64 *Duke L.J.* (2014), 1. DOI: 10.2139/ssrn.2377364

Sunstein, Cass: Nudges vs. Shoves, 127 *Harv.L.R. Forum* (2014), 210. DOI: 10.2139/ssrn.2390120

Sunstein, Cass: *Nudging: A Very Short Guide* (22.09.2014). DOI: 10.2139/ssrn.2499658

Sunstein, Cass: *Why Nudge?: The Ethics of Libertarian Paternalism*, 2014.
Sunstein, Cass: *Nudging and Choice Architecture: Ethical Considerations* (17.01.2015), http://papers.ssrn.com/sol3/papers.cfm?abstract_id=2551264 [referenced as: Sunstein, *Nudging and Choice Architecture*...].
Sunstein, Cass: *Fifty Shades of Manipulation* (18.02.2015), DOI: 10.2139/ssrn.2565892
Sunstein, Cass: *Choosing Not to Choose: Understanding the value of choice*, 2015 [referenced as: Sunstein, *Choosing Not to Choose*...].
Sunstein, Cass: *Forcing People To Choose Is Paternalistic* (01.11.2016). DOI: 10.2139/ssrn.2862694
Sunstein, Cass: *'Better Off, as Judged by Themselves': A Comment on Evaluating Nudges* (09.04.2017). DOI: 10.2139/ssrn.2949855
Sunstein, Cass: The Ethics of Nudging, in: Alemanno/Sibony (eds.), *Nudge and the Law—A European Perspective*, 2017, pp. v–xviii.
Sunstein, Cass: *Misconceptions about Nudges* (06.12.2017). DOI: 10.2139/ssrn.3033101
Sunstein, Cass: *On Preferring A to B, While Also Preferring B to A* (21.03.2018) [referenced as: Sunstein, *On Preferring A to B*...]. DOI: 10.2139/ssrn.3132428
Sunstein, Cass: *The Cost-Benefit Revolution*, 2018.
Sunstein, Cass/Bar-Gill, Oren: *Regulation as Delegation* (25.02.2015). DOI: 10.2139/ssrn.2570669
Sunstein, Cass/Reisch Lucia: Behavioral Economics and Public Opinion, 53 *Intereconomics* (2018), 5. DOI 10.1007/s10272-018-0710-2
Sunstein, Cass/Thaler, Richard: Libertarian Paternalism is not an Oxymoron, 70 *U.Chi.L.Rev.* (2003), 1159. DOI: 10.2139/ssrn.405940
Schwartz, Barry: *The Paradox of Choice—Why More Is Less*, 2004.
Schwartz, Barry: *The Paradox of Choice*, TEDGlobal 2005, 03:20–04:42, www.ted.com/talks/barry_schwartz_on_the_paradox_of_choice/transcript.
Szaszi, Barnabas/Palinkas, Anna/Palfi, Bence/Szollosi, Aba /Aczel, Balazs: A Systematic Scoping Review of the Choice Architecture Movement: Toward Understanding When and Why Nudges Work, 31 *J.Behav.Dec.Making* (2018), 355. DOI: 10.1002/bdm.2035
Taleb, Nassim Nicholas/Sandis, Constantine: The Skin in the Game Heuristic for Protection against Tail Events, 1 *Rev.Behav.Econ.* (2014), 1. DOI: 10.1561/105.00000006
Thaler, Richard: Toward a Positive Theory of Consumer Choice, 1 *J.Econ.Behav.Organ.* (1980), 39 [= in: Kahneman/Tversky (eds.), *Choices, Values, and Frames*, 2009, p. 269.] DOI: 10.1016/0167-2681(80)90051-7 [= DOI: 10.1017/cbo9780511803475.016].
Thaler, Richard: Anomalies: The Ultimatum Game, 2 *J.Econ.Persp.* (1988), 195. DOI: 10.1257/jep.2.4.195
Thaler, Richard: *Misbehaving—The Making of Behavioral Economics*, 2015 [referenced as: Thaler, *Misbehaving*...].
Thaler, Richard: The Power of Nudges, For Good and Bad, in: *The New York Times*, 31.10.2015, www.nytimes.com/2015/11/01/upshot/the-power-of-nudges-for-good-and-bad.html?_r=0 [referenced as: Thaler, The Power of Nudges...].
Thaler, Richard: Behavioral Economics, 125 *J.Polit.Econ.* (2017), 1799. DOI: 10.1086/694640
Thaler, Richard: From Cashews to Nudges: The Evolution of Behavioral Economics, 108 *Am.Econ.Rev.* (2018), 1265. DOI: 10.1257/aer.108.6.1265
Thaler, Richard/Sunstein, Cass: *Nudge: Improving Decisions about Health, Wealth, and Happiness*, 2008 [referenced as: Thaler/Sunstein, *Nudge*...].

Thaler, Richard/Sunstein, Cass/Balz, John: Choice Architecture, in: Shafir (ed.), *The Behavioral Foundations of Public Policy*, 2013, p. 428. DOI: 10.2307/j.ctv550cbm.31

Thaler, Richard/Tucker, Will: Smarter Information, Smarter Consumers, 91 *Harv. Bus.R.* (2013), 4.

Thorndike, Anne/Sunstein, Cass: Obesity Prevention in the Supermarket – Choice Architecture and the Supplemental Nutrition Assistance Program, 107 *Am.J.Publ. Health* (2017), 1582. DOI: 10.2105/ajph.2017.303991

Tiedtke, Klaus/Burgmann, Roland: Gewährleistungs- und Haftungsausschluss beim Verkauf gebrauchter Sachen an und zwischen Verbrauchern, *NJW* (2005), 1153.

Tomer, John: *Advanced Introduction to Behavioral Economics*, 2017.

Tomer, John: *The Emergence and Progress of Behavioral Economics: Does It Constitute a New Paradigm?* (25.10.2017), https://elgar.blog/2017/10/25/behavioral-economics/

Tonner, Klaus/Tamm, Marina: Der Vorschlag einer Richtlinie über Rechte der Verbraucher und seine Auswirkungen auf das nationale Verbraucherrecht, *JZ* (2009), 277. DOI: 10.1628/002268809787748815

Tor, Avishalom: The Next Generation of Behavioural Law and Economics, in: Mathis (ed.), *European Perspectives on Behavioural Law and Economics*, 2015, p. 17 [referenced as: Tor, The Next Generation of Behavioural...]. DOI: 10.1007/978-3-319-11635-8_2

Towfigh, Emanuel: Das ökonomische Paradigma, in: Towfigh/Petersen (eds.), *Ökonomische Methoden im Recht*, 2010, p. 22.

Towfigh, Emanuel/Petersen, Niels: Public Choice Theorie und Social Choice Theorie, in: Towfigh/Petersen (eds.), *Ökonomische Methoden im Recht* (2010), p. 133.

Trebilcock, Michael: *The Limits of Freedom of Contract*, 1997.

Trebilcock, Michael/Elliott, Steven: The Scope and Limits of Legal Paternalism: Altruism and Coercion in Family Financial Arrangements, in: Benson (ed.), *The Theory of Contract Law—New Essays*, 2007, p. 45 [referenced as: Trebilcock/Elliott, The Scope and Limits...]. DOI: 10.1017/cbo9780511570834.003

Tsakyrakis, Stavros: Proportionality: An Assault on Human Rights?, 7 *I.Con* (2009), 468. DOI: 10.1093/icon/mop011

Tsakyrakis, Stavros: Proportionality: An Assault on Human Rights? A Rejoinder to Madhav Khosla, 8 *I.Con* (2010), 307. DOI: 10.1093/icon/moq017

Tsakyrakis, Stavros: Disproportionate Individualism, in: Kochenov/de Búrca/Williams (eds.), *Europe's Justice Deficit?*, 2015, p. 235. DOI: 10.5040/9781474201193.ch-016

Tscherner, Eva: Can Behavioral Research Advance Mandatory Law, Information Duties, Standard Terms and Withdrawal Rights?, 1 *ALJ* (2014), 144.

Tversky, Amos/Kahneman, Daniel: Judgment under Uncertainty: Heuristics and Biases, 185 *Science* (1974), 1124. DOI: 10.1126/science.185.4157.1124

Tversky, Amos/Kahneman, Daniel: The Framing of Decisions and the Psychology of Choice, 211 *Science* (1981), 453. DOI: 10.1126/science.7455683

Tversky, Amos/Kahneman, Daniel: Loss Aversion in Riskless Choice—A Reference-Dependent Model, 107 *Quart.J.Econ.* (1991), 1039 [= in: Kahneman/Tversky (eds.), *Choices, Values, and Frames*, 2009, p. 143]—[referenced as: Tversky/Kahneman, Loss Aversion in Riskless Choice...]. DOI: 10.2307/2937956 [= DOI: 10.1017/cbo9780511803475.008]

Tversky, Amos/Kahneman, Daniel: Advances in Prospect Theory: Cumulative Representation of Uncertainty, in: Kahneman/Tversky (eds.), *Choices, Values, and Frames*, 2009, p. 44 [referenced as: Tversky/Kahneman, Advances in Prospect Theory...]. DOI: 10.1017/cbo9780511803475.004

Tversky, Amos/Kahneman, Daniel: Rational Choice and the Framing of Decisions, in: Kahneman/Tversky (eds.), *Choices, Values, and Frames*, 2009, p. 209. DOI: 10.1017/cbo9780511803475.013

Ulen, Thomas: The Importance of Behavioral Law, in: Zamir/Teichman (eds.), *The Oxford Handbook of Behavioral Economics and the Law*, 2014, p. 93. DOI: 10.1093/oxfordhb/9780199945474.013.0004

Ulen, Thomas: European and American Perspectives on Behavioural Law and Economics, in: Mathis (ed.), *European Perspectives on Behavioural Law and Economics*, 2015, p. 3 [referenced as: Ulen, European and American Perspectives...]. DOI: 10.1007/978-3-319-11635-8_1

Unberath, Hannes: Long-Term Contracts and the DCFR—Interpretation and Adjustment, in: Wagner (ed.), *The Common Frame of Reference: A View from Law & Economics*, 2009, p. 87 [referenced as: Unberath, Long-Term Contracts and the DCFR...]. DOI: 10.1515/9783866538665.87

Unberath, Hannes/Cziupka, Johannes: Dispositives Recht welchen Inhalts?—Antworten der ökonomischen Analyse des Rechts, 209 *AcP* (2009), p. 37. DOI: 10.1628/000389909787443874

Vandenberghe, Ann-Sofie: The Role of Information Deficiencies in Contract Enforcement, in: Ogus/van Boom, *Juxtaposing Autonomy and Paternalism in Private Law*, 2011, p. 43 [referenced as: Vandenberghe, The Role of Information Deficiencies...].

Viscusi, W. Kip: Corporate Risk Analysis: A Reckless Act?, 52 *Stan.L.Rev.* (2000), 547. DOI: 10.2307/1229473

Voorhoeve, Alex: Response to Rabin, in: Oliver (ed.), *Behavioural Public Policy*, 2013, p. 140.

Waddams, Stephen: Autonomy and Paternalism from a Common Law Perspective: Setting Aside Disadvantageous Transactions, in: Ogus/van Boom (eds.), *Juxtaposing Autonomy and Paternalism in Private Law*, 2011, p. 145 [referenced as: Waddams, Autonomy and Paternalism...].

Wagner, Gerhard: Prävention und Verhaltenssteuerung durch Privatrecht: Anmaßung oder legitime Aufgabe?, 206 *AcP* (2006), 352. DOI: 10.1628/000389906782068031

Wagner, Gerhard: Die soziale Frage und der Gemeinsame Referenzrahmen, *ZEuP* (2007), 180.

Wagner, Gerhard: Mandatory Contract Law: Functions and Principles in Light of the Proposal for a Directive on Consumer Rights, in: Ogus/van Boom (eds.), *Juxtaposing Autonomy and Paternalism in Private Law*, 2011, p. 9 [referenced as: Wagner, Mandatory Contract Law...].

Wagner, Gerhard: Zwingendes Vertragsrecht, in: Eidenmüller/Faust/Grigoleit/Jansen/Wagner/Zimmermann (eds.), *Revision des Verbraucher-acquis*, 2011, p. 1.

Waldron, Jeremy: It's All for Your Own Good, in: *The New York Review of Books*, 09.10.2014, www.nybooks.com/articles/archives/2014/oct/09/cass-sunstein-its-all-your-own-good/.

Waldron, Jeremy: Nudges: Good and Bad (Reply to Cass Sunstein), in: *The New York Review of Books*, 23.10.2014, www.nybooks.com/articles/archives/2014/oct/23/nudges-good-and-bad/?pagination=false&printpage=true [referenced as: Waldron, Nudges: Good and Bad...].

Weatherill, Stephen: *EU Consumer Law and Policy*, 2nd ed. 2013 [referenced as: Weatherill, *EU Consumer Law*...]. DOI: 10.4337/9780857936981

Wein, Thomas: *Eine ökonomische Analyse der neuen Verbrauchsgüterkaufrichtlinie zum Gewährleistungsrecht*, 2000 [referenced as: Wein, *Eine ökonomische Analyse der neuen Verbrauchsgüterkaufrichtlinie…*].

Weinstein, Neil: Optimistic Biases about Personal Risks, 246 *Science* (1989), 1232. DOI: 10.1126/science.2686031

Wendehorst, Christiane: Die neue Richtlinie über die Rechte der Verbraucher, in: Schenk/Lovrek/Musger/Neumayr (eds.), *Festschrift für Irmgard Griss*, 2011, p. 717 [referenced as: Wendehorst, in: *FS Griss*].

Wendehorst, Christiane: Das neue Gesetz zur Umsetzung der Verbraucherrechterichtlinie, *NJW* (2014), 577.

Westermann, Harm Peter: Interpretation of CISG 6, in: *Münchener Kommentar zum Bürgerlichen Gesetzbuch, Schuldrecht—Besonderer Teil I, §§ 433–534, Finanzierungsleasing, CISG*, vol. 3, 7th ed. 2015 [referenced as: MünchKomm(BGB)/Westermann, Art. 6 CISG].

White, Mark: Can Homo Economicus Follow Kant's Categorical Imperative?, 33 *J.Socio-Econ.* (2004), 89. DOI: 10.1016/j.socec.2003.12.002

White, Mark: The Crucial Importance of Interests in Libertarian Paternalism, in: Mathis/Tor (eds.), *Nudging—Possibilities, Limitations and Applications in European Law and Economics, Economic Analysis of Law in European Legal Scholarship*, 2016, p. 21 [referenced as: White, The Crucial Importance of Interests…]. DOI: 10.1007/978-3-319-29562-6_3

Wiedemann, Herbert/Wank, Rolf: Begrenzte Rationalität—gestörte Willensbildung im Privatrecht, *JZ* (2013), 340. DOI: 10.1628/002268813x13632601226107

Wilkinson, Martin: Nudging and Manipulation, 61 *Polit.Stud.* (2013), 341. DOI: 10.1111/j.1467-9248.2012.00974.x

Willis, Lauren: When Nudges Fail: Slippery Defaults, 80 *U.Chi.L.Rev.* (2013), 1115. DOI: 10.2139/ssrn.2142989

Willis, Lauren: Performance-Based Consumer Law, 82 *U.Chi.L.Rev.* (2015), 1309. DOI: 10.2139/ssrn.2485667

Winter, Sidney: Economic "Natural Selection" and the Theory of the Firm, 4 *Yale Econ. Essays* (1964), 225.

Wipperfürth, Sabine: *Die Verbraucherrechte-Richtlinie: Eine Analyse der neuen Rechtslage und der Auswirkungen auf den e-Commerce*, 2014 [referenced as: Wipperfürth, *Die Verbraucherrechte-Richtlinie…*].

Wittman, Donald: *Economic Foundations of Law and Organization*, 2006 [referenced as: Wittman, *Economic Foundations of Law…*]. DOI: 10.1057/eej.2007.47

Wolf, Manfred/Neuner, Jörg: *Allgemeiner Teil des Bürgerlichen Rechts*, 10th ed. 2012 [referenced as: Wolf/Neuner, *AT des BürgR*^{10}].

World Development Report 2015: *Mind, Society, and Behavior* [World Bank Development Report], www.worldbank.org/en/publication/wdr2015.

Wright, Joshua/Ginsburg, Douglas: Behavioral Law and Economics: Its Origins, Fatal Flaws, and Implications for Liberty, 106 *Nw.U.L.R.* (2012), 1033.

Wundt, Wilhelm: *Ethik—Eine Untersuchung der Thatsachen und Gesetze des sittlichen Lebens*, 1886, https://archive.org/stream/ethikeineunters03wundgoog/ethikeineunters03wundgoog_djvu.txt.

Zamir, Eyal: Law's Loss Aversion, in: Zamir/Teichman (eds.), *The Oxford Handbook of Behavioral Economics and the Law*, 2014, p. 268. DOI: 10.1093/oxfordhb/9780199945474.013.0011

Zamir, Eyal/Teichman, Doron (eds.): *The Oxford Handbook of Behavioral Economics and the Law*, 2014 [referenced as: Zamir/Teichman (eds.), *The Oxford Handbook*]. DOI: 10.1093/oxfordhb/9780199945474.001.0001

Zimmermann, Reinhard: *The Law of Obligations: Roman Foundations of the Civilian Tradition*, 1996 [referenced as: Zimmermann, *The Law of Obligations...*]. DOI: 10.1093/acprof:oso/9780198764267.001.0001

Zimmermann, Reinhard: Rückabwicklung nach Widerruf, in: Eidenmüller/Faust/Grigoleit/Jansen/Wagner/Zimmermann (eds.), *Revision des Verbraucher-acquis*, 2011, p. 167.

Zippelius, Reinhold: *Juristische Methodenlehre*, 10th ed. 2006.

Zöchnling-Jud, Brigitta: Acquis-Revision, Common European Sales Law und Verbraucherrechterichtlinie, 212 *AcP* (2012), 550. DOI: 10.1628/000389912803571158

Zypries, Brigitte: Der Vorschlag für eine Richtlinie über Verbraucherrechte, 2 *ZEuP* (2009), 225.

Index

Note: Page numbers followed by "n" denote endnotes